D1315285

A Woman Like You

A
Woman
Like You

Life Stories of Women
Recovering from
Alcoholism and Addiction

Rachel V.

1817

Harper & Row, Publishers, San Francisco

Cambridge, Hagerstown, New York, Philadelphia,
London, Mexico City, São Paulo, Sydney

PROPERTY OF
METHODIST UNIVERSITY LIBRARY

FIRST EDITION

Library of Congress Catalloging-in-Publication Data

Main entry under title:

A Woman like you.

Bibliography: p.
1. Women—United States—Alcohol use—Case studies.
2. Alcoholics—Rehabilitation—United States—Case
studies.   3. Alcoholism—United States—Case studies.
4. Alcoholics Anonymous.   I. Rachel V.
HV5137.W63   1985   362.2'92'0926   85-42938
ISBN 0-06-250701-X

85 86 87 88 89 RRD 10 9 8 7 6 5 4 3 2 1

Dedicated to Bill and Lois Wilson, Dr. Bob and Anne Smith,
and the fellowship of Alcoholics Anonymous
Happy 50th Anniversary

A self is made, not given. It is a creative and active process of attending a life that must be heard, shaped, seen, said aloud into the world, finally enacted and woven into the lives of others. Then a life attended is not an act of narcissism or disregard for others; on the contrary, it is searching through the treasures and debris of ordinary existence for the clear points of intensity that do not erode, do not separate us, that are most intensely our own, yet other people's too. The best lives and stories are made up of minute particulars that somehow are also universal and of use to others as well as oneself.

Barbara Meyerhoff
October 6, 1982

Contents

Acknowledgments   xi
About This Book   xiii
Introduction by LeClair Bissell, M.D.   xvii

1. **Elizabeth B.**   1
   "This marriage was going to solve all my problems. . . .
   I gave bar mitzvahs for 800. . . . I never took a drink in
   front of anyone else . . . people thought I was a teetotaler. . . . I would stay in bed for days with the 'flu'
   and drink around the clock . . . just like those men
   under the bridge. . . . But no one saw . . . " Age 42,
   sober five years.

2. **Susan R.**   12
   "I had become the perfect daughter, I made straight
   A's. . . . When I got dropped off at church, I'd call my
   boyfriend. He'd come and get me and we'd go drink
   while my parents went to a Sunday school class on
   parenting. . . . Finally I stopped making up stories to
   cover myself. I got really arrogant." Age 17, sober two
   and one-half years.

3. **Lulu F.**   21
   "When I got out of prison, it was going to be different
   this time . . . I swore I'd never do drugs again. . . . It
   was the drugs that made me so crazy, wasn't it, not the
   alcohol, I told myself. . . . When I started coming to
   meetings, there were only two other black women
   besides me . . . " Age 38, sober eight years.

4. **Gail R.**   32
   "The doctor told me, 'You have such terrible family
   problems, if we just get those straightened out you
   won't have to drink so much.' " Age 48, sober nine
   years.

5. **Shirley B.**   45

"I wanted to become an international lawyer. . . . I
went to Chile on a Fulbright scholarship. . . . There I
was all dressed up in a cocktail gown being 'Lady
Gracious' and suddenly there's a blank . . . and I am out
in the middle of the Atacama desert with the sun just
coming up over the Andes." Age 47, sober twenty-one
years.

6. **Sister Rose**   54

"As a young sister, I became ill on my first mission. . . .
The doctor suggested that my mother superior give me
wine each night to help me sleep and build up my
blood. . . . In the 1960s life in the convent changed, and
we were allowed to wear street clothes. . . . Then I
could go out and buy my own liquor." Age 62, sober
fifteen years.

7. **Malinda P.**   64

"My problem was not being an intellectual or being
a lesbian or a woman. My problem was that I'm
an alcoholic and I was afflicted with terminal
uniqueness. . . . I was the queen of drama early
on. . . . Alcohol ended up being a zone of anesthesia."
Age 37, sober six and one-half years.

8. **Ellen M.**   76

"My father was a Methodist minister. . . . I was
a closet drinker. . . . I wanted to be a perfect
mother. . . . Alcoholism is seen as a moral issue,
especially for black women if their families are
religious." Age 56, sober three years.

9. **Jeanette M.**   85

"At 17 I was the soloist with a major metropolitan ballet
company. I can recall that first drink. It was like a big
sigh went through my body, and all of a sudden I
realized that this is what it was like to feel normal."
Age 49, sober twenty-one years.

10. **Anne C.** 95
"I went straight to medical school to become a doctor. . . . My denial was so great that I convinced myself that vomiting in the morning was what everybody did." Age 48, sober seven years.

11. **Miriam J.** 105
"My first addiction was to food. . . . I was 12 when I smoked my first joint. Within a month I was taking speed, pills, hash, whatever I could get my hands on . . . and drinking. My mother raised a nice Jewish girl, and I ended up packing a gun and selling cocaine." Age 22, sober two and one-half years.

12. **Mollie P.** 113
"I didn't drink until I was 37, and then I only lasted for four years. I was very much a proper matron. The other side of me was screaming to cut loose. . . . I got very involved in the Altar Society . . . and with the parish priest." Age 48, sober seven years.

13. **Marie L.** 123
"Growing up Latin American, we celebrated a lot . . . like first Holy Communions, confirmations, baptisms, birthdays, and whatever else you can think of. . . . That's the first thing I did on confirmation day, got drunk. I was thirteen . . . I was brought up with the saying 'You're born alone and you're going to die alone. You don't need anybody.' " Age 35, sober three years.

14. **Leah G.** 134
"The physical effects of alcohol were so frightening that I was probably only drunk a couple of times in such a way that it was obvious to other people. I never passed out. I didn't have to lose everything before I realized I needed help. . . . I never heard the story that Jews aren't alcoholic until I came in the program and I had to laugh." Age 50, sober sixteen years.

15. **Harriet B.** 142
"I was born on a reservation. . . . I am Chippewah and French. . . . I was sent away to boarding school and taught English. . . . I was torn between two worlds. . . . I entered into a complete denial of my own culture. . . . I didn't want to be Indian." Age 49, sober five years.

16. **Eleanor E.** 155
"When I moved to Houston, I discovered that I was hardly the only gay person in the world. . . . I began to meet people who were like me. Still I was unhappy. . . . Once I began to drink, I could get rid of that feeling that I always had about not being able to fit in, about being different." Age 43, sober six years.

17. **Pearl J.** 166
"Most of the time I was the only black kid in my class. . . . I'd tell myself that I wasn't going to drink, that today's the day I'm doing to go out and do all those things that need to get done and all the while I'm walking to the refrigerator looking for a cold beer." Age 64, sober eleven years.

18. **Jean C.** 183
"I was sober for thirteen years and then I went out, smoked a little dope, and got drunk again. I was in and out of the program for the next five years. I now have another twelve years of continuous sobriety. I learned a little bit this second time around." Age 60ish, sober twelve years.

19. **Rachel V.** 198
"Just as I thought I was 'controlling' my drinking better through running, meditating, and developing good health practices, my tolerance changed and I went downhill fast." Age 41, sober four years.

If You Think You Have a Problem 213
Resources and Books 215
The Twelve Steps and Twelve Traditions of AA 219
An Adaptation of the Twelve Steps and
Twelve Traditions of AA 223

Acknowledgments

I want to thank first of all my husband, who said to me from the beginning of this book, "Do it!"; my children who have not only borne with me through the writing of this particular volume but lived through it all; my family; the General Services of Alcoholics Anonymous staff in New York, who encouraged me from the beginning; and my editors at Harper & Row who from the start understood the needs and ideas herein: Hugh Van Dusen, Clayton Carlson, and Matt Chanoff.

I am grateful to the Hazelden Institute Staff, the Johnson Institute staff, Rutgers Center for Alcoholism Studies. All provided important material and helped direct my research into the area of women and alcoholism.

My typist Sherran went through the entire process of this book with me, inside and out. Her encouragement, comments, and support were invaluable as was the help of my assistant Theresa, who held the rest of my life together while I wrote this book. Cindy also deserves thanks for help with transcription. Naming the tasks performed hardly gives credit to the abiding friendships I have with these women.

Throughout the months of work my women's step study group, Julia, Karen, Dee, Jane, Liz, Loretta, and Patricia encouraged me, guided me, and gave me crucial feedback. My gratitude for our friendship grows. I could not have done this book without their help and support. My sponsor, Betty, provided guidance throughout the process of compiling this book. Margie provided an infusion of energy and help at *the* crucial moment. Mary Lou got me to talk when I was filled to bursting with all the stories I had taken in but not yet put into form. My gratitude to Emma for being the one who listened. This book would not have come into being had it not been for Ella's timely understanding and support. The list of whom I have to thank is endless. There are many more people, women and men alike, who were there for me along the way. To all, I am grateful.

To all the women who so generously shared their lives with the hope that someone might identify with their story, I am grateful. The spirit of the Twelfth Step pervaded everyone's sense and understanding of the need for this book. We need more women's stories. Twice as many women were interviewed as are included herein. Many have held my hand and walked me through the difficult moments. Friends read the stories, criticized, cheered. In the end I was grateful to have had some small part in bringing these stories out into the world. There are so many more that need to be told.

These stories are told anonymously, including my own, in keeping with the Eleventh Tradition of Alcoholics Anonymous: "We need always maintain personal anonymity at the level of press, radio, and films."

Any opinions stated herein are strictly mine or those of the person telling her story and are in no way to be taken as the opinion of Alcoholics Anonymous.

About This Book

I have gathered the stories I needed to hear in order to survive. I hope they will be of help to you as well. Some of you who pick up this book will be wondering about a member of your family whose behavior you can't understand, or a friend or a loved one's change in relationship to you. Some of you have picked up this book because you are wondering if you too have our disease. Some of you may already be in recovery yourself.

You may find a story here like your own, or at least with elements you can recognize. Many of us, in looking back, can see the warning signs of the presence of the disease. It is idle to speculate on how our lives might have been different had we recognized our symptoms earlier, but it might be different for you. We have all shared these stories for the express purpose of their being useful to someone. These stories were told to me anonymously, much like they're told every day and night in AA meetings across this country and around the world.

Fifty years ago, the women in this book would have been locked up in the back wards of institutions, in jails, in the gutter, or dead. We all have the disease of alcoholism, a chronic, progressive illness for which there is no cure. For many of us, the disease of alcoholism is compounded by addiction to other drugs as well. Alcohol is only one of the many drugs available in today's world.

Perhaps my forecast is too generous. As happens with many women, we might have met a worse fate: we could continue to be protected by our families, as well as by society, and some of us would still be drinking and using, caught in the living hell of "a physical allergy coupled with a mental obsession," one of the classic descriptions of alcoholism.

Alcoholics Anonymous (AA) was started fifty years ago, in 1935. Because of that singular event we are all in recovery today and can tell you, in a general way, the stories of our lives before and after we faced our common problem.

Alcoholics Anonymous is a fellowship of men and women who share their experience, strength, and hope with each other that they may solve their common problem and help others to recover from alcoholism.

The only requirement for membership is a desire to stop drinking. There are no dues or fees for AA membership; we are self-supporting through our own contributions. AA is not allied with any sect, denomination, politics, organization or institution; does not wish to engage in any controversy; neither endorses nor opposes any causes. Our primary purpose is to stay sober and help other alcoholics achieve sobriety.*

Of the hundreds of thousands of stories that might have been told in these pages, herein are the ones given to me to pass on to you. This book has been shaped rather than written, the stories witnessed, brought to life in their telling, *heard* into being. This volume is in no way intended to be definitive or all-inclusive. It is simply a beginning of the stream of women's stories as more and more women enter recovery.

If you are like I was, you might think that an alcoholic sleeps on the streets, wears a dirty trench coat and drinks cheap liquor out of brown paper bags in public. That certainly couldn't be a woman like me or a woman like you.

But today we have such an enormous public health problem with alcohol and drugs, we are finding out that the skid-row derelicts are only 5 percent of the alcoholics in this country. The other 95 percent of the alcoholics are wandering around in normal daily life, either gainfully employed or employable, with an estimated 10 percent of those being our business executives. France has the highest rate of alcoholism; the United States ranks only second. *Understanding Alcohol* by Jean Kinney

---

* © Permission to print courtesy of AA.

and Gwen Leaton is a good primer on all facets of alcohol, its use and abuse (see list of resources at the end of this book). Alcoholics Anonymous and the National Council on Alcoholism have brought some startling facts to light as well: it is estimated that 10 million people, out of the 100 million that consume alcohol, are alcoholics. That means one out of every ten. For every problem drinker or alcoholic, it is estimated that at least four more people are directly affected by the alcoholic's use be they family members, co-workers, or friends. This disease knows no bounds and is no respecter of age, young or old. A particularly disturbing statistic is the estimation that there are 3.3 million drinking teenagers between ages 14 and 17, already showing signs of a serious problem with alcohol. Half the fatal accidents on our highways are related to drunk driving. And 80 percent of accidental deaths by fire are related to the use of alcohol; as are 65 percent of the drownings, 70 percent of fatal falls, and 40 percent of fatal industrial accidents. "Studies have consistently shown that a minimum of 20 percent of all hospitalized persons have a significant alcohol problem whatever the presenting problem or admitting diagnosis is. The Veterans Administration estimates that 50 percent of all VA hospital beds are filled by veterans with alcohol problems," Kinney and Leaton tell us in *Understanding Alcohol*.

It is important to remember that these are all *estimated* figures. The chances are that they are on the low side. Alcoholism is a disease of denial and many problem drinkers do not profess to have the illness. Some researchers estimate that as many as one in every seven drinkers is an alcoholic, rather than every one in ten, the figure commonly accepted over recent years. Figures change as the stigma begins to drop away and we talk about this illness more openly. As with all taboos about which we are now beginning discussion, such as rape and incest, questions remain: Are they occurring more often? or are people simply reporting them more, breaking the silence that has surrounded them because the public climate is changing? Our understanding of the disease of alcoholism is in a tremendous state of flux and growth.

Women may be particularly interested in the information we have now about Fetal Alcohol Syndrome, caused by drinking during pregnancy. Of the three most common birth defects in this country, it is the only one that is preventable. Research is showing that the children of alcoholics run a much greater chance of becoming alcoholics themselves than do children of non-alcoholics. As more information comes to light on this disease and its widespread effects, the more important it is to share stories such as the ones in this book.

Storytelling of the kind that goes on in AA meetings is like a subversive activity. It restores value to a life that has been denied and suppressed; exiled dreams are reclaimed. These stories all tell of transformation and another kind of order to be found in life. Community is created between teller and listeners and is love restored. May you find that community of healing open up to you within the pages of this book.

This book accurately reflects my interviews with women recovering from alcoholism and addiction. However, except for one woman who asked that her real name be used, the names I have used in this account are not real names and individual characteristics and locales have been changed to protect the anonymity of those involved in accordance with the traditions of AA.

Introduction

Alcoholism is a chronic and progressive disease, one whose causes are multiple and only gradually becoming understood. The social stigma surrounding the disease, particularly for women, has only in the last fifteen years begun to dissipate in any significant way. Although the problems of alcoholism have been with us throughout history, not until the nineteenth century was it widely talked about as a disease. This understanding has been severely impeded by the social stigma surrounding the disease. Acknowledging alcoholism as a primary disease has come slowly to the medical community itself. By "a primary disease" is meant that alcoholism is itself the illness and is not a symptom of anything else, such as a symptom of a deep-rooted psychological problem or weak moral fabric. A chronic illness is one for which there is no cure, such as diabetes and some forms of arthritis, to give examples.

A turning point came in 1968, when Congress passed the Alcoholic Rehabilitation Act, which declared that alcoholism was a major public health problem and social issue. Out of subsequent legislation grew the National Institute on Alcohol Abuse and Alcoholism. The federal government had joined in the research being done on the disease. There is a great deal more to be learned; however, a few things have become clear. We know that social setting and custom determine exposure to alcohol as well as to the subsequent development of many alcohol problems. There is an environmental and cultural aspect to the disease. A search for the "alcoholic personality" or a particular underlying emotional illness that could lead to accurate predictions of who will or won't have trouble has drawn a blank. There is no such thing as a typical alcoholic personality prior to the onset of the disease. We at last have enough knowledge to be able to say with comfort and conviction that, yes, a tendency to develop alcoholism is truly inherited, not simply learned. That tendency exists quite apart from whether or not one is raised in a home where alcohol is present or is completely absent. It also exists, as shown in studies done on adopted twins, whether or not a person even knows anything about his or her parent's drinking history. A physical predisposition to the disease is present and passed on genetically.

One characteristic of alcoholism is that, though it is very much the same disease, it affects people differently. There is no such thing as Jewish alcoholism, black alcoholism, gay/lesbian alcoholism, and so forth. These are not different diseases, as some would claim. Yet we are just now beginning to understand the different ways in which the disease manifests itself in women and men. A woman's experience of the disease is markedly different from a man's, and the response of the world around her is very different as well. It is still much more unacceptable for a woman to be an alcoholic than a man. The stigma further delays recognition and treatment of the disease, meaning that often women have deteriorated much more than if the disease was recognized and treated early on. A woman who falls prey to the disease may seem to have forsaken her expected societal role of virtuous wife and mother. There is an almost universal assumption that the woman who drinks heavily must be promiscuous as well. That is one of the reasons why in certain Moslem countries a woman discovered to have been drinking could be killed on the spot by her male relatives. In ancient Rome, she could be starved or stoned to death.

Over the years there have been various theories as to why women become alcoholics. These include the "bird theories," such as the "empty nest" syndrome (the crisis precipitated when a woman's child rearing is done and she is left at home alone) and the "over-filled" nest syndrome (in which the woman is trapped in her child care role). Some have said that the modern woman is too liberated and try to explain the increasing incidence of alcoholism among women in terms of her attempts to manage in a "man's world." On and on the theories go—none of them able to explain why in spite of all the "reasons" some women become alcoholic in these situations and others do not.

One study found that women who work full time, and also have to fill the homemaker role as well, drink more than the single working woman. There is a real paradox faced by the woman who is a high achiever in our society. Her success may provoke fear and rejection of her role as a woman. She may have to give up her personal goals of achievement in order to be accepted as a woman. While this conflict can certainly add stress to a woman's life, again, it does not explain why some women become alcoholics and others do not under the same set of circumstances. For that we may have to look to the genetic and biochemical aspect of the disease for which one either has or doesn't have an inherited predisposition.

Most people start drinking for similar reasons; it's a common and acceptable thing to do in our society. It often makes us feel less shy and eases a variety of situations. The woman who uses alcohol to solve problems is the one who gets in trouble, not the one who is a heavy drinker. The plan is not to develop a serious life-threatening illness, to wreck lives, families, and careers, to drink against one's better judgment. Like other illnesses, alcoholism arrives unbidden and unwanted. It happens to people. As in other major and potentially fatal illnesses, denial is a part of the disease complex and creates odd complications in its own right. The prolonged denial allows the disease to progress much further and do much more damage than is necessary now that we know some of the telltale signs. Everyone gets enmeshed in the alcoholic denial system—family and friends as well as the alcoholics themselves. They all cover up, make excuses for, give other names to alcoholic behavior, and in doing so only aid in the inevitable and inexorable progression of the disease. Each of the stories in this book reveals warning signs that can be heeded, if they are recognized for what they are, symptoms of a disease.

For many years studies of alcoholism were done on men with the assumption that what was true for men was true for women also. In recent years these assumptions are increasingly questioned. There are some obvious differences. Men are larger than women; therefore when a man of 185 pounds matches a woman of 105 pounds drink for drink, she will be more drunk than he is because she will have a higher blood alcohol concentration than he does. This rule simply reflects size, not gender, but many a "scientist" has failed to allow for this fact.

Men and women also have a different distribution of fat and water in their bodies, so that women are indeed more affected by drinking than men. Women seem to be more vulnerable to the toxic effects of alcohol on the body, because the liver is more sensitive to alcohol in the presence of estrogen and thus more likely to be damaged than a man's. There is a "telescoping" effect of alcohol that has been noted in women. The disease tends to run its course more rapidly in women, so that the time from the onset of regular drinking until the development of serious problems with drinking occurs in a shorter or "telescoped" time span. In studying over four hundred men and women who are sober members of AA, I found that the median time interval between the onset of regular drinking and the time they were forced to stop drinking altogether was six years shorter for women than for men.

Another difference in the experiences of alcoholism in women is the phenomenon of "cross-addiction." Men can be and are cross-addicted as well, but it seems that there are more reports of this among women than men. Since most of the tranquilizers in this country are prescribed for women, it would not be surprising to have this problem. The terms *cross addiction*, *dual addiction*, and *polyaddiction* refer to multiple dependencies such as on alcohol and drugs whether prescribed by a doctor or procured on the streets. Cross addiction is a growing problem, particularly with young people.

We still lack a lot of simple, basic information. We know that both men and women are drinking and using drugs at an earlier age. It is now more socially acceptable for women to drink. Women can go to bars without a male escort and not necessarily have it assumed that they are there to pick up men. Some people claim that there are as many alcoholic women in the United States now as there are men. While initially women were rare in meetings of Alcoholics Anonymous, recent surveys showed that one out of every three newcomers is a woman. More women and younger women are beginning recovery in AA. It has been suggested that the mode of inheritance is at least partially through a sex-linked genetic pattern, but attempts to prove this hypothesis not yet convincing. Absolute numbers? No one can be certain. There appear to be at least one alcoholic woman for every two alcoholic men.

We are now in a position to understand that drinking is one of the three most common causes of birth defects in this country and the only one that is preventable. This information is tremendously important news that every woman today needs to be aware of. Fetal alcohol damage is so common that it affects one in every two hundred live births in the United States. For American Indian women, the figure is one out of fifty live births. Damage can range from mild mental retardation to severe physical deformation as well. The full effect of fetal alcohol syndrome (FAS) is relatively rare and primarily affects the children of very heavy drinkers. There is increasing evidence that heavy drinking on the part of the male can result in damaged sperm and probably in an abnormal fetus as well, yet women are the ones who must carry the possibly alcohol-damaged fetus to term or make the difficult decision not to do so. A knowledgeable physician can say with certainty that there is no known safe amount of drinking for a woman who is pregnant or who is trying to conceive. This is recent knowledge, and far too many women were and still are uninformed. They will live with the tragic consequences.

We know now, too, that alcohol appears in the milk of the

nursing mother and is retained there well after she has stopped drinking and the levels in the blood have fallen. We do not yet know what effect this retention has on the newborn child.

On the one hand, talk about efforts to prevent a disease like alcoholism from occurring altogether rapidly leads to the admission that we don't know how to prevent it. Certainly education alone is not prevention, although it is important and useful: facts and figures are hardly enough. On the other hand, secondary prevention is entirely possible. It is no longer necessary, if in fact it ever was, to stand by, wringing one's hands and waiting for the alcoholic to "bottom out" spontaneously, in order to have recovery become an acceptable course. Too often that "bottom" can mean death itself in an accident, suicide, or an alcohol-related illness. Alcohol is a toxin, a poison that acts as a depressant on the central nervous system and that damages every organ system. And this is to say nothing of the damage to one's loved ones, one's work. These realms are damaged beyond measure.

Recovery from alcoholism can begin by attending AA meetings or by entering a treatment program specifically designed to treat chemical dependency.

Traditionally most treatment services have been designed by and for men. Most diagnostic tests and questionnaires used to screen for alcoholism were standardized by men. They may work for women as well, but they have rarely been tested to see if they do. Opinions that women alcoholics are "sicker" and harder to treat than men still abound, although there is little evidence to bear this out or refute it.

Despite some of the difficulties this overview implies, women respond well to treatment, particularly when thought and attention are given to their need for services such as child care and to the importance of the presence of other women as attractive role models of successful recovery. Treatment groups made up entirely of women are found to be particularly effective. This approach helps women avoid the trap of choosing self-censorship over open discussion of sensitive issues. It also eliminates the tendency many women have to take on the task of nurturing and caring for the men in the group rather than working on their own recovery.

Women in treatment often need to work on issues of sex roles, assertiveness, dependency on others, and social stigma in ways quite different than a man. More and more stories of having been the victim of incest, rape, sexual abuse as a child, and battering are surfacing in women's treatment. These topics are often impossible for the newly sober woman to begin to talk about with men present in a group.

More differences: It has been shown that women are more likely to have another alcoholic in the nuclear family than are men. A man's response to his wife's alcoholism and a wife to her husband's alcoholism are quite different, in cases where both parties are not alcoholic. Men are more reluctant to seek or accept outside help for a wife's drinking problem or to attend a family self-help group such as Al-Anon or a treatment program. They tend to try to control the situation themselves and, when that fails, they see divorce as the only solution.

The reverse is true of women. For a variety of reasons, some economic as well as emotional, the wife tends to stay with the alcoholic husband, seeking help and trying to cope with the impossible situation. Much more research and study is needed to answer the questions now being raised about the family system.

Some of the most important work of the last decade has been in developing an understanding of alcoholism as a family illness. Although it may only be one person who has the actual physical dependency on alcohol and/or other drugs, it takes a whole system for that person to continue drinking and using. The non-alcoholic is *unwittingly* involved in enabling the alcoholic to continue to drink. Family members, in response to the unpredictable behavior of the alcoholic as the disease progresses, develop their own means of coping with the stress of living with an alcoholic. This coping is necessary in order to survive. But in doing so, and without realizing it, they themselves develop a very unhealthy system of coping. A small example would be excusing, as "the flu", someone's absence from work because of a hangover. They end up participating in the denial system of the alcoholic. The family develops unspoken rules, such as no one being allowed to talk about feelings. A family member who breaks out of the alcoholic family system through participation in a program such a Al-Anon or Alateen has often precipitated an alcoholic's recovery because the family system that supported the disease is no longer intact.

One of the most successful ways of motivating people into treatment has been through employee assistance programs (EAP) at the workplace. An important part of the denial system is the belief that there is no serious problem because the individual thinks he or she is still able to function on the job. Hearing from a colleague or employer that this is not the case makes a deep impression. When a worker is told that the job performance is not satisfactory and that if it does not markedly improve termination is probable, the message can be strong and clear. If this confrontation is linked to accurate diagnosis of the disease, a sensible treatment plan, and adequate monitoring to ensure against or deal with relapse after treatment, the outcome can be excellent. Some of the better programs claim recovery of over 80 percent. More and more companies realize that such programs are in their best interest.

Although these programs have been in existence for over three decades, most have paid little attention to the needs of women. Those industries and unions that deal primarily with male employees were the first to offer EAP. Physicians, for instance, have impaired physician committees in every state, while the nursing profession still offers less than a dozen. Airline pilots had their own program through ALPA, their union, while flight attendants did not until over five years later. When an EAP serves a mixed population and is theoretically available equally to men and women, even after allowing for the total numbers in the workforce and assuming only half as many women as men to be alcoholic, women are still much less likely to be referred for alcoholism treatment and hence less likely to have this opportunity to find recovery. Explanations for this difference have varied. Some reasons are obvious. Women in office work and in the whole "pink-collar ghetto" are less likely to be unionized in the first place. Traditionally, alcoholism has been thought about as a man's problem, and planning has been done on the basis of that assumption. Even when a female employee is in obvious trouble, the problem is more likely to be explained as "depression" than as alcoholism, a combination of ignorance, of old stereotypes, and sometimes misguided chivalry. Women also report that they are more likely to substitute tranquilizers and sedatives for alcohol during work hours than are men, so are somewhat less likely to be observed as drinking. More subtle may be the notion that work is less important for women who tend to marry, bear children, and drop out anyway. The woman may represent a smaller investment on the part of an employer. Less may have been spent on her training. If for a variety of causes she is taken less seriously as an employee or is seen as of less value than are men, it follows that less effort is made to treat and salvage her. It may seem easier just to fire her and be rid of the problem. When she is fired, she is said to be less likely to fight back or to hire an attorney. This response is then explained as due to fewer financial resources, a greater sense of guilt and stigma, and/or to women's tendency to be less self-assertive in general.

Another route into treatment for many men has been a collision with the law enforcement system. In recent years, this has increased through the programs designed to address the drunken driver problem. It is common now to find at least some primitive screening for alcoholism after arrest. There is usually some sorting into groups of people who require warning plus driver education and others who are alcoholic and need treatment as well. Again, more often it is the man who is arrested, convicted, and perhaps treated. Women are less likely to be arrested or jailed than are men in general, and usually make up a fairly small percentage of the people in these programs. Again, the explanations vary. If man and woman share a car, he is likely to be the driver. He is more likely to own a car. Even if she is alone and is stopped by the police, she is less likely to be booked. A recent study in New York showed that those women who were charged with drunk driving usually had been in serious accidents and that evidently the more minor episodes were being ignored. Too often the police escort a "lady" home or let her off with a verbal warning. Although jails do not cure alcoholism any more than does mandatory sentencing, the failure to act firmly with the woman who is driving drunk works against her and can deprive her of this route to treatment.

A third most common way into recovery is through the personal concern of friends, family, and professionals such as physicians and clergy. Again, people may fail to think of and acknowledge alcoholism in a woman. The doctor is reluctant to speak words that feel more like an accusation than diagnosis. A husband is perhaps more reluctant to seek help than is a wife. Too often he conceals, protects, and attempts to control the situation by himself until it is totally out of hand. Home remedies are rapidly abandoned when they fail to manage other illnesses, but the persistent notion that alcoholism is a result of stress, or is due to some inherent weakness rather than being a legitimate disease, continues to delay treatment.

In these pages you will meet a variety of alcoholic women, enough to demonstrate the futility of easy explanations. You will find a variety of ages, of ethnic groups, of social and economic backgrounds. All are different, but the fabric of their lives shows common threads. They show pain and puzzlement, despair and hope. Finally they meet AA and begin recovery. And they reunite with the community of other women and find self-acceptance and new dignity.

LeClair Bissell, M.D.

1. Elizabeth B.

I come from a family of alcoholics. My grandfather and father were alcoholics as well as a variety of other relatives. I maintain that I was born an alcoholic. In any case I am told that I was given my first alcohol at 3 weeks of age, because I had colic. Daddy was a doctor and prescribed a teaspoon of bourbon in four ounces of water. I was given it regularly as an infant. I grew up in a small town in the Midwest where both my father and grandfather were doctors. We were a prominent family, if you can be prominent in a town of 4,000. Both men were respected citizens, pillars of the community, highly credentialed in their professions, looked up to and active in civic and charitable affairs. They both absolutely terrorized the family. It was a sort of Jekyll and Hyde situation.

There was a lot of physical and emotional abuse in our home. Most importantly, I never knew what to expect. Sometimes my father was loving, witty, wise and full of praise; other times he would be a monster and get physically abusive. I went through what almost every child of an alcoholic goes through. There were secrets in our family, and we were constantly admonished that some things were never to be talked about. What went on at home stayed at home.

Though Jewish, we were not raised that way. Being raised Jewish was hard to do in a small midwestern town. My father was scornful of any religion.

When I was very young, I was terribly happy. I was bright, precocious. I did everything early and was reading by the age of 2. At 3, I recited long passages from memory and performed for friends. I adored my mother. She was beautiful, loving, and extremely intelligent.

One evening when I was 5, my parents were getting ready

to go out. I had been told that I had to stay at home and promptly threw a tantrum typical of a 5-year-old. I was furious with my mother, hit her, and told her that I hated her and that I wished she would die. My father took a firm hand and told her not to indulge me and they walked out the door. My mother never came back. They were in a car accident and my mother was killed. My father had been drinking. He was crippled for the rest of his life.

As a child I believed that my wishing her dead had caused this. I lived with terrible guilt. My grandparents moved in to our home to help raise us. I became obsessed with my father and terrified to let him out of my sight. When he left the house I would often run into his closet and hold onto his clothes and cry. I no longer felt safe. I felt on the outside of everything. There was a hole inside. His drinking continued to progress over the years, and by the time I was an adolescent he was beating me. Then there would be a lot of remorse. Apparently I looked just like my mother. People showed me pictures to prove it. It must have been very difficult for him. Still, there was a lot of love and caring in our family. It was very confusing, because the caring and the affection was somehow all mixed up with the hitting.

My father remarried when I was 12. I thought everything would be fine. I wanted a mother so much—she even had the name I had always wanted. We would be a family again. But it just wasn't that way. I had been my father's surrogate spouse for years. I had traveled to New York with him when I was 9 and 10 years old and took care of him when he was drunk. We would go to the Algonquin Bar and he would tell the bartender, "This is my daughter. She is with me, so make sure that when I'm ready to leave she's in the cab too." He would tell me to remember the hotel we were in, the room number, and he'd give me the key. I was around adults all the time and used to having a very important part in my dad's life. He shared his secrets with me. I was part of his life rather than of my peers. My stepmother walked into a very difficult situation. I was impossible for her.

At the same time of their marriage I hit adolescence. Between the two events, I found myself consumed with rage. I still carried around both the rage from my mother's death and the fantasy that my anger was so powerful that it could kill people so I'd better not let it out. I became a really vicious teenager. I lied, cheated, seduced the basketball coach and got him fired and run out of town on a rail. Good grades were no effort. I was a behavioral problem with my mouth. Inside I was scared and alienated.

I began to drink in high school, always to excess. I had a tremendous capacity for liquor, but I knew from the first time I drank that there was something different about how it affected me. I knew that I had to control it. I could see that my reaction to it was different from other people's. I had three times the capacity of any of the boys. I could drink the football players under the table, be stone-cold sober, and drive everyone home. I only drank on those occasions when I wanted to do something indulgent. I used it as an excuse for my behavior which I could then dismiss because "I was drunk." Having seen the disease in my own family, I knew enough to have figured out that somehow families passed on drinking and that I would have to be careful. I was never going to be an alcoholic, it would never happen to me.

Having a new mother didn't fix things, so then I decided that my problem was the small town we lived in. I was destined for better things. I was really educated at home, with lots of reading, lecturing, and quizzing at the dinner table. I did well on the college entrance exams and was accepted at the most prominent of the Ivy League women's colleges. But that didn't fix me. I was terribly unhappy. Other girls had been groomed in fine preparatory schools. I had to compete. Grades were hard to get, so I transferred back to the state university where I could make straight A's with little effort. And there were men.

My father dropped dead about this time. He was 42 years old. How he had functioned that long I'll never know. I saw him get up in the middle of the night when he'd been drinking and perform emergency surgery. He was never sued for mal-practice, he never killed anyone. The town knew and tolerated it. A policeman brought him home one night when he had found him passed out on the ground next to his car in the hospital parking lot. Now he was dead, a heart attack. My world came to an end.

The night before the funeral, my grandmother lined the children in the family up and told us, "Now there are going to be people here tomorrow from all over the state. There will be straight backs and dry eyes. Do you understand?" That was the way our family operated. I was devastated and for the first time I knew that feeling that other people have described as "nothing." There was no grief, no pain, just deadness. I was 19. That lack of feeling went on for months. I knew that I was in serious trouble and that something would have to change quickly or that I would die or go insane. So I got married.

It seemed perfectly logical to find someone else to replace the loss of my father. When I look back, I can see that it was doomed. I searched out the man I wanted, found him in a space of three months, nailed him down, and we were married three months after that. On paper it was a very good match.

We married and left the Midwest. He went to law school and drank occasionally, sometimes getting drunk. By this time I knew that alcohol was bad for me and his drinking frightened me to death. I was not drinking at this time and had become firm that alcohol was bad in our family. So I focused on con-trolling him and his drinking. I had big expectations of this marriage, that he would do well and accept work with a ven-erable law firm on graduation. Unfortunately I had not checked this out with him. Once he graduated I discovered that I was married to a radical lawyer who let his hair grow long and rode a motorcycle. We were both miserable. He kept trying to leave, which was even more terrifying. So I decided to have a baby—that would take care of everything. It did help momen-tarily, but he started running around, disappearing for days at a time not long after she was born. I hid this from everyone. I was ashamed.

When my daughter was only a few months old, doctors discovered that I had active tuberculosis. I wound up in a TB center in the Southwest, the youngest woman in the place and the only one under 85 who spoke English. I was there for six months, with hardly anyone to communicate with, slowly going crazy. I tried to learn Spanish but I was under a lot of medication, one of which was a drug that gave me hallucinations and to which I reacted violently. Between my mental state and the medication, my attempts to connect with anyone were fruitless. But they said I had to have this particular kind of medicine, and they started me over with a dosage to desensitize me and build up my tolerance to it. It also worked as an antidepressant. I was still not drinking at this point.

I arrived home six months later to a husband who did not want to see me and a baby who hardly knew me. I continued on the medication. I was told that I could not take it and drink, so I was careful not to. Within one month my doctor at home decided to take me off the medication and my husband walked out on me. I began drinking immediately. I had no money and a small child I didn't know how to take care of, and within a few months I was drinking alcoholically. I found a job, and would come home at night exhausted and drink myself to sleep.

Within a year I was taking off time from work to drink, telling myself all the while that I needed it to sleep, that I was an insomniac and that if I didn't sleep I would get sick again—and who would take care of the baby? I had to drink, because I used alcohol medicinally. It was a central nervous system depressant and that's what I wanted. I can honestly say that I never took a drink in my life for refreshment, conviviality, or making myself more comfortable in a social setting. I took it as a drug and I knew what it was.

I limped along this way, supporting myself and my child. People who say that alcoholics have no willpower have no idea how much willpower it takes to maintain a miserable life like that. After a year and a half, what was going to fix me forever happened. Prince Charming rode into my life. He was good-looking and funny. Bright, powerful and wealthy as well; he had a huge family that was just like mine with everyone yelling, screaming, and kissing each other. I describe their attitude toward things as this: "If it moves, kiss it, if it stands still, eat it." This marriage was going to solve all my problems.

He had children from a previous marriage who lived with him. I was going to be Florence Henderson with the Brady Bunch, just like on the TV show. We got married. I had hot and cold running servants, I was on all the right charitable boards. He's president of a major multinational corporation. I had arrived. I set out to be the Renaissance woman I always knew I could be. I was room mother for the seventh grade, I gave bar mitzvahs for eight hundred people. I never missed a carpool or a board of directors' meeting, I never went face down in my enchiladas or tripped at the country club. And I never took a drink in front of anyone else.

I drank only in private by this time, usually in the middle of the day, only in my room. I would get all my errands and meetings out of the way before noon, because at noon I would lock myself in my room, turn off the phone, and tell the maid to say that I wasn't there. Then I'd pour a tumbler full (that's a large iced tea glass) of vodka from a bottle in my closet, and lie down with a good book until I could go to sleep or pass out. Having set an alarm to wake my up, I would be passed out for a couple of hours, wake up with the alarm, eat some sugar to get my blood sugar up in an attempt to sober up, and then go drive the carpool. I'd come back for dinner with the family, have social engagements in the evening, wait until my husband was asleep to sneak out of bed, go back to the closet and pour myself another tumbler full of vodka to drink.

I would not drink when we went out for the evening because I knew from the past that I couldn't control it. So it looked as though I didn't drink. People thought I was a teetotaler. But my husband knew that something was wrong with me. My behavior began to get more and more erratic, and I couldn't control my rages and reactions to things. Yet he didn't see me drinking, and he was very preoccupied with his own concerns with business and was gone a lot. I think the children and the maid knew, but he didn't.

I began to make the rounds of doctors and therapists. I decided that I was drinking because I was depressed, therefore I should take antidepressants. That didn't stop me, but I discovered that they were good for the shakes from my hangovers. I tried tranquilizers. It was no use. I never told anyone about my drinking, though, just about my terrible family problems. We also talked about all the symptoms of alcoholism—disturbed sleep patterns, free-floating anxiety, and so forth. But nobody ever saw through the denial, recognized the symptoms and the pattern.

Every morning in the shower I would promise myself that I would stop drinking. One morning I was sitting in front of my makeup mirror shaking, not having had anything to drink. I had been shaking since 4 A.M. I did not want to drink. When my husband would get up to jog in the morning, I would pour a shooter because by this point I couldn't walk without alcohol and was drinking through the day to stay "normal." Sometimes I would throw up two to three times before I could keep it down. But here I was in front of the mirror shaking, and I knew I would have to have a drink even to make the morning coffee. What kind of horrible degenerate has to drink at five in the morning? And I flashed back to when I was sixteen and my stepmother was taking my father out of town so that he could dry out. I had gotten up early that morning to say goodbye, and he had to have a drink to get over the shakes before he could say goodbye. I relived that scene as I looked into the mirror. I knew that I had become my father.

My husband's company has an Employee Assistance program for their own personnel who may have drug or alcohol problems. I called the man who ran it and told him what was happening to me. He came right over and told me that I had to go to Alcoholics Anonymous. But I said that I couldn't because my husband would find out and leave me.

He gave me the Big Book of AA to read. I just knew I could do it all by myself. I didn't drink for a month, but I couldn't keep it up and I knew it. When I stopped drinking I also noticed that there was something terribly wrong at home. My husband was rarely there. I began drinking again, periodically. Ironically, my husband would inevitably show up or want to see me just at that point. He was furious. One day he called and asked me to come downtown and meet him for a movie. I had just started drinking the hour before. I couldn't drive drunk. I knew he would know if I showed up. I called his employee again with the assistance program and told him that I needed help. He moved quickly. He went to my husband's office, told him that I was an alcoholic and needed help. He called some other people, who came out to the house, picked me up and took me to the hospital and *bam*! I was in a treatment program. I was terrified. I got in touch with my feelings and nothing else. I came out of there a basket case and a festering sore that had just been opened up. I came home to children who would not speak to me and an irate husband. My recovery was not greeted with great rejoicing. My family had not taken part in the family week at the treatment center. I was a mess.

I knew that I had to go to AA to get well. I went to three meetings a day, all over town. People in AA were the only ones who would speak to me. Even my maid would have nothing to do with me. My husband was home less and less. He sent his children back to his ex-wife so that I could "concentrate" on getting well. My daughter went back to her father.

I was approaching my recovery just like I had lived my life. I did everything right on the surface, but it was a shell with nothing underneath it. I went to all those AA meetings, talked a lot, absorbed the concepts and sounded wonderful. I had a sponsor. Yet underneath I was on a very insidious path toward relapse. I only shared selectively. I never talked about what was going on inside. I didn't want anyone to know that my husband hated me; I was ashamed and embarrassed about that. I would tell one part of my story to my treatment-after-care group, another part to my sponsor, and talk about something else in meetings. I skipped around to meetings just like I had to liquor stores so that nobody knew what was really going on with me. There was no home group that I went to consistently, nobody that could put the whole story together, and no group that was totally involved in my recovery and me in theirs. I became more and more terrified.

I came home from a meeting one afternoon and found a note from my husband saying that he had left me, at least for the time. Every trace of his existence in our house was gone. He must have had a moving crew in the minute I left that morning. After two weeks, I drank again.

People in the program saved me. The man who'd first given me the Big Book came to see me, called me a spoiled brat, and put me on a plane to a treatment center in Minnesota. That was six months after I had first gone into treatment. The second time through a program like that is no day at the beach. My counselors at the two centers talked long distance and really had my number. I had intellectualized myself right into a relapse. I began being forced to open up this garbage can with all my horrible little secrets in it.

The turning point came when I was sent to talk to a little nun who ran a grief therapy group. I told her my story and she said, "You certainly have made a lot of unfortunate choices." I thought that was very rude, particularly for a nun to say. I replied, "I've always had my shit together, it's just always been too heavy to pick up." And she said, "Whatever made you think you had to carry it?" I asked her, "Who else is there?" "My dear, that is your problem," she told me. And she was right. I thought I could recover by myself. I began to make a turnaround and really started working the steps of the program. I took the fourth and fifth steps just like the Big Book tells us to do. Then a miracle occurred. My husband showed up for family week after telling everyone that there was no way he'd come. When he arrived, he announced that he wasn't staying. The second day he was irate because they'd put him in the group therapy. The third day he wanted to talk about feelings, and the fourth day he broke down and cried and said that he didn't realize how sick he'd been as a co-alcoholic. He was in Al-Anon. I couldn't believe it.

When I got out of treatment a few weeks later, things were still rough, despite the progress. I came back to an empty house. My husband still lived in a apartment by himself. But I looked around. I was alive, functioning, and sober. I had a chance. Treatment helped me recover my ability to give and to love. The compulsion to drink did not return.

The one person I thought I needed for my survival had left. Although still married, we were separated. He had become involved in an affair that he was having a hard time breaking away from, though he kept saying he wanted to. That's when I learned to pray. My sponsor kept telling me that I had an unhealthy addiction to my husband, that—like many women—I had made him my higher power, and I was going to have to break my addiction to that relationship if I was going to stay sober.

We got a family therapist who knows about drugs and alcohol and who refuses to serve as the primary therapist for alcoholism. The only thing he's seen work is Alcoholics Anonymous or a similar twelve-step program, and he won't see people unless they are also going to A.A. He was a great help. We saw him for six months, and it was just like my sponsor told me, I would have the relationship with my husband that I'd always wanted once I didn't need him. The day came when he didn't "have" to be there for me to be OK. I was not excited or encouraged when he was affectionate, and I was not frightened when he wasn't there. All of a sudden, things began to change. I began to get well in the program. I stopped getting my self-worth through my husband. I learned to say no to people.

My husband came back home. The children came back. I had to learn to do things differently. He no longer goes to

Al-Anon. The children are not in any recovery program like Ala-teen. But I had to want to get well whether they did or not, so I just went right on ahead with my own recovery. There's been a tremendous amount of improvement.

I've learned to wear life loosely. I was always so intense, everything was such a big deal. I thought suffering was something you had to bear. I learned that life included pain, but that I have a choice about whether or not I'm going to suffer. My spiritual experiences have been of the educational variety, just a growing awareness that I am not alone now. There is a quiet awakening going on. No rushes or highs of spiritual experiences, and I'm grateful for that. I'm tired of the high sick excitement. That was such a big thing for me. I could wrap myself up and get motivated for three weeks on one remark. The highs of internalized anger are just like the same rush I got from six ounces of vodka before the depressive part of the drug set in. Today I'm ready to give that up.

I used to consider myself a high-bottom drunk because I was never drunk in public. No one knew. I would stay in bed for four days with "the flu" and drink around the clock, wet the bed, burn cigarette holes in things, just like those men under the bridge. No one saw, except my maid, who stopped speaking to me. Like Job, that which I feared most came upon me. AA gave me the tools for living, and today I can walk through whatever happens.

2. Susan R.

I'm 17 and have been sober almost two and one half years. My parents are not alcoholic, though my grandparents and some of my uncles were. But it was very well covered up, you would have never guessed. I was born on the East Coast, and moved when I was going into the fifth grade. By that time everybody was well established in their cliques and I didn't fit in.

I was always hyperactive. When I was in third grade, I would come home crying from school every day. The teachers would tell me and my parents that I had problems. They said I couldn't get along with my peers. I got bored real easily in school, too. So there I was in a new school, not fitting in anywhere. My solution, from the third grade on, was to get real snobby and say "I don't want to spend time with you anyway."

When I was eleven, we went away to the South to visit my grandparents. They had a summer home on an island off the coast of Georgia. That's the first time I remember drinking. All of us kids would be down at the beach, and everybody down there drank and a lot of them did drugs, so alcohol was OK. It was no big thing, I didn't get drunk or anything. I came back home that fall and started the seventh grade. I'd finally made a few friends.

Although I was more comfortable socially, for some reason I thought I was really terrible. That was always in the back of my mind. But seventh grade was normal. From the first time I started school up through seventh grade, I always made straight A's. My parents thought I had become the perfect daughter. I went to church four days a week. I was in the choir and had a lot of practices to go to. I rode horses, probably three times a week. And made straight A's. I was your ideal child.

I went back to the beach again next summer and just quadrupled my drinking. I drank a little during the seventh grade but not much. Now things were different. I stayed with the choir because I wanted to go on the ski trip. I began to drink screwdrivers. Orange juice was good for you and you couldn't smell the vodka. They would never guess that a 12-year-old was drinking at choir practice. I took a lot of booze from my parents. I always looked a lot older than I was. I could pass for 18 when I was 13. I had this wonderful rapport with older guys. It was real easy for me to get booze. Things were also a little looser then.

I think that part of the reason I drank so early was that I was bored stiff in school. It was so easy for me. Straight A's, and I never studied. I'm no brain—I just work fast and I'm compulsive. The other reason is that I'm an alcoholic. The way my drinking took off that second summer might have told me something about how alcohol affected my system, but what did I know?—I was 12 going on 13 years old.

My parents were very plastic at that time. We had moved because my dad had gotten a big promotion. Mother got these fancy charge accounts at Saks and all, and got all involved in the Junior League and all the "right" things. So I'd come home and here was this plastic family. Nobody talked about anything. Everybody had their role worked out, and I stayed busy with mine, trying to keep up the front of being the "perfect daughter."

My boyfriend in the eighth grade was a real druggie, did acid all the time. He was so freaked out on acid all the time that I got scared to death of drugs. Now he says he's a controlled drinker and drug user. Wonder how long he'll last. Anyway I broke up with him, and the summer before my freshman year in high school I hooked up with a guy who was 28 years old, a part-time golf pro at the local country club. I told him I was 18 but I was 13. I'd tell my mom that my girlfriend and I were going over to the club to play tennis and go for a swim and to pick me up at 10 P.M. Actually, I was going over to this guy's apartment and fooling around and drinking. I wasn't having sex yet, but I was getting close. I got away with all kinds of stuff real early. My mom never suspected a thing, or if she did she never let on. School was just out and I had done well that year, despite the drinking that I had started. I had held down a job after school to pay for boarding my horse. I was still riding and going to church on Sunday morning.

When I got dropped off at church, though, I'd go in the kitchen and call my boyfriend. He'd get me and we'd go drink, and then he'd take me back and Mom would come get me from church. This was a different boyfriend now, but it was OK because he drank a lot. My parents left me at the church so that they could go to a Sunday school class on parenting. That's how it was, going into high school.

Then I got a boyfriend who had the worst reputation in school. He was what we called a "shit-kicker." They wore boots, drank beer, and carried a shotgun. They were very protective of girls. Shit-kickers didn't like people who smoked pot. My boyfriend wouldn't let me smoke pot. You could only smoke cigarettes, drink beer, or Black Label Jack Daniels. There were also other groups, the socials, freaks, jocks, and nerds, but I liked the shit-kickers. It was a very small select group.

I was still working after school, my grades were A's and B's. The first exams I ever took in high school, I was so drunk I don't remember. I just remember sitting down to a biology exam thinking, "How am I going to get through this one?" I got a B, and I don't even remember taking it. That's the way I did a lot of things. You had three exams during the day and an hour break. We'd ride around in my boyfriend's big black truck and drink in between it all. I sat up front with him. In back we had about fifteen people, all drinking too.

One night I was out with my boyfriend, and we jumped a curb or something and got pulled over by a cop. That was the first time I went to jail. My boyfriend was 18, still a sophomore in high school. It was a lot worse for him. My parents came down and got me, and my grandmother—I hadn't even known she was in town. I had told my parents that I was spending the night at a girlfriend's. I started running away from home not long after that.

A friend of mine got a new car. We were sitting around drinking and decided we'd go to Wyoming. That was a Sunday night. We didn't get back till Thursday. We almost got killed. We never stopped driving. It was me and two guys, and we all fell asleep, and we woke up and there's a telephone pole coming at the car. The speedometer's at 120. Out in the middle of nowhere, nothing to see but telephone poles. That was the first time it occurred to me that, Hey, I might have a real problem. Something was wrong. We ended up in Kansas City. We got pulled over by the cops in the middle of the night, and we made up some story about how we were all cousins and we were going home and had just had car problems. Up until I pulled that little stunt, my parents had thought I was doing OK. I had been making my grades and working. I was still riding horses, too. But after that, the trouble began to break out in the open. For the next three months or so, I just kept skipping school, getting drunk, and running away from home. My parents went through hell. They had been married for over fifteen years and they had never talked.

Things started to get bad. I was 14. We started going to family counselors, we talked to the minister at the church, and I just walked all over them in about three visits. They couldn't deal with me. No one could believe or even imagine that I might have a drinking problem. I was too young to be an alcoholic. They kept thinking it was psychological. None of these people knew anything about alcoholism and addictions, much less in somebody my age. By then I was even getting my horse drunk and riding him drunk. I had a friend who had a farm in the country, and I'd run away out there some-times: we'd have parties in the middle of nowhere, and I'd just sleep it off in his truck. He left me alone.

Finally I stopped making up stories to cover myself. I got

really arrogant. They'd say that I was grounded, and I'd just flip them the finger and say that I was going out for a few beers. They put up with that for a couple of months. I was planning to go to Mexico with this guy at school who drove a Porsche and dealt cocaine. My boyfriend found out about that and flipped out. We were over at some friend's talking about it, and my mom called. She said we've made an appointment with your psychiatrist, and we'd like for you to come. My boyfriend said, "Go ahead." She gave me some story about why we had to meet at the doctor's office at the hospital. It never clicked until I got in there and they closed the door. I had just been committed.

I didn't really get introduced to AA there. It was some totally different program, nothing like AA. It was run like a real business. It was hardly anything like AA. Nobody stayed sober that I knew of that went in there. I was in an adolescent treatment unit. Finally I ran away after a month, told my parents I was going crazy. They talked me into going back. They ran a lot of tests on me, said that I was a schizophrenic, severely depressed, and that I should be hospitalized for two to three years. We had a big conference with my parents. They were really torn up about it. We all knew I was an alcoholic by this time, but these folks had some different way of dealing with it. My parents brought in a nutritionist that said she was going to cure my alcoholism with vitamins. I had liver damage from all the drinking, my body was shot to hell. I had only been drinking for two years. This lady had me on television. I was supposed to be the guinea pig for this new experiment. She was really sweet. I took a lot of vitamins and nothing changed. Finally I told my parents I had to get out of that program. They let me come home.

I changed schools and went to a small "druggie-drop-out school," I call it. One teacher to every eight kids. Cigarette breaks. It was in a house. We had off-campus lunch so my mother would come every day and take me to lunch. I was not allowed to eat with anyone else. But every forty-five minutes on our cigarette breaks we'd drink beer and smoke pot. I used a lot of breath freshener there. This went on for about three weeks. There was a big party coming up. I said, "Mom, there's a big party for a friend of mine tonight. I've been really good and haven't had a drink in three weeks," lying through my teeth. She relented. She said, "OK, you can go." She said I could drink. We all thought it was a matter of "control." I was to be home by midnight.

The last thing I remember clearly was playing a game of quarters. My drinking had progressed to the point where I was drinking a lot, but I'd never get that drunk feeling—and then my body wouldn't move. Somebody threw me in the swimming pool, and I didn't move, no response, couldn't swim. Finally somebody came in after me.

From what I've been told they tried to talk to me, five guys, all good friends, tried to tell me I was getting into too much trouble and I was going to get them in trouble. They knew what time I had to be home, so they deposited me on my doorstep and left. I couldn't remember anything. I had on somebody else's clothes. My parents must have put me to bed. I woke up late the next afternoon, and there was throw-up everywhere. It was a mess. I had a hangover all of the sudden, and I never got hangovers before. That was a kind of bottom for me. I had been taking diet pills the last couple of months there too.

They put me back into treatment, a different program this time. Still not an AA program; this one was psychiatric-based, but if you wanted to go to AA they would take you there. This program was out in the middle of nowhere, in the woods, literally. I lived in a tent in the woods for the next eleven months. I was still in a lot of denial about my problem. We had therapy, but I also had to sit and think a lot, out there in the woods. They said I had to start going to AA for after-care once I got out. They got me ready for AA, as I look back on it now. I might have had another four years of drinking if I hadn't had time to sit and think like that. When you're that young and you've got so many people around you doing just what you're doing, drinking and doing drugs, you're not aware that for you the use is different. Most teenagers don't get pulled out of their environment like that and get a chance to get some perspective, think about things a lot. I think that has something to do with why a lot of people, especially teenagers, drink a lot—it's so "normal." I had one more drunk after that. I had two beers, which totally wasted me. Slept in a park that night. All that time to think, the change in the way alcohol affected me, I knew I couldn't drink anymore. When I finally got back home, I just started coming to AA meetings and it just felt right. I could relate to every single person there. Fortunately there were a lot of young people there, 20 years old or so. I don't know how I would have made it that first year if they hadn't been there. I'd go to school, come home, and go up to the club for a meeting. I basically lived there. People got used to me being around and got over my age because I had only just turned 15. That was a big jump.

Recently there have been more and more people age 15 to 16 coming up to the club. When I came in, the closest person to my age was 19. When you're as young as I was and caught up in alcohol and so stubborn, that's the way you identify yourself. It takes you a while to get to really be friends with the older folks in the program, but you do.

There's a big taboo about kids being alcoholics and addicts. People want to think you have to be a certain age to be an alcoholic or drug addict. They don't want to talk about kids needing to go to AA. They talk about children who have "emotional" problems. They don't want to call them "alcoholics." I tell you, I got to the point with my drinking where I really couldn't get drunk, just like those winos under the bridge you hear about.

Things have just fallen into place in my life since I came to AA. Feels like I'm talking about somebody totally different. That doesn't mean I never get depressed anymore, it's just now I have the tools to live life with. That's what the program is all about. It's not about not drinking. It's about living and how to do it sober, one day at a time.

I've gotten superinvolved in the AA young people's stuff. I went to an international convention in Chicago that had two thousand young people there. There were some 12-year-olds running around with more years of sobriety than me. Some people say that it's not regular AA to have a young people's meeting, but I don't think so. We had fourteen young people's meetings that weekend. I think we need young people's conferences like that, dances, things that younger people can relate to more. If a young person walked into a typical AA meeting, they might have a hard time if there's nobody under 30 or 35. At least in the beginning that's real important. It's not as important now that I've been coming around a while, but I still have to work with young people. That's what keeps me sober. I'm a special interest group. I have gone to more schools to talk to kids than I can remember. I've done volunteer work at the hospital, I've taught some drug education classes for parents and kids. The kids have to go to these classes if they get into trouble at school. It's just different from working with older people. It's like if you were the only woman in a group of men and it was your first few AA meetings, you'd have a hard time thinking it was for you. When people first come in, they're looking for a reason to tell themselves that they don't have to be here, that they're not really an alcoholic. This is a disease of denial. It's a disease that tells me I don't have a disease.

When I first came in, I got tons of praise for getting clean and sober at my age. It was a big deal, and after a while it wears off and you're not so special any more, and you gotta grow up. Sometimes it's like leading a double life when you're as young as I am. I went to a high school party not long ago, and what do you do but check out all those beer cans and stuff. It felt really strange to be there. It's like I'm still a kid in high school, but when I step out the door, I'm a grown-up.

Believe it or not, this saved my parent's marriage. Now we

all can really talk. They would have gotten divorced had we all stayed in that plastic world. My mom loves the Al-Anon program and has gotten real involved. My dad is in Families Anonymous, which is an extension for parents that grew out of treatment centers in Minnesota where they've done so much pioneering on alcoholism as a family disease. Life is real simple now. Sure they still want me to go to Harvard and become a doctor or a lawyer like a lot of parents, but they know I'm my own person and they accept me now.

3. Lulu F.

I was born in the South. There were five of us. I was the baby. My mother never drank, but my father did. I remember when I was real young my mother had taken us to church on Sunday morning. My daddy had been out drinking the night before. We came home and she put some rolls in the oven. I was out on the front porch playing, and she was sitting in the big porch swing, talking with some relatives, when I looked up and seen him coming at her with a broom. He broke that broom right over her because she'd burned the rolls. He used to beat her quite a bit, but that was the last time. She left. Next Tuesday we were all in school, all five of us and we got called in to the principal's office and told to go home immediately. We just flew out of there.

When we got home, Momma was there to get us. She hired a man and a truck to help get us and all our things and moved us off to a big city not too far away, where she'd found work and a place for us to live. The man who owned the cafe at the bus station where she was waitressing got real sick and she was able to buy the cafe from him.

We all had to work. I was the cashier. I must have been all of 8 years old. They would have to stack up those big wooden pop bottle cases so I could run the cash register. That's when I really started to learn how to manipulate men for money. I used to dance real good, and I had long, pretty red hair. It's my natural color, even though I'm black. The men would give me money to dance, and I'd just keep the jukebox going, and the more money you put in the jukebox, the more money was ours. My mother remarried and I did not get along with my stepfather. I was standing at the kitchen stove one morning when he walked in with an erection in his pajamas and said,

"If I did something, would you tell your Momma?" I said "I wouldn't have to tell her because when I get through pouring this boiling water on you she'd know all about it!" So he never touched me but he made me pay for that. He'd pick fights with me just so he could whip me. We'd fight like two men. Sometimes I'd be beat up so bad I couldn't go to school. He'd swear to my mother that I was lying and that that's how I came home from school. My brothers finally beat him up, and I moved out to a cousin's in another town altogether. I started to drink with my brothers when I was 10.

I was real bright, it turned out, so they sent me to a private school, a Catholic school. But I never wanted to be a good student. I just wanted to play hooky and drink. I was the basketball star, and I loved to play football. I'm a pretty big woman, always was. One of my street names was Big Lu. Well, here I was at this nice Catholic school, and I was always getting in trouble for stuff like teaching some girls how to shoot dice in the bathroom. Finally I got kicked out for drinking.

While I was going to this school, I was living with some other relatives. Moved in with them to go there when I was about 12 years old. My relatives let me drink and smoke. But occasionally I'd have to surrender to one of the men. That was the tradeoff. Incest. It always took alcohol to do that. But finally I got fed up with that situation and that kind of a tradeoff, and I left. Fell in love with a baseball player and got pregnant. I drank all through that pregnancy. I was so ignorant—about everything. Well, I lost that baby, and then I drank about that. I had started into labor and the baby started coming out on the elevator when the intern who was with me on the elevator pushed the head back in. I finally got up there and delivered. Later on that night they came in and told me that my baby died. He had lived about three hours and I never got to see him. I named him after my favorite saint. That's about the most painful thing I can share with you even today all these years later. I left town immediately after that, drinking and running with the ball players. Stayed in North Carolina a while, came back through the South, and ended up with a sister out on the West Coast. That's where I got into drugs.

I'm about 18 by this time. Got introduced to marijuana. Met a lady at the store. We just started talking, and then I started going over to her house and we'd smoke grass and drink. She was a married lady, and a lesbian. That was my first. It was through going down to visit her sister in the county jail that I met a couple of pimps and that's when the other stuff started. I started picking pockets. I got real good at it. I'd say I was a prostitute to pick up a man, then we'd start toward a room, and by the time we got there I'd have already picked his pocket and had some good excuse why I couldn't go in there. Because I had his money and then I didn't need to go through all that. It was much easer than going in a whorehouse. I started stealing out of stores too, minks and diamonds, all kinds of stuff. Had a new car every year. Went to Vegas a lot, traveled. Of course I was drinking all this time and smoking marijuana too. Sometimes you'd get too hot, and you'd have to leave town. The police knew what you were up to and who you were, so I'd have to cool off somewhere else. I got my first jail time from some checks I got from picking pockets. When I got out of jail, the guys I was running with were selling drugs. I started snorting cocaine with the pimps. They made it look real glamorous. But I wasn't so interested in that. I really needed to drink. I couldn't be without alcohol by this time. I always kept a bottle in the glove compartment and a flask in my purse. I remember a girl that nobody wanted to bother with. They called her Boozie. She was a good pickpocket. I liked her because she drank just like I did. We would just drink and fight. She was my kind of girl.

I got involved with a dealer who was on a run bringing back some cocaine and heroin from Mexico. We got busted. I got off and he had to do time. They brought me back to the town where I'd been living because there were three bench warrants out on me for picking pockets. I had to stay in jail a while more. When I got into court, the judge said that I was a menace to society and the only way he'd let me out of jail was if I left the state entirely. So I did. That's when I moved on and really began to get into heroin.

No more pimps. I was too slick for them. I had a Chinaman now. I was his mistress. That didn't last too long. A girlfriend introduced me to her man, and we went off and got married. He was a heroin dealer. Every husband I've had, and that's four, has been an alcoholic-addict. I knew from what I saw with my daddy that that was bad, but that's always who I ended up with. Funny thing was, they never wanted me to drink or use drugs. Here's this guy cutting up heroin, snorting it all the time, and he doesn't want me to use. I'm still drinking, and I start sneaking the heroin. Finally he let me start snorting it. Three days later he locked me up in that apartment, and when he came back I had torn the place apart looking for more. This stuff was real pure, came from the Orient. He was a merchant seaman so he could get it. I was really hooked. Alcohol wasn't enough any more. Then I started selling it with him. We got busted, so we left town.

At this point I hadn't started shooting yet, I was just snorting. That's how we could tell ourselves that we weren't bad, that we weren't dope fiends. I still couldn't go anywhere without a drink. By this time we've been all over the country, and we're in Colorado. I told my husband that I was going to the store to get some groceries and that's really what I meant to do. But I had to walk past a bar on the way, so I thought I'd have just one drink, then I'd get the groceries. I hadn't picked pockets in years, but there's a guy in there who buys me a drink, and when he opens his wallet and I see all the money he has I end up picking his pocket, getting caught by the police and taken to jail. That pattern just continued and got worse. Got out of jail, went to Frontier Day in Cheyenne, Wyoming. Everybody was just getting drunk and having a time. Now I was picking pockets in blackouts. I went into a bar, and the next time I looked I had five wallets and I didn't even remember picking them. I went into the bathroom and looked, and four of them were sheriffs. They were going to this bar after duty and getting drunk with the girls. The next morning my husband and I are sitting down to eat breakfast when the sheriff drove up. They were real nice about it, and they just sat in the car and waited till we finished breakfast, and then I went to jail. After that we went up north. I started shooting heroin. Still smoking marijuana and drinking and using cocaine. More blackouts, busted again. This time I got sent to out of state because there was no federal prison for women there. I got out with good behavior after a few months. I never got in any trouble there. I shot drugs, sold drugs while I was in prison. We made hooch and drank. I smoked grass. The police brought us drugs. I played softball and helped coach the team. That was the first time I ever went to an AA meeting or started hearing about Alcoholics Anonymous was there in prison. But I'd go in there to laugh at their drunk stories and eat donuts. I'd hang around and drink coffee, but I didn't get it.

Then something happened. When I had been arrested for smuggling years before and was in jail waiting for trial, there was a lady that they put in the tank with us who got busted for drunk driving. She was real drunk, and everybody laughed at her and didn't want to bother with her. She woke up with the shakes and I could see myself in her, but I couldn't admit that to myself or anyone else at the time. She was an older woman, a professional woman, and I took care of her. Here it is now years later and I'm in prison again, and I'm walking into one of the AA meetings and I saw that lady come in. That got my attention. That was the first time I went to a meeting and listened. I was scared to death. She was in Alcoholics Anonymous, and she was bringing the program into the prison. I sat down and really listened, and a seed got planted. We hugged. I was so glad to see her. I was so glad for her that she was sober, because God knows she needed it. I was still denying how much I needed it too.

When I got out of prison, it was going to be different this

time. The insanity of this disease! I swore I'd never do any drugs again. It was that man's fault, wasn't it? If I just stayed away from him and drugs I'd be OK. It was the drugs that made me so crazy, not the alcohol. I tried to go back South, but even my home state wouldn't accept my parole, so I went back north. Despite all intentions, in less than a week's time I'd sold everything I could for drugs. I did not want to go back out on the streets. I knew something bad was happening. I talked to my parole officer but he couldn't really help me get a job. I couldn't tell him about the drugs but I asked him to please help me get work. There was no halfway house. I was real frustrated. They always told us in prison that if we would just get a job, get you a family, and get married then everything will be all right. But they didn't tell you about how you're going to feel or why I had to have alcohol to get up in the morning. It was everybody's fault but mine what was happening. I just couldn't see it, and no job was going to help what was wrong with me.

No job, addicted to everything, and so my husband and I are dealing again. Another dealer calls us up, wanting drugs to sell that we won't front him. He gets mad and threatens us, tells us to be ready, he's out for us. Everything's getting real crazy. We're walking down the street one night, and he walks up to us with one hand behind his back. We thought he had a gun. I pulled a pistol out of my boot and handed it to Merril—and he killed him, shot him. Threw the gun in the ocean. We didn't know he didn't have anything until he fell. In the street they call it "selling wolf tickets," bluffing like that. We got arrested and beat the case.

I met a guy in the military, dumped my husband, and left town with him to get married in his home state in the Midwest. I got out of jail, went straight to the airport as the judge had ordered, and was drunk by the time I arrived. When I got there I discovered that his mother was an alcoholic too and that was all I needed. I really want to make this marriage work. I am sick of my life. He wants me to stay home and be a wife, and I'm trying, and I'm going nuts. My parole officer was a former captain in the service and we drank together. He gave me some leads and I got a job in a chicken factory; but between my asthma and my drinking I couldn't keep a job. I'd keep a bottle in the car and was out there every break. My drinking was a lot worse now because I was trying to be good and wasn't doing any drugs. It was drugs that were the problem. If I just stayed off the drugs, I'd tell myself, I could just drink a little and it would be OK. I'd drink, and I'd go for a loaf of bread at the store and might not come home for two or three days. My husband was a nice guy, but he was alcoholic too.

Finally I met the dope lady at the bootleg house one day and started snorting again. This kept me away from home a lot. He swore I had another man, and one day when we were in the car he was drunk and mad and decided he was going kill us both. He wrecked the car, but it didn't kill us. Broke both my jaws, cut my throat, broke my leg. I just laid there. I had a spoon of dope in my bra. I managed to put it in my purse, wouldn't throw away any dope. The woman I got the dope from came to the hospital when I first got there. I told her the heroin was in my purse, and she got it out and fed it to me. Even with all the medication they gave me when the doctor got there I never passed out, that's how bad my tolerance was.

I end up going home to Mother to get well. I'm just getting worse but I don't know how to let loose of all this. So it's one year later, and I'm sitting at a red light, me and some girls that had been out stealing and drinking and drugging all day, when a truck comes up from behind and totals the car. I had just started to walk from the year before when this happened. Next day I'm hurting and I call my mother and ask for help for the first time. She said, "I'll take you to my neighbor. This man used to go outside naked and fall down all the time and he went somewhere for two to three months and he came back OK, and he's been all right ever since." I said, "You don't understand, that's not what I'm talking about. I have this physical problem from this accident. I don't know why you're talking about this neighbor." I know that neighbor had gone to treatment and is now in AA. I got referred to a doctor who examined me, and I finally said, "I think I have another problem. Alcohol and drugs." He knew all about it and arranged for me to go into a women's halfway house after I got out of the hospital, where I'd ended up again. We called AA, and somebody came down to the hospital to see me. That's when I really got the message.

AA people are the only people in the world that had come to me for anything, and they gave me something and I didn't have to do anything. Just be me. I really used to act up. My mouth was real bad, foul. I only knew the way of the streets, and that's the only way I knew how to express myself. They tolerated me at any and all levels. They brought AA to the hospital, and they took me to meetings when I got out. That's the first time I remember saying a prayer since I was a child except when I was drunk. People made me feel like I belonged, no matter what I had done.

There was a speaker at the first meeting I went to out of the hospital that I could identify with. I started hearing about feelings. I didn't know anything about feelings, I had drowned them with alcohol and drugs so long ago I didn't know I had any anymore. I didn't know anything about resentment. I didn't "resent" people, I just didn't like them. I didn't take the time to just "resent" you, you know. I did not know that anger motivated me to function all my life. And I didn't know that anger is a form of fear. I learned all this in this program. I didn't know what those knots were when I woke up in the morning—the ones that feel like donuts in your stomach they're so big. I didn't know that was fear. I didn't know that I was always scared of what was going to happen that day and by the time I got through with that day, something *had* happened. I sure didn't know that *I* was my problem. I thought it was everyone else. I didn't know that every single problem I had, I had in some way or another created. It's my attitude toward a particular situation that makes it a problem for me. I'm a crisis junkie, most alcoholics and addicts are. If I didn't have a crisis in my life, I'd go out and create one, then I'd be fine. I had you to blame for the way that I was feeling, then I could get drunk, get loaded, and it was somebody else's fault. I didn't know that I didn't have to worry about everything. Today the God of my understanding shows me that I don't have to worry, that all I have to do is get my ego out of the way, and that I'll be taken care of. Any problem I have, I don't care how upset I was with it, if I just let go of it long enough and ask God to take care of it for me and to help me, it always turns out better than anything I could have made of it.

When I came in to AA—eight years ago now—there were only two other black women coming to meetings. Now this is a big city. One of them was dropping pills, so I couldn't turn to her. The other one was too damn nice for me. She had over twelve years in the program, but I couldn't relate to her, our experiences were so different. She was middle class. I came off the street. So here I am a black woman in this big old town, and the only people I got to identify with is the people they always told me were fucking me over all my life, and that's white people. Keeping me without nothing. Even when I go to meetings now, there often aren't black people unless I bring them with me. But it just doesn't bother me. I talk and share just the same because AA works no matter what the color of your skin. I was never taught to be prejudiced. But when you're looking for an excuse not to change, the first excuse the black person has is "I can't identify with or relate to those white people." I heard Betty Ford talk one time, and we felt exactly the same way; she just had more money to spend than I did. Thank God I didn't have it or I would have been dead. That's just an excuse, saying, "I can't identify, I can't relate, this is a white folk's program." I took a young woman into a meeting with me and she said, "Oh, but look at all those white people!" And I said to her, "Where did you see a sign that says, 'No Niggers' are supposed to be here?

Did anybody ever tell you that in AA?'' After the meeting she couldn't get over how nice everybody was and how many white friends I had that had come up and hugged me, wanted to know how I am. I can't tell you how good I have been made to feel in the program of Alcoholics Anonymous.

I went to an AA convention not too long after I came in the program. I was sitting in the hotel lobby talking to a lady from that town, telling her that AA was different in her town, that back at my home people were really friendly. She asked me how many people I had gone up to and introduced myself to, and she was right on. I wasn't reaching out to anybody. I thought because I was one of the six blacks out of six hundred people that they were supposed to make me special and come up to me.

I've learned how to have friendships with men in this program, that means without sex being involved, just as people. You know, it made me feel real good to understand that I have a disease and that it took being a drunk and a dope fiend to take advantage of people and do the things I did because I can't do that sober. I have changed so much through working this program that it's almost like talking about another person to tell all this.

My way of staying sober is continuing to work with drunks and addicts. I started a residential treatment program. That business about sharing and giving away was imbedded in me. People and God have given me so much that I have to keep giving it away. That's the way to keep sobriety, give it away. So I just went out and got a building and some drunks and started working with them. I've always wanted to give to people; we all do, I just never knew how before, too busy doing myself in. All I've got is me and my experience, strength, and hope, and that's enough today. God loves me just like he loves you, and he has forgiven me for what I did. It's today that counts.

Today we don't turn anybody away here. We're getting involved with kids. We've taken the parolees, all sorts of folks that nobody else knew how to handle, but I do. The elderly alcoholic woman. Nobody wants her. But we take them. If we don't have room, we make room. I didn't have anywhere to go when I got out as a parolee and I haven't forgotten where I come from. The elderly woman has nowhere to go either. Nobody wants to mess with you when you get old. Regardless of why they end up here, the bottom line is almost all of them had some kind of alcohol problem or they're hooked on pills. We see so many now of the elderly hooked on pills. Pain medication. It's more loneliness, sometimes, than anything.

I hope I never go back out again and drink or use, because I don't think I'd make it back. I'd wind up dead. God has been so good to me. Everything that I need as a human being to be happy has been given to me through this program, just like people told me, if I would just be patient. I'm happily married, I have a child. One day at a time. I just got an big award for outstanding community service, can you believe that!

4. Gail R.

I was born with a platinum spoon in my mouth. And though I was thoroughly convinced that I was extraordinary and different, I never felt that I belonged. I am a twin, 48 years old. My sister Maggie and I are the youngest of the several children in our family. I'm from the Midwest.

The feeling of not belonging was so strong in me that as a child I used to think that I was adopted and that only my twin sister was part of the family. I was terribly afraid of my father. It was the kind of household where children were really a display item. We would be brought downstairs by our nurse to say "Good evening" to our parents' dinner guests and then after whatever number of minutes it was that my father thought was enough, he would clap his hands and we would be removed.

My parents didn't compare my sister and me particularly, but we compared ourselves. I always felt that I didn't measure up. I spent most of my life wanting to be my twin, Maggie.

When I was 16 years old, I got pregnant by a very nice young man. I was so frightened that I couldn't tell my parents, and finally the doctor told them. They were shattered. People like us didn't have things like that happen to them. My mother had lost several babies before she finally had us, so the thought that I was pregnant and would have to give up the baby for adoption undid my parents.

No one knew about this, not even my twin sister or my other brothers and sisters. It was simply announced that I was ill. They must have felt that in order to save me that they had to send me away. I was whisked away to Detroit, where I lived with a doctor's family. They were very good to me, and this doctor delivered the child. It was all terribly confusing, upsetting, and frightening. Suddenly I had a baby boy and then it was gone. There was never any question about keeping the child. The baby's father never even knew about the pregnancy. No one knew. The baby was given up for adoption. I went home for my junior and senior years of high school and tried to pick up where I had left off. My parents never discussed this experience with me. It was never talked about.

Having a baby haunted me all through my life, through my own marriage, having my own children, through everything. You don't "forget" something like that. The feeling that I did not fit, that I was not OK was engraved on me by that experience. I had now proved to myself that I was not acceptable. I went crazy in a kind of quiet way.

After that my relationships with other young men were very racy. I drank insanely from then on. I loved it from the beginning. Alcohol filled an enormous hole in me. I thought, "God, I have found the answer to all that pain!" I was looking for the wipeout.

I started into college back East, but again I felt that I could not fit in, and my parents let me quit. I joined my sister who was skiing in Europe. We came back, went to work, and shortly thereafter my father became ill and died.

After his death, someone decided that Mother needed to take a trip. Since my sister and I were the only two left at home, it was decided that we should accompany Mother on the grand tour, around the world.

I was 19, and in those days the big Pan Am jets had a first-class section with a bar downstairs. I walked down those stairs and saw a man at the bar with prematurely gray hair, a suntan you only get when you play golf every day, dressed in a white silk suit with a martini in his hand. He was an American businessman who lived in Ceylon, which is now Sri Lanka, who was twenty years my senior and thought I was just darling. He wooed me and pursued me and ended up asking my mother if he could marry me in Rome. She said no. So we eloped. I got my passport, left the hotel, and we took off for

Ceylon where we were married. Mother was left with my twin sister to finish the trip.

When Mother got back to the States, she made up an entire article that appeared in the society column of the paper about my "wedding in Rome." It said what my sister wore as my bridesmaid, what flowers we carried, everything. She made it all up. She was covering her tracks. She had no idea where I was.

Two years later I went back. By this time we had made up, and everything was fine. She said to me, "It's wonderful to see you, darling, and just remember that you got married in Rome and this is my bailiwick, so get your story straight."

Phillip, my husband, turned out to be an alcoholic. And I am sure as I look back, that I was alcoholic as well from the time I first started drinking. I always drank more than anybody else. All the children in our family turned out to be heavy drinkers. Though I don't recall my father drinking, I always heard stories about his drinking when he was younger. He seems to have just stopped. You know, some people are alcoholics waiting to happen. My mother didn't drink until my father died. But when my father died, somebody handed her a drink, "for her nerves," and within two weeks, she saw that she could use it to help take away the pain. I never saw her with a drink before his death, and I never saw her without one after that for the next twenty years. She was under a lot of emotional stress.

I came from a wealthy family, married into another wealthy family, and in Ceylon, where we lived for almost twenty years, it was very easy to have a grand lifestyle whether you had money or not. If you did, it was just that much grander. My husband and I had our own business in international trading. There was no one to answer to, no controls on us, nothing. Everyone we knew drank and partied all the time, just like us. We had a lovely family over the years. I had all the servants in the world, and I didn't have to do anything. I was my husband's business partner because I wanted to be.

Fortunately for the children, there was a lot of affection in our house and the children somehow understood that they were loved. But they really raised themselves. Oh, the servants were there to care for them, but they raised themselves. They never knew when they came home from school whether or not we'd be there, or whether or not one of or both of us would be drunk, or whether or not we had flown off to Hong Kong.

In those days in Ceylon you didn't have to have a prescription for Valium. We just keep a big bottle by the toothbrushes. Both Phillip and I would take them every morning because we'd have the shakes so badly. With my oldest children there was still some semblance of order to life, but by the time my youngest was born, we were both full-blown alcoholics.

In the AA Big Book it says that if you drink like I did, you either go insane or you die or you get sober. Those are your choices. I went through the mental hospital route.

It was easy for me to see my husband's alcoholism. I told him that if he didn't do something about his drinking that I was going to leave him. So off he went to a psychiatrist, who hospitalized him for his drinking. He had done just what I told him to do, and I couldn't stand it. I took a lot of pills, drank a fifth of vodka, and ended up in the adjoining suite in the hospital on the top floor. Within three years I was in the basement of that hospital, locked up in the psychiatric ward. Alcoholism is a progressive disease. It always gets worse, never better.

I was hospitalized several times over the years. I knew that drinking was my problem. I remember saying to one of the doctors, "I am an alcoholic," and his reply was, "Gail, you have such terrible family problems, if we just get those straightened out you won't have to drink so much." They gave me more and more medication to help me get off of liquor, tranquilizers, antidepressants, you name it. I would leave the hospital having been instructed not to drink and to take my medicine. I would do this for a few days, even weeks at a time, but eventually I would pick up a drink again, on top of all the medication. My husband was progressively getting worse with his own drinking and drug use. Twice he beat me up so badly that I had to be hospitalized. He was drunk. I tried to press charges, but since we were married and we were in our home when it happened, he was within his rights and I could do nothing. I was suicidal and utterly without hope. I had no idea what could be done for me. I thought I was hopeless. The periods between hospitalizations grew shorter. I tried to kill myself.

I remember standing in the bathroom in front of the mirror, really drunk, full of alcohol. I was standing there at the sink with a razor blade in my hand, cutting away at my wrists, when I saw a shape behind me in the mirror. I knew someone was watching me. I turned around and saw my youngest daughter standing there in the doorway. I will never forget the expression of horror on that child's face. In my mind's eye that was the worst moment of my drinking and the most hopeless moment of all.

I was taken to the hospital where they sewed up my wrists. They kept me in for observation. The next day I got a call saying that my oldest son was on his way to see me. He was about 16 at the time. He had been out of town when this happened. I was feeling a little better, got out of bed, combed my hair, put on a peignoir and climbed back in my bed, carefully crossing my wrists so that he couldn't see the bandages. I heard his footsteps coming down the hall. He walked up to the door of my room, banged it open against the wall and did not even step inside. He just stood at the doorway and yelled, "Oh, Mother, haven't you watched enough television to know how to do that yet? The next time, if you really want to kill yourself, you take the razor and start toward the back of the neck, going down, coming around the front. Be sure you're in a tub of hot water and then you'll bleed to death."

He turned around and stormed off down the hall. I burst into tears, "How could he say that to me?" I thought. I was terribly upset. When we talked about this many years later, he told me that he had run down the hall into the bathroom and thrown up and that he had cried all the way home.

I realized, looking back, that his treatment made an impression on me. Everybody else just said, "Oh, poor Gail, poor thing," which is what I had wanted him to do. But he refused to play in to my self-pity, and I never forgot that. I didn't stop drinking yet, but that was a crucial moment.

The psychiatric treatment of my problems continued with an even greater variety and heavier dose of drugs. As was the pattern, I would drink again at some point. It was a terrible downward spiral, and I knew it. I was terribly frightened and told the doctor that I had to go into the hospital and be withdrawn from the pills and alcohol together, not just the alcohol. I was there for two weeks to detoxify my system. Withdrawal from alcohol can be dangerous. Convulsions, even death, can follow if it's not done properly. When you've got drugs involved too it's more complicated medically.

I had not had alcohol in two weeks, no drugs for one week, and they thought I was fine and sent me home. I was there for a few days, not drinking, not taking anything and I remember walking into the living room—and that was it, I went unconcious. I was out for ten days. Apparently my body and mind were so severely dependent on the drugs and alcohol that the withdrawal in the hospital had not been long enough, and my brain and my body just short-circuited. I came to in the locked ward in the hospital. My motor reflexes had all been affected, my speech was slurred, I was staggering. It was not a stroke. The doctors said later that they didn't know if I would ever come out of it, or if I did, if there would be much of me left.

I was in the hospital for six weeks after that. I was so scared that it got me to Alcoholics Anonymous. My priest, my psychiatrist, my husband, my children, my friends, everybody thought I should go. Everything else had been done for me, and nothing worked.

The AA group there was tiny. I would go to meetings, not

drink, get a little better, and then start drinking again. Then I would crawl back to AA until I was better again. I would hide my drinking from my friends. I would go to parties and not drink, and everybody would tell me how wonderful I was. Then I would go home and drink a bottle of liquor by myself. I became very secretive and crazy. It was easy for me to see my husband's terrible drinking problem, and I kept thinking that if I just get away from him, then I'll be all right. *He's* got the drinking problem.

I scooped up the children and took them back to the States and went to my twin sister's home. Within five days I was locked up in the county medical detention ward. My sister had had me committed because she thought I had gone round the bend. I had come 10,000 miles, and all I had done was change nuthouses. I was the problem, but I could not see that. I kept bringing me with me and these terrible disaster areas of my life, because I was the disaster area. Everybody else in the cast of characters had changed, the locale, everything but me.

I went back to Ceylon and went to AA on my own this time. I left my husband for good at this juncture, and returned to the U.S. to stay wanting to get sober as much as I could at the time. I wanted to stop hurting so much and to stop having such terrible disasters. I moved to a city in the States where I had a friend who was willing to help me. By this time, I had burned out my family and friends. But my friend knew about AA and knew of a women's recovery house, and she helped me get into it. My children went back to Chicago to live with my mother, and I stayed in the recovery home about six months. I wanted to take care of my children, but I just couldn't handle them. They ended up living with my mother for almost a year and a half. That probably saved my life. I have heard about these incredible women who get sober and go straight home from the treatment center and pick up where they left off with their families and work doing it all. I couldn't begin.

I needed a lot of time to get sober away from the family that I had never truly been responsible for and away from the man who I had been married to and drank with all those years and away from that environment altogether in Manila.

One night I left the recovery house and went out on my last drunk. That was nine years ago to date. I was angry. I felt that I was not understood. I was feeling sorry for myself. It wasn't that I suddenly thought I wasn't alcoholic. I was just wallowing in self-pity. I holed up in a motel, got drunk, and in a lot of trouble. I got kicked out of the recovery house and ended up in a hospital detox unit and treatment program.

I had been in and out of AA for three years by the time I ended up in that hospital program. I kept fighting the program and the idea of surrender and the steps. I used to think that the whole idea of alcoholism being a disease was a cop-out. It was just a matter of willpower, and if I was going to get sober it would have to be me that did it. When people tried to talk to me about the steps, I thought of religion and the Catholic Church and I'd tell them, "I've been through all that. Don't talk to me about a God, don't talk to me about the Church." And they would try to say to me, "Gail, this is a spiritual program, not a religion," but I couldn't see the difference. I refused to accept what they said, and I wouldn't work the Twelve Steps, and that's quite simply why I couldn't or wouldn't stay sober.

Now I realize that we don't get sober by ourselves. We need each other and the program. Meetings are wonderful, but without working the steps we are in deep trouble.

What was different for me this time in the hospital was that I discovered that I really wanted to live. I hadn't felt that way in years. And if I was going to live, I knew in my mind that that meant sobriety, there couldn't be any half-measures. And if I was going to be sober, it would have to be Alcoholics Anonymous.

That insight was so wonderful, even with all the resistance, I knew exactly where to go, exactly what I had to do and for the first time in my life I asked for help. I was instantaneously relieved. I remember that feeling the moment I asked for help,

I just said, "God, I cannot do this alone, please help me." And even with all the fear and confusion, I felt peaceful and I knew that I was all right.

I went straight back to the recovery house after I got out of the hospital and talked to the woman who ran it. She had thirty years of sobriety at that time. I told her, "Mary, I really mean it, I want to be sober. I want to live and I want to try. And I know that I have a terrible track record and I don't know if I can do it."

"Tell me something, Gail," she said, "Do you believe in me?" And I told her, "Of course I do." And she said, "Then I'll tell you what: you believe in me and I'll believe in you until you start believing in yourself." Then she got up and came around from the table and hugged me and said, "Now we begin the first step."

"Oh, Mary, I've already done that one." I told her.

"Gail, if you had really taken the steps, especially the first one, you would not have had to go back out and drink again. Go to meetings, open your mind and your heart to this program and let the people who always loved you love you now and we will love you into sobriety."

And that is exactly what happened to me. It was marvelous. I remember a couple of weeks down the line after that something went wrong and I went to Mary and said, "I can't stand it, I have to drink!" And she said, "No you don't, Gail. You are a recovering alcoholic, and with that goes a tremendous responsibility. One of those responsibilities is to stand there and let it hurt."

After I had been sober a couple of years, I went back to Mary and told her, "I'm sure that you must wonder if anything you say stays with us after all the thousands of women that have gone through this house, with how insane and crazy we are when we get here. I can tell you that when I need to remember something, I still hear it in your voice, and I can feel you standing here with me."

There are people who say to me, "I have never known Mary,

but I feel like I know her through you." She told me that sobriety wasn't going to be easy, but that it was possible, yes, even for me.

I got a little apartment right across the street from the recovery house when it was time for me to leave there. Here I am a 40-year-old woman, and I had never been alone. I had never done anything on my own, and I was terrified. I thought that I could run the world—the far eastern division—because of the big company my husband and I had had and the important position I held in it. But I didn't do things that other people did. I couldn't type, I always had a staff. I came here thinking that with my experience in the international trade business that I would get a wonderful job instantly. Not only did I not get a wonderful job, I couldn't get *any* job. I went on an interview at one of these employment agencies, and the woman told me that I was going to have to get some marketable skills. "We have to be able to put something down on this application but you don't have any qualifications." That was very hard for someone like me who wanted to think that I was the Second Coming. There I was being told that I wasn't really able to do anything.

I went back to Mary and said, "They want me to take an accounting course and to learn how to type. I don't think I can do that." She said, "How much is the school going to cost?" I told her, "Nothing," and she said, "Don't you think you can afford to try?"

So after all these years I went back to school and did wonderfully. Came through accounting with close to a 100 average. It was great to learn that my brain still worked even though I didn't want to run out and become an accountant. I learned to type. I finally got a job, and I got fired. Then I got another job and I got fired, and I think back, "Thank God for AA." I had learned early on in the program when things were hard not to run around saying, "I'm fine, I'm just fine," but that I was to go to meetings and talk about how I really felt. That's what I did. I would go all the way across town on two buses just to sit in this meeting and cry. It was a little hole in the wall, a place we call "The Divine Dump," with people from all walks of life. But they all knew me, and I knew that it was a safe place to be.

I was confused about my children. My husband and I were in the process of going through with a divorce. He had gone completely off the deep end with his alcoholism and had become terribly ill. It was terribly hard. He's now back in the States in a nursing home. He's had over forty strokes, and both his legs have been amputated because the alcoholism accelerated his diabetes. Sometimes alcoholism kills people or like in Phillip's case, is just maims them, for the rest of their life. It was a terrible time. He was so sick. My youngest son said that he had said goodbye to his father in Ceylon and that now he went to visit a man who could be his great-grandfather. It was hard on everybody.

Two of my girls came back to live with me. They were in their mid-teens. I had been sober a year and a half, and I finally had a little tiny job, and we got a tiny place, and we were all going to live together and be able to talk, and it was going to work out wonderfully.

Well, they stayed about four months and then said that they wanted to leave. What a blow! I was cleaning houses because that was the job I could get.

Someone said to me, "How can *you* clean houses?" And I told them that I had lived in a fantasy world all my life and that I am somehow getting to look at the reality of my situation. "If that is the only job I can get, it's the job I have to do." I worked with another friend in the program, and we cleaned houses for $3.35 and hour. I hated it. I did a good job, though, and as I look back I know that that was important for me to do. You have to clean a lot of houses for $3.25 an hour to support a family. I had to apply for welfare as well. It was very hard to bring myself to do that, but I wanted my family. I thought I'd gotten it together now, and I should be a responsible mother, a good homemaker and productive worker.

The children were right. I wasn't ready to be a mother. It was all too much at once. I was still learning how to be sober, how to have some reality in my life. The girls went back to my mother's. Nine years later, I have a marvelous relationship with my children. I have a good relationship with my ex-husband. The children and I visit him in the nursing home. Just seeing him in his condition reminds me of what alcoholism does to people.

Now I have a job in a brokerage company. I went in there as the afternoon receptionist. I was terrified to even go for that interview. I had been wearing nothing but blue jeans and sneakers for a year and a half cleaning houses. I had gone from being so confident of who I was and what I was to thinking that I was not going to be able to do anything but clean houses for the rest of my life. That was four years ago. I just took the exam to qualify for a broker's license and passed. Now I'm a licensed broker.

Today I have a great life. It took every single one of those experiences to get to where I am today. It has taken me a long time to be able to say, "This is who you are" and let that be all right. It took years to build up the facade, and it's taken years to tear down those walls. I had all the money, property, and prestige you could want, and it's very easy to hide behind all that. When it's stripped away and you have to be who you are because you can't buy people off or buy your way into things or use your money to get you where you want to be, you just have to be yourself. And today that's who I want to be. I don't want to be anybody else any more.

I have more friends than ever and also a level of friendship that I never knew was possible, especially with women.

Mary told me, "You will get to know women, and you will learn to love them." And I thought, "Not me. I don't trust them." I was a "man's woman." I had never really felt close to women in my life, save one or two. I was the one who always got drunk with the boys, flirted with the husbands. I used to go to lunch with my husband and six to eight men.

We'd go to the bars where I was the only woman who shook dice. Most women didn't like me, and I loved the fact they didn't approve of me. But what Mary said has come true. That's what's happened. The friendships I've discovered with other women are profound. Part of learning to like and care for women was really part and parcel of learning to accept myself as a woman. I couldn't like other women as long as I didn't accept myself.

About that child I had when I was 16 years old; I found that I needed to go back and close that loop, put the past to rest as best I could. After eight years of sobriety I decided that I wanted to at least make an effort to find that young man and have him be able to identify us, my children and I, if he were looking for us. I didn't know where to begin, but I soon found an agency that helps people in these circumstances. I realized that I was going to go back and ask my mother for some of the facts I needed. She was 86, and I was 47. We had never talked about this episode to that day, over thirty-one years later. It was terribly hard for me to go back home and do this. Once I was finally able to bring it up, we talked the whole thing through. Thank God we had that talk. I had blocked so much from my own memory and by now the doctor were dead, the housekeeper, everyone else who could have remembered which hospital, the exact date, all the facts I needed was dead except for Mother. She told me how terrible it had been for her too, and we cried and held each other, after all these years.

When I sat my children down to tell them about this brother that they had, I thought I was giving up my deepest, darkest secret—but they already knew about it. I was dumbfounded. I had told them when I was drunk and not remembered. They didn't know how to handle it at the time, so they never brought it up themselves. But when I finally sat them down to tell them this they said, "Oh Mom, we knew that a long time ago!" They were so relieved that I could finally talk about it. Now it's not half a story, it's a whole story.

5. Shirley B.

I was born in Virginia and grew up all over the country. My parents moved twenty-one times in my first ten years. My father was an alcoholic and one of my uncles died of alcoholism. I started drinking when I was 17 and had left for college. If I had known then what I know now, I would have realized that when I had my first drink I was an alcoholic.

I had gone to a wedding. I was very shy, a wallflower, and had no idea how to be comfortable socially. Then I had some champagne. I remember that first drink of champagne going down. It was absolutely wonderful. Suddenly I was OK. I looked around for the best-looking man in the room, waltzed over, and said, "Hi, Honey, let's dance." He danced. I had discovered the secret to social success.

The next time I drank I had two drinks and blacked out. I went on with the rest of the evening, but I could not remember what happened. Now I'm aware that this is another sign of the disease of alcoholism, but then I did not know that. I was disturbed by this event, so I went to the school psychiatrist at the university and told him that I had had a couple of drinks and then had amnesia. He told me that I was very neurotic and would have to undergo treatment. This was in the early 1950s. So I began a course of psychotherapy and treatment that went on in various cities off and on for over ten years. This proved helpful with many things, but not with my drinking.

I wanted very much to become a lawyer. I went to law school at a time when a lot of women did not do that sort of thing. Fortunately I was a periodic drinker, not a daily drinker, so I could go throughout the week studying and working to put myself through law school and be fine. But on the weekends I would get drunk and behave like the alcoholic I was. I did well in law school, but I had a lot of trouble with my romantic relationships. Of course it never occurred to me that maybe my problem was alcohol, not the men.

I had latched on to a nice young medical student. He knew I drank too much, and so did I. I told him that I needed him to help me control my drinking. I said, "After two drinks, will you please cut off the booze?" He agreed. Not long thereafter we became engaged and went to a party together. After the two drinks he said, "No more." I then proceeded to go around to all his medical school colleagues and inform them that my fiance was too cheap to buy me a drink, and would they please buy me another one? They did.

He put up with that kind of behavior and I lost respect for him, fell out of love, and broke off the engagement. It never occurred to me that my own conduct was immoral; I thought it was all his fault.

After I came into Alcoholics Anonymous, I heard people talking about alcoholism as a physical, emotional, and spiritual disease, and it really turned me off. I had no use for a word like *spiritual* when I first got sober, and I certainly had no use for a concept like morality. I could not see that I had ever done anything immoral.

But when I look back on the things I was doing and the attitudes I held at this time in my early twenties, I have to now clearly label them as immoral.

I remember driving over to see friends at night and drinking with them. I was always afraid that in driving home I might hit somebody and kill them. What bothered me about this idea was that if I killed someone I might be found guilty of a crime involving moral turpitude. That would mean that I couldn't take the bar exam and practice law. That's what really disturbed me, the idea of not being able to take the bar exam, not the fact that I might kill somebody. Now, after over twenty-one years of sobriety, I see this as immoral though at the time it never occurred to me that there was anything wrong with such thinking.

I wanted to become an international lawyer, a dream which everyone considered very impractical, but I was a very determined young woman. When I finished law school, I got a grant to do graduate work at a top Eastern Ivy League school for an advanced degree. I was very fortunate in being there because there was also a center for the study of alcoholism there at the time. I had continued my course of psychiatric treatment, but the psychiatrists told me that I described myself as one would an alcoholic. I was not told, as were so many people, that my drinking problem could be cured through psychiatry or psychology. These doctors knew better.

I knew that alcohol was causing me tremendous problems by now, and I was honest with these psychiatrists. They told me that in their experience the only thing for an alcoholic to do was to stop drinking altogether. So I did. For a while. I even went to some AA meeting, but I quickly decided that it was not for me. I had absolutely no interest in any silly organization that talked about God. I was a militant agnostic.

So I finished up a degree and spent the next few years abroad. I went to Spain that winter. I studied art and literature, a wonderful relief after five years of studying law. I was fighting my alcoholism and trying not to drink. But it was cold that winter, and we had very little heat. I discovered Spanish sherry, which was very cheap and that seemed to solve the heat problem, at least for a moment. Then I would stop drinking, then I would start again. Back and forth, always aware of my drinking, even when I wasn't doing it. I was a true periodic, still not a daily drinker. Yet.

Then I went to Chile for more law school, on a Fulbright scholarship. They had marvelous good wine in Chile, very cheap. I thought there was something very elitist about drinking good wine, and I liked it. I would get up in the morning, have a little breakfast and then within a few hours the maid would prepare lunch. At this point I proceeded to indulge in my fondness for wine, daily. Then I would go to class in the afternoon and later meet my boyfriend for drinks and then take off for the evening parties. I was extremely bright, and somehow I got by with all this. I floated through that year.

The American Embassy sent me out on a lecture tour. I went to northern Chile, to a copper mine in the Atacama Desert. Here there was the largest open-pit copper mine in the world at that time. I gave my lectures and speeches in the afternoon, and of course they gave a cocktail party for me. My ego loved all this. There I was, all dressed up in a cocktail gown, being 'Lady Gracious.' And suddenly there is a blank. It's roughly 4 o'clock in the afternoon, and the next thing I know, my consciousness comes back and it's about 5 A.M. and I am out in the middle of the Atacama desert with the sun just coming up over the Andes. There is absolutely nothing and no one around me. No copper mine. Nothing. I'm still dressed for the cocktail party, complete with my high heels and elegant dress.

That desert is one of the most dramatic places in the world. It is so dry they say that it hasn't rained for a hundred years. There are not even flies or mosquitoes. To the east are the Andes Mountains, to the north, and south the desert is 600 miles long or about 70,000 square miles, to the west the Pacific Ocean. I am standing there lost, without the vaguest notion of how I got there. Obviously I had been at the cocktail party and just took off, something I tended to do when I got drunk. Fortunately I had lived around the desert at one point and had heard a lot of desert lore. I remembered being told that if you're ever lost in the desert, don't walk in a straight line, walk in a spiral. If there is anything there, you'll eventually find it. So began to do that. It was a little slow in my high heels. I did that for several hours, and eventually I came across some Chilean workers and I said, "Donde está la mina?" ("Where's the mine?") They must have thought *they* were drunk. Here they are out in the desert and here's this red-headed, white-faced woman in a cocktail dress and high heels asking for directions.

I like that story because somehow it's symbolic to me of where we all are when we are drinking as alcoholics. Alone. Talk about being alone—that was the most intense feeling I had during my alcoholism. I felt completely alone, no one understood me. And then there I was in that desert. I had managed to get myself physically out there—alone, lost, and deserted.

After that year in Chile, I went back to the East Coast for more graduate work. I was 25 years old, working on my doctoral degree, and the alcoholism was getting worse. My drinking was getting out of control altogether. I went into intensive therapy and was able to become a little more controlled with my drinking. Even though I finished at the top law school in the country people weren't eager to hire women law professors at that point in time, so I had some legitimate complaints about my situation. But everything was compounded by my alcoholic craziness. Finally I took a job in Washington, D.C., and managed to go one entire year without a drink. After that year, my psychiatrist pronounced me "cured." Two months later, I was drunk. I would go to my office in the State Department, work all day, not touch a drop, then come home at night, slam the door, and drink. I went back to the psychiatrist thinking that the only thing left for me to do was kill myself. He told me that he believed that we had worked through my neuroses and that all that he could suggest was Alcoholics Anonymous. I said no, I could not take their talk about God. But he was clever. He appealed to my intellectual snobbery and said, "Look, Shirley, they know an awful lot about alcohol. Why don't you just look at it as a research project and give it a go?" I went.

At that first meeting I went to in Washington, it turned out that the speaker was a man who had been sober ten years and was an agnostic. He said that it was possible, even if you don't believe in a God, for AA to work for you. I was flabbergasted. I went up to him after the meeting and said, "Is that really true?" He assured me it was, that he had been a ship's captain and had traveled all over the world. He'd also been an actor and a naval engineer. He had the right kind of personality for me to be able to identify with. He became a good friend and guided me through that early time in the program. I haven't had a drink since, over twenty-one years ago.

That was it, for me. I was home. I finally found people who understood me and a few of whom, just enough, didn't believe in a God. There weren't too many like that, but just enough that would tell me that the program could work even if you didn't believe in God. A lot of people tried to tell me that I couldn't get sober if I didn't believe in God, and that really scared me. Thank goodness Jack was there and told me otherwise.

So I began to get sober, and one of the joys of being sober is going ahead doing all the things you wanted to do in your life. Jack encouraged me to start going back to the symphony. "Go back to the symphony again. Isn't that what you used to love to do? Now you can hear the music. Go!" He was right. I went back to listening to music, back to the symphony halls. When I was drinking, I could hardly wait for intermission, but now I could really enjoy the music again.

My job with the State Department involved a fair amount of travel, which I enjoyed. But how was I going to stay sober while traveling overseas? I had to go to Egypt, so I talked with Jack and he told me that I should contact AA overseas, that it existed in many of the countries where I was going. But some of the countries didn't have AA, so he told me that I'd just have to find a drunk to work with. *Fine—where am I going to find a drunk in Cairo?* I thought.

A friend in the program gave me the name of a reporter to look up when I was in Cairo. I did. We began to date, and I soon discovered that he was a practicing alcoholic. There was my drunk to work with. He was a very nice person and being around him really helped keep me sober. I saw this very talented, valuable human being slowly destroyed himself, and it was very clear that I didn't want to be like that. I don't know if he ever got sober, but perhaps I planted a seed. I told him about AA. At least he had living proof that sobriety was possible.

I have been to AA meetings all over the world, Lebanon, Peru, Bolivia, even Turkey. It's incredibly inspiring to find AA in all these places. After a couple of years in the program I wanted very much to take a job in Rio de Janeiro. The only time I really came close to drinking again was over this job.

I had been trying for months to get this position in Rio. The State Department kept telling me that they couldn't send a woman there for this job because it involved investments and that Brazilians would not deal with a woman on so masculine a subject as that. But finally they could not find anyone with my qualifications who had the language and interests I had. They gave me the job. And that's when I wanted to take a drink, the day they told me I had the job. Fortunately, I had AA friends in the State Department whom I phoned immediately. We got together over coffee and talked the feelings out. One of these AA friends had been in the State Department for a long time. I asked him what to do about staying sober on an extended assignment like this. He said he'd had two experiences overseas. Once he stayed sober. Once he got drunk. The difference was whether or not he kept working the program. He told me that if there was no meeting where I went I simply had to start one.

The first night I arrived in Rio, I found an AA meeting. It was in Portuguese. They asked me if I spoke Portuguese or Spanish. I told them Spanish. They said, "Say a few words to us in Spanish and we will understand some of it." There was such warmth in their reaching out, though they had never seen me and I could not speak their language. I began to learn Portuguese.

My two years there taught me something incredible. Most of our AA groups here in the United States are fabulously wealthy compared to the rest of the world. Our groups in Brazil were so poor that we did not serve coffee at the meetings because our groups could not afford the donation that it would have taken to provide it. Remember, this is where the coffee's grown. Those of us who had American-style incomes donated the money to pay for the room where we held the meeting.

One meeting we had was on the twenty-first floor of a downtown office building. A mountain had fallen on the city's only power plant, and so there was no electricity for over four months! We had to walk up the twenty-one flights of stairs. The meeting got very small. At one point all of us who attended there regularly were out of town except for Bill. He was an older man, quite overweight, and not in very good physical condition. Getting up those twenty-one flights of stairs was quite an effort for him. But I found out that while we were all gone, he had walked up those twenty-one flights three times a week and sat in that room alone. I asked him why he did that, since he knew that we were all out of town. He said, "Somebody might have come up those stairs looking for an AA meeting, and I just had to be there in case that happened." I've never forgotten that. That's the kind of spirit and concern you find in AA.

An Anglo-Brazilian friend of mine had spent some time in the United States a few years before and had gotten sober. She was very much in the upper class. When she had returned to Brazil, she spent her own money going around to start AA. She went all over the country, going into hospitals saying, "Take me to your alcoholics." Everyone thought she was absolutely crazy, but by God, she got a lot of thriving AA meetings going in that country.

Some years ago I spent a year in Indonesia teaching. There was no AA member on the island of Java. The people there are very moderate. They are mostly Moslems and basically just don't drink. So I ended up corresponding with an American Catholic priest on another island who was in AA. Just through writing back and forth, I stayed sober. He certainly helped me, and I hope I helped him too.

Now AA is opening up so much everywhere! Now I'm teaching law here in the United States again, and I've got four women law students in my courses who are also in AA.

I have come to some sort of spiritual faith over these years, but it's very personal and my own business. I just think it's critical that people realize that they can get sober even if they're not a believer at the time. Anyone, male or female. The way AA gets talked about in this country sometimes, it might seem that you have to be a Christian. But that's not true either. Years ago they found out that AA flourished particularly well in Southeast Asia, which is a Buddhist culture. AA is not a religion. You don't have to believe in a particular God in my opinion. You just have to have the desire to stop drinking, and in time you will develop your own understanding and relationship to a power greater than yourself. If I can do it, anybody can.

It's also important that people who are new to sobriety, or are worried that they may have a problem, know that you can experience joy, release, and gaiety without alcohol and drugs. I used to say, "Yes, I know I have to stop drinking. I accept that. But if I do, I can never dance again." I love dancing. Sobriety sounded like a good but dull prospect.

My sponsor said, "Hold on, and someday you'll dance again." Eighteen months later I was dancing madly in the streets of Rio de Janeiro during Carnival, having the time of my life— sober. What a marvelous discovery that was! I've had more fun these past twenty-one years than I ever dreamed was possible. My street dancing has continued. Last spring I did a wild cha-cha-cha with a group of Cubans in the streets of Santiago de Cuba. Life is more exciting now because I can *feel* it.

6. Sister Rose

My name is Sister Rose, and I'm a recovering alcoholic. The first thing that anyone asks when they hear that I'm a sister is "How can a nun be an alcoholic?" And I always say, "Very easy." I am first and foremost a human being subject to all the diseases that people have, therefore I too can have the disease of alcoholism. I believe that I was born with it. I also know that if you are an alcoholic like I am, it is very easy to get alcohol when you need it no matter who you are.

I was born in a very small mining town in the West, into a very loving, caring Italian family. My mother and father were not and are not alcoholics. Wine was served at the table sometimes, though I did not drink as a child; it never interested me. We did not drink much as a family except when other people came over.

I entered a religious community right after high school at 17, and didn't drink there, of course, for a long time. As a young sister I became very ill on my first mission and kept getting thinner and more and more sickly. They didn't know what was wrong with me. The dear doctors thought that it might just be stress, tension, and overwork so they gave me a tranquilizer, Librium. They also gave me sleeping pills because I couldn't sleep. This is a long time ago now; I have been a sister for forty-five years and sober for over fifteen.

My difficulties continued until finally one doctor suggested to my mother superior that she give me wine each night before I went to bed, because that would surely help me sleep as well as build up my blood. At first when she gave it to me I poured it down the sink. I don't know why, but I suppose that deep down something inside me knew that it was not for me. But after a while I began to feel guilty. When you enter the convent, you take a vow of obedience, so not obeying my mother superior became a moral issue for me. I felt underhanded, and finally began to drink the wine each night. And what I found was that it worked. At last. It was a panacea for my pain. It was better than the drugs were, and I knew from then on that I had something that would help me. It didn't cure me from my illness, and I also didn't begin to drink in any quantity at that time, but I knew that relief was there. Over the years they finally discovered that I had a disease of the adrenal glands. They didn't produce enough adrenal, so if I became overtired I became very ill. This condition improved once they started the correct medication.

What I had learned was that when I got sick or things were not well for me emotionally or when I was under stress, I could take something to drink. There was always wine or some kind of beverage in our convent, kept in the closet for visitors, people who might get colds, or some special occasion. Of course, it was not served regularly. But I did know that it was there and I would use it as "necessary," "medicinally." I never drank, even when it was served on those rare occasions in the community, such as Christmas, I would save my glass and take it to bed because it helped me to sleep.

Over time I was given more and more responsibility, and the stresses increased. I became principal at a large school and the mother superior of a large house myself. The greater the stress, the more I would drink. Fifteen to twenty years had passed now, and I began to need it more. When I finally did really begin to drink alcoholically, it lasted a very short period of time. I went down the drain fast, within four years. I have heard that in women the disease can progress quite rapidly and that often women cannot drink for the number of years that men can without getting bad.

Not only did I begin to need my alcohol very badly and begin to look for it, but I pulled away from the community. I felt very strange. I tried to keep as far away as possible from the other sisters. I isolated myself. I had always been sickly, so they never thought anything about it. They would say, "Well, Sister Rose is sick, so she went to bed early" or "She was sick today so she didn't get up, you know she's never been very well." So I had a ready excuse for my behavior and they respected that. I used it all the time. I got worse and worse, and nobody ever said anything. No one had that kind of understanding of the disease or that kind of courage, I think. I was the superior. It would have been very difficult for anyone to confront me even though they may well have wondered what in the world was going on. No one ever asked, "Where has all the liquor in the cabinet gone?" In the 1960s, life in the convent changed and we were allowed to wear street clothes and remove our habit. Then I could go out and buy my own. I was always very careful to drive way to the other side of town to buy it and get what I needed, and now I needed alcohol more than anything.

Even up till the end of my drinking, I never drank until the evening. I would get up in the morning, be really hung over, and go through the day at school. God, was I miserable! But I had to do this in order that people not notice how bad I was. They had to have noticed, when I look back on that time, but no one said anything.

When I talk to anyone now who says they have a sister in their house that they think has a drinking problem, I always tell them, "If you have finally noticed it, it is already in full bloom." I believe that the sister who is drinking is already at a crisis point if someone is finally coming to me and asking if I think there is a problem. The denial of the disease can be astonishingly strong in the convent. A lot of sisters don't want to be involved and they don't have to be, unlike the family situation where often people are so tied to one another that you can hardly avoid being swept into the maelstrom. But in our situation in the convents, you are living with maybe twelve or fourteen other women or more; you can come and go without people noticing. If they do notice, they will rarely say anything, much less face you with a comment like, "Sister Rose, I think you drink too much." What an embarrassing thing to say to another nun!

My behavior continued to change. I became very irritable and quick-tempered, whereas I am usually a calm person by temperment. People excused this on the basis that I was "sick."

As we alcoholics often do, I decided that moving would solve my problem. We call them "geographics," a change in geographic location in order to solve our difficulties. I went to work at a school in my home town. A sister who was a very dear friend of mine was the principal, and she had a brother who was in Alcoholics Anonymous. She knew what was happening to me, she could see it. But before she said anything to me she contacted a priest that she knew who was in recovery himself. He was working with other priests. She went to some AA meetings on her own. She found a treatment center that would be suitable for me, and then she said, "Sister Rose, I think you have a drinking problem. I think you need help."

By this time I had been hoping and praying that someone would help me. The week before I had gone to teach my religious education class at a school nearby. I drove myself there and back, taught the class, and could not remember ever having done it. I was in a complete blackout. I heard later that it was a good lecture, but the fact that I had no recollection of it scared me to death. I knew that something was terribly wrong. I had evidently had something to drink that evening before dinner. I thought I had only had a little, but apparently I had had quite a lot. Or perhaps my tolerance had changed— that happens sometimes too, as the disease progresses. In any case I knew that I needed to do something with myself, and I didn't know what to do. I felt that I would die if something didn't change and I had no idea about how and where to begin. I was in a waking nightmare.

Over the years I had continued to always be in some doctor's care, that's for well over twenty years. I always had tranquilizers, and for the periods of time that I tried to control my drinking, even stop altogether for three months here and there, I would continue to take my tranquilizers.

You know, being intelligent and educated has nothing to do with knowing anything about alcoholism. I had gone back to school, gotten a master's degree, but still I knew nothing about alcoholism and could not recognize the withdrawal symptoms. I would feel ill, have to vomit, have terrible shakes. I could hardly hold a pencil in my hand. I didn't know what was happening to me, I just knew that it was bad. The tranquilizers would alleviate the withdrawal, balance it out. If I was especially shaky, I would just take an extra tranquilizers. I was terrified. Then the pressure would build up and I couldn't handle it, so I would drink, of course, thinking that I would only take a little bit, and then I never did, because that's the way it works. I could no longer control or predict when I would stop once I took the first drink.

So after that blackout, when my friend sat me down and told me that she thought I had a problem and needed help I just grabbed on to her and said, "Yes, I know that I do, and I know that I need help, and I don't know what to do." At that moment she called in the priest who was in recovery, and they sat me down and explained what they saw and asked if I would go into treatment immediately. I said yes. They made the arrangements, and I was on my way to a center in Minnesota.

When I went into treatment, there were no nuns on the staff of this particular place, like there are now, but there were priests, and they were very fine to me. The first thing they did was tell me that I needed to be a human being, first and foremost. They told me to get out of my nun's clothes that set me apart and start dressing and acting just like the other women there. They didn't say that in a nice way either. I found treatment very difficult initially. I thought that because I was a nun, I was much worse than other people there. I was in a religious order, I was supposed to be perfect. I was a very bad person. It was all right for the "normal" woman to be an alcoholic, but not me, a sister.

My counselors had to work very hard with me to get down off that pedestal. For a while I would say when I introduced myself in a meeting, "I'm Sister Rose, I'm chemically dependent." But for myself, I had to get to a point where I could look myself in the mirror and say, "You are a drunk." I had finally realized and begun to accept where I was. I had broken the pedestal on which I had kept myself so elevated above everyone else.

I realized that I had a disease, that I wasn't guilty, that I was probably born with the disease, that it became active when I took tranquilizers and alcohol, either or both, and that that's what had happened to me. It was a tremendous relief to finally discover that I wasn't a morally bad person who had no self-control. That was the biggest relief I had ever experienced in my life.

Another difficulty I had in treatment was with anger.

When I was a child, I was allowed to express a lot of feelings. Our family was very volatile. Very happy or very sad, we always knew who was happy and who was sad. Feelings were not hidden. That was the way we lived. But when I entered the convent, I thought I had to give up those emotions. I knew that anger was a sin. I would have to admit to a priest in the confessional that I had been angry, so I wasn't about to do that. I worked on it so that I could no longer feel my anger. I became a great hoarder of anger. People who would do things to me, I would just say, "That's OK," and it wasn't OK, and I never learned to say that it wasn't.

I was the kind of person that everybody came and talked to about their problems. If two sisters were having difficulties with each other, they would come to me and I would try to help them both. Often they would walk out of the room fine, but I would be stuck with the anger. I didn't know how to begin to deal with my feelings. They worked with me a lot in treatment on my anger. At first all I could acknowledge was that I was "a little upset," when I was actually quite angry. Finally I got angry with someone during a group session and blew up. After that I was able to acknowledge it and at least be able to say, "I am angry." I think that anger is particularly difficult for women to express openly in any case, and being a sister compounded my inability to deal with it in a positive way.

Getting rid of the guilt, acknowledging that I could be angry were big breakthroughs for me. The rest of treatment went very well after that.

When I left the treatment center and came back, I began to have another problem—reentry. Because I work with nuns so much, I see this over and over again. It is very difficult for a sister to come back into the community. I have a dream of someday soon starting a halfway house or a safe place for sisters to go when they are coming out of treatment, for possibly a year's length of time. It takes some time in sobriety to begin to discover who you really are. When you first come out of a treatment center, you are acutely aware of yourself as an alcoholic, but chances are that your community doesn't want to hear about that. Being a sister and an alcoholic isn't considered nice, and most of the nuns will never mention it to you. So many people are still in the dark about the disease of alcoholism.

If you're a nun and you go to a regular AA meeting when you're very new in the program, it can be problematic. It was for me. If you let people know that you're a nun, you are often treated differently than everyone else. When I got out of treatment and went back to the small Irish Catholic mining community in the West where I'm from, there were hardly any women. It was mostly miners, almost all male meetings, in other words. They swore like troopers, but being such a small town, they knew of course that I was a nun—so when they got up to tell their story, they were constantly interrupting themselves, apologizing to me, saying, "Oh, excuse me, Sister Rose." Pretty soon they couldn't get a full story out if I was around. I felt like a fish out of water, and I finally stopped going to those meetings for both their sake and mine.

For a long time I had no one to talk to. There was one priest in this town who was really great, though. He began sending women to me that he suspected were having problems with alcohol. Mind you, this was a mining town, so it wasn't easy for the women to come out about these matters. But then more and more of them would come to me to talk about their problems and I began to feel that that was my niche, working with women and alcoholism.

I left my home town finally, and took a position as the director of a retirement center in a large city, and began to take night classes to get my certification in alcoholism counseling. Then one of the priests in the program asked me if I would work on retreats for alcoholic women, and I began to do that. Finally the women's residential treatment center asked me to come and start as the resident manager. I have been here ever since and love my work.

People began to hear about me after a while and have sent more and more nuns to me to help get into treatment. I do a lot of intervention and counseling with sisters and have started an AA meeting for nuns. We have quite a group that meets regularly. We do things together and support each other a lot. We all go to regular AA meetings as well—it's imperative. We need to get comfortable with ourselves and be able to go to meetings and say, "Yes, I am a sister," just in the same way that the next person can say they are a doctor or a truck driver or a teacher, whatever they might be, it's no different. But when you're fresh out of treatment or just new in the program, it's very helpful to be able to talk AA with other nuns as well. It's really important not to feel alone or isolated or unique.

I never thought about leaving my community, even when I was very ill. I have never been unhappy in community life. A lot of people think that if you drink you must be unhappy. I wasn't, not with others. I met some wonderful people along the way and have had close ties with many of my religious sisters, and I feel good about being in the community. So coming into a spiritual program like AA was really fine for me. I already believed in a higher power, so I didn't have to go through what many do who have rejected any notion of a power greater than themselves. My problem was that I thought that my higher power had left me because he thought I was so bad, he didn't want me. What I discovered was that I had pulled away from God, not God from me.

Now I find that the work I do is bringing me closer to God than ever before. I sit here and can see and participate in miracle making every day. When you see women walk into this recovery house, very ill, some close to dying, having no connection whatsoever with a higher power, angry, full of fear and hatred and turned off to life, when you see them begin to turn their lives around and you can have some small part in that, it is the most wonderful thing I know of to do. If you can help people get a realization of their own personal God, that's where it's at. You don't need a religion for that. God is within us, and it's how we need this power and how we interact with it that really counts. I believe that God is total love, and the love that each of us gives the other person is that kind of love. I also believe that you will never see God unless you can learn to see God in other people. That's my philosophy and my experience as a result of working with this program.

I have to be careful about my language. It's a mistake to limit the idea of God to "Him." I sometimes use that term because it's hard to say what I mean simply, and that's the way we were brought up. I really like to call God "Yahweh" which means "I am who am." It's a Hebrew word from the Old Testament, and it implies no he or she. I believe that for us to limit God in any way is an error on our part. God is a much more spiritual power than anything we can name. We are hamstrung by our humanness. God is beyond and includes all the qualities of human beings, male and female.

A priest from India came and said a mass for us once at our convent. He talked to us about the rainbow. He said that at his home in India they believe that God is female. He said that they describe her as a loving, generous, caring person who wears the rainbow as her cloak, her many-colored cloak that reaches down to protect all her people. I found that to be a beautiful and helpful image of God.

7. Malinda P.

I was born in a small town of about 5,000. For all I knew, I grew up in an absolutely normal environment, normal for a white, middle-class girl. I did not fit in from the start. I was a little too tall, overweight; my hair was curly—everyone else's was straight, or so it seemed. I was just an odd kid and I took it personally. I always felt like I was missing something, as if the directions had been given out and I just hadn't been at school that day.

There was alcoholism in my family, and as so often proves the case with the children of alcoholic families, we each assumed certain roles. Mine was to be the family hero and I took it very seriously. I worked very hard at achieving, that was how I got love and what made me feel acceptable. I remember coming home in grade school with a report card of nine A's and one B. The comment was about that one B and nothing more needed to be said to me. I continued to judge myself in terms of a perfect score, and I always, always failed. That carried through my growing up. There were always people around me telling me how much I was accomplishing, but I was always focused on what I hadn't done well enough.

In school I didn't feel comfortable with boys. I was always taller. I didn't feel comfortable with my body, but I knew that I excelled intellectually so I put all my attention on developing my intellect. That's how I learned to move through the world. People who frightened me I could intimidate by being articulate. I developed a kind of aloofness and sense of intellectual superiority. At the same time I always had the sense that I was failing at what I was supposed to be doing, at being a daughter and girl. I was not excelling in terms of dating and all the stereotypical specifications of a well-rounded, well-adjusted, well-liked girl. I was already at my full height of 5'7" by the seventh grade. Before I ever took my first drink I was a perfect example of someone who felt like I was a piece of shit at the center of the universe, not only my own universe, but everyone else's. It has been such a great gift in AA to understand just how self-obsessed we all are and to know that, at least within the confines of the meeting rooms that we all sit in, that everyone is going to be honest about just how self-obsessed they are. Once I got into drinking, I just carried all those strange feelings, feelings of alienation and apartness with me.

When we were in third grade, many of my friends were trying to figure out whether or not they were adopted. I never put any energy into that at all. I knew I wasn't adopted. What I thought was that I had been put in my family from outer space. I thought that when my mom was giving birth at the hospital there had been a trade and that in fact, I was a facsimile, delivered from outer space, and my mom's memory was erased so that she didn't even know the difference. So there was no way to talk to her about it, because she couldn't remember it. It was a perfect closed alcoholic system. There was no use talking to anyone about it because nobody could help me, no one could understand my very special experience. It was so heavy for me. What would there have been for me to say? I carried that terror and that certain knowledge that part of my problem was that I wasn't human. That was the reason that I didn't have the directions and the codes—of course I wouldn't, because I wasn't human.

When I first realized that that's what I had done, while it made a good story, the longer I'm sober the more I realize that fantasy had informed and shaped my life. As I grew older and started using alcohol and drugs, I put more and more of my life into that category of "they will never understand what I am talking about." By the time I hit my bottom, I had put most of my life in that category: "they can't understand so there's no point in talking about it."

When I sat in my first AA meetings and heard people talk

about psychic pain, I was offended. I'll never forget the first time I heard someone use that term: how could that person understand about psychic pain? You want to talk psychic pain? I am the queen of psychic pain. I had used that exact phrase and it shocked me to hear someone else use my unique, special language.

I'm not really one who thinks I am recovering anything. I think of myself as "uncovering." I spent a whole large part of my life re-covering something that started out perfectly beautiful, shiny, and bright, and I slowly covered it up. I don't need to "re-cover" it, I need to "un-cover." The process of that uncovering for me has been acknowledging in one situation at a time and one experience at a time and one day at a time that I am really a common, garden-variety drunk and even more so a common garden-variety human being. Before I came in the program I had no peers. I was always "better than" or "less than" everyone else. I had such a high level of contempt for most people because to them I was passing as a healthy, independent woman out in the world making social changes, helping other women to take power. I was a public figure, passing every day, and I was dying.

There was a part of me that was so glad that I was getting by, and then there was this other part of me that took it all in, just as I had all my experiences growing up where no one understood: "You really want to know why it is I feel weird? Well, there's no sense in telling you because you wouldn't understand." That was the dialogue that went on in my head all the time. You just couldn't understand, so I didn't even try to communicate with you.

I developed a facsimile personality, which I projected into the world and which was so close to my idea of who I wanted to be that no one could tell that it wasn't real. The distance between who I was inside and who I was projecting on the outside was so far apart that finally, in my drinking, I couldn't straddle those two canyon edges any more, and I just fell in. That's what happened.

My drinking began as a teenager in high school. I had gone to my father's office party, and on that particular night I decided that I wanted to have a gin and tonic. So I just went ahead and drank as many as I wanted and went over to a friend's house for a slumber party. Her mom opened the door, and I just passed out cold, right on the floor. One of my friends took me home, and I threw up all over the place and then went back to the party and offended everyone there. I ended up out in the middle of the street, lying face down wishing that a car would come along and kill me. The queen of drama early on. All my behavior that I proceeded to do for the next sixteen years I did that night. I was totally out of control. It was a preview of everything to come but I didn't know that then. I blamed it all on my friends. That was the way I began my drinking, and it had happened within two weeks of my having come out as a lesbian.

What alcohol did for me was distance me from all my feelings of anxiety and despair and feeling so separate from everyone else. It put me on the other side of those feelings, and it made it possible to act as if I were more comfortable than I really was. Alcohol became my problem solver for feelings. I've heard it said that we become alcoholics because we don't have a coping mechanism for our feelings, so alcohol does that for us. It ended up being a zone of anesthesia between me and all those painful feelings, a palpable zone that gave me a physical feeling of protection.

I know today, with over six and a half years of sobriety, that dealing with feelings is always going to be my major issue. The program teaches us to live with our feelings one day at a time and to live with more than one feeling at a time. As an alcoholic, whenever I would have a choice between a positive feeling and a negative feeling, I was going to focus on the negative. That of course reinforced my reasons to drink. Positive feelings didn't. When I focused on the negative ones, then I could say, "Look, if you had my life, you'd drink too!"

The last part of my drinking is stuffed with ironies. I had

heard that if you drink a lot that you'll gain weight. I was obsessed with my physical appearance, and I didn't want that to happen. I essentially stopped eating and took vitamins all the time so I wouldn't get sick. Of course I kept drinking and using cocaine. I remember being at a friend's house, really hung over. I hadn't eaten in a day and a half. I had two or three lines of coke, took my vitamins, and then threw up over her balcony. I thought to myself, well now, I'm cleaned out, ready to start my day. I went in, washed my mouth out, and went on.

The insanity of that last month is shocking to me now, that none of my friends thought that that kind of behavior was weird—and even more so, that I wasn't more concerned about what was happening to me. I was just in despair. I wasn't concerned, I was desperate. It never occurred to me to quit drinking. I thought, "I have to watch out that I don't kill myself." I thought about suicide all the time.

In the meantime I felt increasingly isolated, because my career was blossoming at the same time I felt worse and worse and was becoming more desperate and out of control. Finally I found myself with my hands around the throat of my lover, my partner, and my closest friend. I was just trying to get her to shut up, I thought. That was my idea. I just wanted her to be quiet. I was ripped out of my mind and I was in the middle of strangling her.

I had not seen myself as a violent person, especially to other people. But I was getting more and more physically violent in my own world. I just started breaking things. I would take whatever was nearby and just break it. I would sit in a restaurant with people and pick up a spoon and just bend it. A surge of rage would pour through me and I'd start breaking things. I remember walking through our house knocking the glass out from all the windows with my fist. I turned around and was amazed that this woman I'd been living with was shocked. It was just what I had to do, couldn't she understand? And then there I was strangling her. I wanted her to shut up. Fighting for her breath, she managed to get out the words, "How can you support battered women?" That got me. I knew I'd gone too far. I was totally ripped. She got out of the car we had been sitting in and left, got in her car, and drove away. I started up my car and drove away as well, in a different direction. And before I'd gotten ten miles I was already justifying my behavior, thinking to myself, "She is always nagging me, we have so many conflicts. I need more space, more time alone." What I really wanted was an unimpeded environment in which to drink. I was isolating from my work, my lover, my friends, family, everyone. Then I would find myself with people whom I did not know, telling them about my life while I was drunk in some bar.

I kept driving that night, on back to my house, where I knew I had some pills. A friend had given me a handful one night, telling me that "this is the closest thing you can get to heroin without getting addicted." Don't even remember the name of them. Now it's about half an hour after I've tried to kill my lover, and I keep thinking, "If I can just take these pills, I can get just a little bit higher," that's how I thought of it, that's what I told myself, but in fact I was about to attempt suicide. I took all the pills I had and passed out.

I woke up the next morning, very groggy and unnerved at my behavior. I remembered it all. I knew that I was really out of control, and I knew that I could no longer predict when that kind of behavior would happen once I took that first drink. Somewhere I had known that, but now it was beginning to sink in. I was on my way down fast.

My solution was to just drink more and more by myself toward the end. I just drove around in my car, did a lot of errands, and drank and drank. Thought about how rotten my life was, how I didn't have any friends. What work I did was about getting off the stage so that I could drink. People talked about the incredible intensity of my performances in those days, but what they didn't know was it was me in withdrawal.

It took me a long time to figure out that if you really want to get high don't drink beer, so I switched to wine. When I got to gin and tonic, it took me a long time to figure out that you don't put tonic in it if you're really going to get high. That was like a moment of revelation, standing in my kitchen thinking *"Why waste this tonic? I'll just have the gin. It makes things a lot easier."* Then it was *"Why dirty this glass? Just drink out of the bottle."* Then I discovered vodka. Vodka had something for me which no other alcoholic beverages had and that's that it was brutal. In that last period of my drinking I used alcohol to really beat myself up. I would wait to take a drink until I couldn't stand it any more. I wasn't conscious of this at that time but now I can see what was happening. I was putting myself right up to the edge of the terrible physical withdrawal and then giving myself a reward by drinking.

My whole life was built around this dance that I was doing with alcohol. Alcohol had become my lover now, my higher power and I did everything that was necessary to have a totally bonded relationship with that bottle. I used cocaine and almost entirely cocaine at the end to take the edge off so that I could play out the dance a little bit farther. It was like making love. How long can you stretch this out?

The real hit was not the rush of taking the first drink, the real hit was feeling the bottom coming at me, going down. That's what became a hit for me. I was at such a level of self-hatred by the time I was ready to stop drinking that I can hardly believe it. Alcohol—my tender lover, my best friend, the one thing left that had become everyone and everything to me—turned on me. When it turned, it turned totally. With what little self-control I had left, I used to inflict tremendous physical, mental, and emotional pain on myself. When I heard of alcoholism as being a mental obsession coupled with a physical addiction, I got it exactly. Nobody had to explain that to me. I understood.

I hit the point where I couldn't get drunk and I couldn't get sober. I knew that I would have to deal with what was happening to me around alcohol. I decided that I was going to have one last evening of drinking with my favorite bottle of wine. I was going to finish this relationship with some dignity. I was breaking up a relationship. That had been the most important thing to me, I could always say, "I'm not a sloppy drunk. I am articulate to the end. I'm going to do this slowly and deliberately."

I was going to buy my favorite $45 bottle of wine and have a friend over for an elegant steak dinner. I was lying on the beach, working on a tan to keep up appearances, thinking this evening through when I realized that my friend wasn't really a wine drinker. "Why am I allotting her half a bottle of this really extraordinary wine? But if it's on the table, I don't know that I'd feel comfortable drinking the whole thing by myself. Maybe I should just buy the wine and drink it by myself." At that I sat right up on the beach and said to myself, "You're an alcoholic."

Through a friend whose father had gone into treatment, I found out the name of a place nearby where I could get help. I went in and met a woman doctor and immediately started to discount her. I took one look at her and thought, "Well, she's not an alcoholic. She won't understand."

I told her that I may have had a problem with my drinking over the last six months, that I didn't know if I was an alcoholic and that I thought maybe if I came into treatment, I'd be able to put the brakes on, so to speak. She looked right through me and said, "You don't have to lose everything in order to be an alcoholic. In your case, if you're not an alcoholic, you could sure use thirty days off to rest in any case."

I liked that. I didn't have to make a commitment. She went on to explain, "Alcoholism is like an elevator going down. You can get off at any floor you want. You don't have to go all the way to the bottom." I thought about that. Then she took out her business card and wrote her home phone number on the back and said, "Call me, any time." I said, "What are you hours?" She said, "I mean *any* time. This is my home phone. There will be a bed for you here whenever you call." That was the beginning of my connection with AA, though I didn't even realize yet.

I believed her, and I was totally overwhelmed. Somehow this woman got what I was talking about, and I didn't have to go through all my stuff. I sensed from her that she knew how I felt, she knew what was going on with me, that was undeniable. I didn't have to explain anything. She understood. I've since heard that the most powerful five words in Alcoholics Anonymous are "I know how you feel."

It was a week before I called back and asked for a place. They took me in immediately. At the same time I was signing up for the twenty-eight days of treatment, they kept saying to me, "All the doors are locked from the outside in, but we don't lock the doors from the inside. If you ever want to leave, you are free to do that. But if you leave, you can't get back. The doors are locked. It's up to you. It's always up to you."

They kept stepping out of the authoritarian role with me. I kept looking for things to find wrong, ways to put them down. "Who the hell did they think they are, trying to help me get well?" I had all my own reverse sexism, my own reverse homophobia, reverse heterosexism, all my judgments running, and I walked down the hall into the main room just before dinner and on all the tables were these big blue books that said *Alcoholics Anonymous*. I said, "Oh, shit! I'm not this bad. Not this bad. Wait a minute, there's been some mistake!" And that's how my recovery began.

It took a while to really accept my powerlessness over alcohol and drugs, to accept that I had really been insane and that it was not going to be my self-will that was going to restore me to sanity. As I read the Big Book of AA, I saw this "God" business and I saw "he" this and "he" that. Where were the she's? Weren't women alcoholics, too?

I was fortunate to have a couple of woman friends who were feminists, who had come into the program ahead of me. It was a good thing they were there. I'd see them during that first year of sobriety, and I'd ask them, "Hey, how do you deal with the patriarchal bullshit in the Big Book?" And they'd tell me what they did. One of them had taken White-Out and gone through the book whiting-out every "he" replacing it with "she." Another said that she had found it necessary to change the language when she read out loud in meetings, saying "he *and she*." She said that she found it necessary when a meeting ended with the Lord's Prayer to say "Our Mother" instead of "Our Father." And I did that, too. I found it necessary to change the language. There were some guys and women who laughed at me when I'd do that, but what I heard said at meetings was "Take what you need and leave the rest." That's what I needed.

I came into the program with a big argument around not wanting to deal with the God concept because it was so patriarchal. I really wanted to use that as an excuse to be able to say that the program didn't work for me. To my surprise, everybody said, "Great! Don't worry about God. Just worry about staying sober." Every rationale, every excuse that I had that would make this program not work for me, people would say, "No problem. Just keep coming back."

I kept waiting for someone who was my age, with my life-style, who had my politics, to tell my story. I kept coming back because I didn't want to drink. My life was in shambles and I didn't want to drink. The most important things to me was my art and it had been taken away by the disease of alcoholism.

It took a while to realize that I had gone through a major physical, emotional, mental, and spiritual breakdown. I was going to have to go back and dig down deep in recovery if I was going to get my art back. So I kept listening, kept doing what was suggested, kept talking, kept looking for that person who was going to tell my story. One day this guy with a jellyroll haircut and pack of Marlboros rolled up in his sleeve sat down at the table and told my story. I couldn't believe it. Here was somebody that was completely unlike me, I thought, but the feelings he described were just like my own. I identified so strongly with his story. That changed my life, kept me sober, and from then on, I realized that it was possible for anyone to tell my story regardless of how we might differ in outward circumstances or appearances. Not only was that true, I could use that truth to help get me well because there were people who had been around longer than I had and they knew how to feel comfortable with all that stuff that I'd been drinking over. Not only were they sitting in meetings sober, they were not stupid, boring, or glum. Some of them were actually happy, joyous, and free. They were men and women who I would like to be. Some of them had what I wanted. And the Big Book said that I could have sobriety too if I was "willing to go to any lengths."

Some of what I was told I would have to do to stay sober I rejected out of hand, thinking, "*That* I will never do!" like the idea of praying for someone you resent. But when I got pushed up against the wall and had to choose between a drink and taking action in the direction of sobriety, I did a lot of those things I thought I could never do.

When I first came into the program of Alcoholics Anonymous, I thought some of the people were just total bullshitters, self-righteous, book-thumping, sometimes inarticulately racist, sexist, homophobic, and every conceivable 'ism' going on in this so-called fellowship. There were maybe two people that I could identify with. Now that I've been in the program for a few years, it's extraordinary how much those people have changed.

When I got out of treatment, I went right into mainstream AA. My life had been very separate and exclusive at the end of my drinking. Even though in my own work I had always stood for the inclusion of all people, women and men alike, I wasn't doing it in my life. In my head I knew that what equality was about was making the circle big enough so that everyone could be a part of it and that feminism was about making that circle complete. But that was all in my head.

I went to the most mixed community I could find, mixed on all levels. I feel as if I've had an opportunity to get sober and grow up with America. I didn't go to the most intellectually hip meetings. I always knew where they were if I really wanted to run my stuff. If I wanted to go and be a lesbian, I knew where the lesbian AA meetings were. If I wanted to be a woman among women AAs, I could go do that. But my problem was not being an intellectual or being a lesbian or being a woman. My problem was that I was an alcoholic, and I was afflicted with terminal uniqueness. I needed to sit with the family of the human community and learn how to be human among humans, peer among peers. I needed to learn how to be a practicing human being.

8. Ellen M.

I was born in the Southeast in 1930; my father was a Methodist minister. I am one of two children. My life in growing up was very loving, caring. I was raised with my mother, her sisters, my father, and my brother. I did not come from an alcoholic family, I am the only person in my family that is an alcoholic, and sometimes I think that it's because I am the only person that drank.

I went to high school and got married when I was 17 and graduated from high school in May. My daughter was born in October of the same year. I call 1947 my big year. From that marriage I had two children.

When my son was 2 years old, I left the Southeast and my husband. I remarried, and from that marriage I had three more children. My second husband drank heavily and at the age of 30, I decided to join him. I did not drink until I was 30. Little did I know what I was doing. I had the attitude of "if you can't beat them, join them." I was tired of fighting with him about his drinking. In just a couple of years, I was an alcoholic. I would drink and I would say to myself, "OK, I am an alcoholic." First I would take care of my children and do what needed to be done before I would proceed to drink myself out. After the children were in bed, I would drink. I went through my day first.

Typically, I would get up, get my children ready for school, make breakfast and lunch. If there was anything that was going on at school I went up with the children because I didn't work, my husband didn't want me to work. By this time I had my third child to take care of. When the kids came home I would have dinner ready. We'd eat, they would do their homework, and then when they went to bed I would proceed to drink by myself. My husband would always be asleep. I was a closet drinker, as they say. Then I'd go to bed. This happened for a long time and my husband didn't realize I was drinking that much. I would get up the next morning and go through the same routine.

I had a fourth child. But I would have times where I would go for a month or so and say to myself, "I am not going to drink." And I wouldn't. Then I had my youngest child, my last one. Somewhere in there before he started to kindergarten, I decided that I was going to leave my husband and I did. I got a job, I got a house, I left him.

I worked hard, sent the kids to parochial school, and took part in all the school bazaars, everything that went on. I was a room mother, I cooked for the church dinners that we always had, and the bake sales. I did them all, and then I would go home and drink. By this time, my two oldest children were grown, so I only had the three kids. By the time my middle child reached 13, I decided that I had to do something about myself. I felt that I could not be raising teenagers and still drink.

I went into the hospital and stayed eight days. I wanted to be a perfect mother. And if I was going to, I would have to have all my senses about me. So I sat the kids down and I talked to them, and I made them understand that it was just the three of us. I would pay for them to go to school, but I would not pay lawyers, I would not come to court, I would write no one if they went to jail. For some reason they believed me, and I never had the problem that some parents have faced with their children.

When I decided that I needed to stop drinking, I stayed in the hospital and I stopped. I did not go to AA at that time, and I did not go to therapy. I have been a practicing alcoholic, a dry alcoholic, and now I am a sober alcoholic and I can really feel the difference. For almost seven years, I was dry. I did not drink. I went to work, did things with the kids at school. Two of my sons played Little League baseball; one of my sons was into classical music and concerts, and I went with him to those things. I worked in my yard, in my house, and just didn't drink.

When I was sober six and a half years, my youngest son was 17 and was going to graduate from high school. He was very independent, so I was beginning to feel like I had no purpose. So the day after Thanksgiving I started back to drinking. I decided that when the new semester started in January I would go back to school. My youngest son just didn't need me anymore. I needed to do something. I had to quit my job because I had developed an allergy. I went back to school in that January and I did OK—I was surprised, my grades were good. I was studying business, which I hate. I would go to school in the morning, my son and I would leave at the same time. I would go half a day to school, then I would leave school, stop at the liquor store, go home, do my homework, and drink. This went on until the Easter vacation. I was able to maintain without anybody knowing I was drinking, even my son.

Then at Easter it just got out of hand. I don't know what happened, but one day I didn't have to leave home to go to school. It was some holiday, so I just proceeded to drink all day. When my son got home he found out that I was drinking again, real heavy. Alcoholism is a progressive disease, and even though I didn't drink for the six and a half years, the progression did not stop. When I started drinking again it progressed right away; it got me.

I went into the detox unit at the hospital and stayed three days. I knew I was an alcoholic, but I thought that meant I could just not drink and that then I would be OK. I was in control as long as I didn't drink—that's the way I felt for six and a half years. It wasn't hard not to drink because I stayed so busy. I had the most beautiful garden and flowerbed on the block, my house was spotless, never a spot of dirt anywhere, and I had held a full-time job. I stayed so busy that that's how I stayed dry. But that's all I was—dry, not sober. There's a big difference. I was a very unhappy person. I know that now, but I didn't then.

I was in detox those three days, went home, and in two days' time I was back in detox. I went home that afternoon and I walked the floor all night. I could not sleep, I could not sit down; and the next morning at 6 A.M. before my son got up, I was at the liquor store. So in two days' time I was drinking again and so sick. They talk about a bottom in AA, and I know that the day that I could not leave the bathroom I had reached my bottom. I could not stop drinking, no matter how much I wanted to.

When my son came home and found me drunk again, he called around and for some reason he got hooked up again with the detox unit that I was in two days before. Back I went and stayed five days this time, and in the process another woman told me about a women's residential recovery program that was very good. She suggested that I try that, so I came to an interview and they accepted me. They called me and told me that I could come.

I called one of my sons. I tried to get him to convince me that I could not go into the program, that I should just go home like I did before. Every reason I came up with about why I needed to go home, he had an answer for. He kept telling me that it was not necessary for me to go home. The last reason I gave was that Robert needed me, and he said, "Robert's 17 years old, he's graduating from high school, he's extremely independent, and it's high time for you to do something for yourself. You're always doing something for someone else. That's part of your problem." So the next day I went into a long-term residential women's recovery home for drug and alcohol addictions both.

I was told that I had to study and do the Twelve Steps of Alcoholics Anonymous. And at that first step-study meeting I was in, the lady chairing the meeting explained that I had a disease. Being an alcoholic did not mean that I was a weak person. It was an illness, not a moral issue. That was the thing that I could immediately accept, that I was not a weak person. I had always known that I was a strong person. That's why I couldn't understand why I couldn't control my drinking. I found that there were other women like me. I didn't know, until they told me in detox, that there were even programs like this. I knew nothing about these things.

I believe at that point, had I been told in the hospital that I could go home and go to ninety AA meetings in ninety days, I would not have gone to AA. "Ninety meetings in ninety days" is what they tell newcomers, so that they'll hear enough stories of people's lives that they'll be able to find ones they can identify with. I just never would have done that. I didn't really know anything about AA, but I just couldn't stand the idea when I heard it. I don't think I would have made it without being able to come into AA through this women's residential program. It was just what I needed.

The first AA meeting I attended was in our house at the residential center and, boy, I felt displaced. I felt like it wasn't for me. They weren't talking to me. They were talking to somebody else. There were about twenty-five women in the room and only two of us were black, the rest were white. It was not my cup of tea.

It was very hard for me to get into AA. It took me a long time. There were a lot of different reasons. One was that I had a hard time with the first three steps of the program. I had to go back again and again to that first step where we have to admit that we were powerless over alcohol. I knew that I was a strong person, and I took it all the wrong way. I thought "powerless" meant that I was weak-willed or something. I would say, "OK, I'm powerless when I drink, but I'm not powerless if I don't drink. OK, I agree that my life is unmanageable when I drink, but now that I don't drink I can manage it, control it."

I thought what I needed was an all-black AA meeting, but I found that I was uncomfortable there too. At the particular meeting I found, it happened to be a lot of street-wise blacks, and I felt misplaced there too. So I kept looking.

I don't think it was the women that I was so uncomfortable with in those first meetings at our recovery house, so much as I was just uncomfortable with the whole AA approach at that time. Everything in the literature seemed to be geared to the white, middle-class male. It was just hard to relate to, to feel connected with. There were not too many stories about women. I needed to hear about women recovering, how they did it and what went on with them.

But I kept attending the meetings. I had to. I knew that I couldn't stop drinking by myself. I had tried that. There was a kind of wonderful feeling about the meetings, but I was told that to get sober I would have to forget about my race. Well, I could not do that because I had been raised to be proud of who I was. I was told that I was an alcoholic first and a black woman second. It doesn't work that way for me. I am a black woman who also happens to be an alcoholic. That's the way I have to deal with who I am. When I say that, some people think that I'm angry, but I'm not—it's just that this is who I am. I am not this nice, quiet, little, soft-spoken woman. I love meetings now, especially ones that are racially mixed. That's how I'm most comfortable.

I care about all people, but women alcoholics have a special place in my heart, especially the mature woman. It does my heart good to see young people getting sober, but when we interview a woman that is, say 45 to 55, I have a special place in my heart for her. I see a lot of women at this age say, "There is nothing left." And *I* know that there is a wonderful life out there. It is wonderful being sober. I still have my problems, that's part of life. People that are not chemically addicted have problems too. I do the things now that I wanted to. I have known for a long time that I would like to live by myself—I'm doing that. I knew when my children were growing up that I wanted to go back to school—I am doing that. I found out business school was not what I wanted to do, so I went back to another school for two years. Next September I'll enter the state university. They asked me what am I going to major in. I don't know. It's not really important. The important thing is that I want to go to school and I am going to go.

I told one of my sons, when I started back to school a few years ago, that I'd be 58 years old when I graduated, and that was too old. He just looked at me and said, "If you don't go to school, you'll still be that age." He's right. So I'm going back and I am going to take my time.

I completed the program at the women's residential center two and a half years ago. I never left. I was asked to stay on as senior resident, and I did. By the time I had a year of sobriety, I was given the job of resident manager, and I started to school. Since then I started to do workshops and groups on my own. I have been here since and I love it. I always wanted a lot of girls, and now I've got them.

I think a lot of women think it's hard for them to get into recovery. Our families come first. We don't have to lie for ourselves, our families lie for us. When friends would call, one of my sons would always tell everybody I was sleeping, but I would be drunk and passed out. He would never say that.

I think it's important for women to know that if they need a residential treatment place, there are places out there. Everybody doesn't get sober the way I did. I think this was the way for me, but there are lots of women out there that I have seen get sober by just going to AA. And there are all-women AA meetings, so that any woman that feels self-conscious about a mixed meeting can attend those as well as the regular meetings.

Now I go to AA meetings and I have a sponsor. I was talking with her not long ago when it came to me that I missed my youngest son's first holy communion. I was devastated. I remember I had been drinking the night before. I got up, I got him ready to go, and I said, "I'll be along in a little while" (because he had to be there early). And I was feeling so bad that I took another drink. And before I knew anything, he was back home. It was over. It meant so much to me to be a good mother, and there I was, letting my own child down. In AA they talk about with this disease how we begin to violate our own standards. Yes, that happened to me.

Sometimes I get frustrated at work. I see families be unwilling to take a child so that the mother can come here, and then they'll fight her putting the child in a foster home when they won't help. I see this with women of color especially. That makes you less than a woman. You do not give up your child for any reason. It's seen as a moral issue, especially for black women if their families are very religious. They are told that they're not serving God and that all they have to do is get strong in their religion and they won't drink. That is not true.

I don't care how religious you are, you need something else in order to stay sober. I know that everybody doesn't get sober in AA and stay sober, but I think it's one of the easiest ways to do it. Religion is not enough. My people so easily confuse religion and spirituality and think that religion is the answer for everything. Oh, we're not the only ones that think that way, I know that—but that's sure strong in the black community. What they forget is that religion is man-made, but that AA is a spiritual program.

A lot of times when you are new in AA you will confuse AA with religion and that's not it. There's a big difference, but it takes time to understand that. I believe that the principles of AA and the way it's set up, that anybody, whether they are alcoholic or not, will be a much happier person if they live by these principles. AA gives us a program for living, a how-to, a blueprint, a way of life. Organized religion often tells you what you're supposed to be, but not much on how to do that.

AA works, regardless of who you are, whether you are a woman of color, and that means the Indian, the Oriental, the Latino woman or a black woman, or if you are male or female—the principles work.

The way I stay sober is that I go to AA, I work with the women here in very close contact. I do a lot of outreach. I believe in order to keep it you have to give it away. I really believe that as a black woman I have a duty to the black community to let them know what goes on in our communities with alcohol and drug use. I also believe that any black woman that is recovering has a duty to reach out and let the other women know what is going on and how they can help, that she is not alone and not a bad person because she drinks. She has a disease. I fight a lot of the time with the black women that have recovered and don't want anyone in their neighborhood to know that they are recovering. That really gets me. I'm not saying that we should confine the outreach to the black community, but I believe that as a black woman it is my duty to let the community know that we are alcoholics. And that there is a way to recover. I want us to stop saying to people that you have "had a nervous breakdown"—that's one of the ploys that we use. Too often we won't say that we are alcoholics. Then the rest of us don't know that there's hope, that there's a way out.

My family used to tell me that it was the people I was running around with. How could that be? I was a closet drinker. I was not running around with a crowd. I was too busy raising a family and working—I had my children and drinking, and drinking is almost a full-time job. So I didn't have any friends, really. My children, that's all.

Today, it's really different. I have a lot of friends and I'm doing things I have always wanted to do, with my friends from AA. When I get up in the morning and it's raining, I still can see the sunshine.

9. Jeanette M.

I grew up in a brilliant family. Both my parents were outstanding in their fields. My sister was classified a "superior child" by the age of 3. Then I was born. Though my own parents were not alcoholics, at least one, if not more, of my uncles was. I believe my alcoholism was inherited genetically and that what caused my alcoholism is very simple. It was Jeanette's body combined with the substance alcohol.

I do not believe that what happened to me as a child caused my alcoholism. Why people drink and why people become alcoholics are two entirely different matters. So in talking about my past, I try to be careful. Someone might hear this or that part of my story and try to grab on to it as an explanation and say, "Aha, *that's* why she became an alcoholic!" Other people who have had similar backgrounds to mine . . . indeed, worse . . . did not become alcoholics. Anything I tell you must be taken in that context.

So here I was in this dazzling family of achievers. I needed to find a place for myself and I chose, for whatever reason, to find my place in the family by being the stupid one, by being the one who didn't succeed. By the time I got out of the third grade, I still had not learned how to read. I think there were some physiological problems as well, but forty years ago, we hadn't discovered dyslexia, which I suspect I had.

So I grew up feeling less than and inferior to other members of the family, but nobody "did" that to me. That's just how it turned out. At that time nobody knew what was wrong or what to do about it, but my parents fell on the appropriate thing accidentally. They took me out of the school I was in and put me in a school that emphasized phonics. They also got me involved in ballet and dancing on the basis that everyone in my family excelled in something, whether it was sport, art, or intellectual pursuits and that they had to find something for me, some place where I could excel. That only thing that nobody else in the family did was dance. Since I was an infant I had tried to dance to music whenever I heard the radio playing. I would knock over my high chair from bouncing to the music. So they felt that there was something in movement for me, that direction was already there. So I began studying ballet.

These two things caused incredible change in my life, the school transfer and starting ballet. At first I could not pay attention to the classes. I was hyperactive as well as dyslexic. (I think that these are often precursors of alcoholism.) My ballet teacher asked my mother if she couldn't find something else for me to do. My mother said, "No, this is it, we've tried everything else." So we hung in with ballet until somewhere about the age of 10 something shifted inside of me. I saw a great ballerina dance, and I was transfixed. After that I wanted to be a ballerina. I became very serious and intent and worked terribly hard on my dancing.

When I was about 11, I became anorexic. By the time I was 12, I was 5 feet 5 [inches] and I weighed all of 90 pounds.

Anorexia affects many women alcoholics as does bulimia. I think it was self-induced drug addiction. I was addicted to my own substances and I never felt better than when I was anorexic, never had more energy, more get up and go. I was high. It was like being on amphetamines. I was high from starvation.

Our family doctor was brilliant, and he got together with my family and together they told me that I could not go to ballet class until I had gained 10 pounds. That's how they handled it. I loved dancing so much that I gained the weight.

By the time I was 14, I was a member of a major metropolitan ballet company. By 17 I was a soloist. My dream was to go to New York and become a member of the New York City Ballet Company. So when I was 18, I went to New York for the summer to take classes there. There were about forty people in the class and I was in the back row. I had gained some weight and I didn't feel good about myself and was sort of staying in the background.

The ballet mistress had worked with me when I was with the other city ballet before I came to New York. She came in that day with George Balanchine and they watched the class. I didn't think much about it except that I didn't want Balanchine to see me the way I was, overweight. After class I walked out the door and they were waiting for me in the hallway. Balanchine walked up to me and said, "We would like for you to join the New York City Ballet Company, will you do that?" This was my dream come true, so of course I said yes.

The summer before this when I turned 17 I had my first encounter with the substance of alcohol. And though I didn't know it at the time, now that I look back, I realize that what it did for me was to physically normalize me. It did something to my metabolism, it did something to my blood sugar level, it did something to my endorphin levels, something not dissimilar to what the anorexia had done. I can recall that first full drink of alcohol. It was like a big sigh went through my body, and all of a sudden I realized, "Oh, so this is what it's like to feel normal, to feel OK!" I didn't literally tell myself that, but that was how it felt. I remember it so clearly.

There I was, 17, dancing with a professional company, a soloist. I had a very high capacity for alcohol almost from the beginning. I hardly got drunk. I would go out with other members of the company after a performance and we would get something to eat and drink as well. When I look back I realize that that was the beginning of the end of my career. So there I was a year later, now I was 18 and I was in New York City Ballet and I began not to feel very good physically.

What I didn't know was that when I *didn't* have alcohol in my body I felt abnormal, more and more abnormal. I couldn't pull all this together then. I just didn't feel like going to classes sometimes, I felt so bad; and I was one of those people who never missed a class. My eating began to go haywire and I started losing my self-esteem. Starting out as a child I had not felt very good about myself, but then all the things that had happened subsequently with dance had made me feel really good about myself. I had become successful. I had learned to read, made very good grades in school even though I was traveling with the ballet company. I had felt good about myself, and then these things began to happen. Just before I had moved to New York while I was back home I would find myself going down the hall sneaking wine out of the refrigerator. Now at 17 no one would have called me alcoholic, but in fact I was already manifesting signs of the disease with my high tolerance and need to sneak drinks.

So once I was in New York the drinking after performances increased. We would all go out together afterwards to get something to eat and drink. Some nights I'd go home after that with a bottle of wine and polish it off, or sometimes I'd go home with a quart of ice cream. It seemed to be one or the other. I did not do this every night by any means, but the point is that this disease was beginning to progress. The problem at that point was not the drinking, but it was what happened when I wasn't drinking and the difficulties and conflict that set up emotionally and physically.

My motivation began to deteriorate. Here I am, in my dream of being in this ballet company and I can't get to class every day. Here I have an opportunity to work with the greatest choreographer of all time and I can't understand what is wrong with me. I don't feel good. I thought it was all emotional, because it feels like it's emotions. You feel depressed. You feel anxious. I thought I was going crazy, that I must be emotionally disturbed. Mind you, I'm not ever drinking during the day. I'm not even drinking every night or getting drunk, so it never occurred to me what was happening had anything to do with alcohol. Besides, I know what an alcoholic is—they are 45, they are male, and they live on skid row.

All I know is that I'm going crazy and that this opportunity is slipping through my fingers, I can feel it going. Mr. Balanchine is beginning to give me more and more roles. He keeps watching me from the wings. He says that he has plans for me, and in my head I am saying, "I can't do it. I can't do it." This man never saw me dance well like I had with the company before. I know that I'm going to let him down. I'm having a nervous breakdown is what I'm having, and I can hardly get dressed to go to the theater. I'm wandering around, I'm starting to fall on stage and pass out at strange times, not when I'm drinking but when I'm sober. Strange things, yes, there is a tremendous emotional conflict going on. You see people think that the breakdown is what caused my alcoholism. That's backward. Alcoholism caused the breakdown.

So I called my mother and said I have to leave New York and I have to come home, something is terribly wrong, I have to see a psychiatrist. I talked to Mr. Balanchine and told him that I had to go home. He said, "No, see one here in New York," so I said OK. But the truth was I needed to leave, I had to leave. I just couldn't stand what was happening, so I gave notice to the manager of the company and told her not to tell Mr. Balanchine I was leaving because I knew he would talk me into staying again. I could not say no to this man, I could not turn him down.

I was dancing in what was to be my last performance. The company manager told Mr. Balanchine anyway, and he came up to me in the middle of the ballet while I was backstage. He said, "I hear you are leaving us?" I said, "Yes." He just turned on his heels and walked away. My whole world was shattered. And though I didn't know it at the time, it was because of alcoholism.

I went home and saw a psychiatrist and continued to drink. We never talked about drinking. That was twenty-five years ago. After doing the logical things, like teaching ballet, I finally took six months off and did get over the worst of the breakdown. In a way, I was at least functional again.

Then I decided to get married. I wasn't real happy being married and the drinking was progressing. Again, I'm not seeing any of that. "My husband likes fine wines," I tell everyone—but he doesn't really like them, *I* like them; so we drink wines. I'm turning into a "winette," but I didn't know that. Still I would never drink during the day, but I don't feel very well. I'm not happy in the marriage, so I have a baby—that seems like the logical thing to do. As things aren't getting much better after the baby, I get a divorce and now I'm a complete failure. I failed at my career, failed at my marriage, I am failing as my child's mother, and things are just falling apart all around me. I am still going to the psychiatrist four times a week and have been for five years now.

I'm dating again, and I meet a guy who has thirteen double martinis on our first date. Now up to this point, nobody has ever confronted me about my drinking. No one except my first husband, who said, "Jeanette, you can't drink martinis because they make you mean." So I don't drink martinis, but of course as soon as I get rid of him, I find myself a martini drinker, which is what I like, martinis. He's the youngest vice president in the history of his company. He's adorable, handsome, everything I want, and we fall madly in love. He has some drinking patterns I notice and he forgets things a lot. He has blackouts. You see, I've never had a blackout that I could remember, so I didn't understand, especially when he would forget me. That's what really upset me—when he would not show up for a date. I decided that he was an alcoholic. One day on the way to my psychiatrist I discovered an information center right in the same building so I sneaked in and got all this information to prove to my boyfriend that he was an alcoholic. I got out my red pen and starting marking off all his symptoms and found this thing called the "controlled drinking test." I thought, "Oh, this is just what he needs to take." The controlled drinking test is very explicit and says that you have to limit yourself to one, two, or three drinks, and they make very clear that it's not three bottles or three tumblers of whiskey. It's very clear what a drink is, including beer. You have to choose a number and stick to it for a minimum of six months on any occasion when you'd ordinarily drink. You can't say breakfast, lunch, and dinner are all occasions; you just get one occasion a day. They are very clear, and I'm reading the test, and I'm thinking, *This is the stupidest thing I've ever read. They must have written this for people who don't drink. This is really a dumb test. I wouldn't really want to walk across the room for three drinks, much less one drink.* That was really stupid. I get down to the bottom, and it says, "If you're saying to yourself that this is really stupid, and that you wouldn't walk across the room for three drinks . . . " and everything that I'd been thinking . . . then guess what? I'm going "wait a minute!" I'd done the twenty questions for *him*, and, of course, he flunked.

Then the whole thing came together like a flash. It was like, my God, I was 27. I have one child. My life fell together. I had made three suicide attempts. I'd been hospitalized with my wrists cut open and almost severed a tendon in one. All of this, and never ever until this moment did I put it together! It's not that I am depressed, I realize, it's not that I am a basket case, it's that *I am an alcoholic.*

I presented this test to my boyfriend, and we decided to go on a controlled drinking test together. The only reason I decided to was because he was willing to. I already knew I didn't want to do it. I already knew I didn't want to drink that way, but I went on it so that we could do it together. The nights I was with him, I cheated by not having the full amount because I began to see that I could tell if I had just a little more I wouldn't be able to stop. Something inside me said, "Oh God, there is something, there's a point here." But it would be different every time. One night I felt I shouldn't drink, shouldn't even start, and another night it would be "Well, I better not have the second one." Sometimes I could have the three and I'd be OK. I began to tell there is something to that test. People say that alcoholics can control their drinking. Well, maybe if you wanted to try to live your life in that kind of way you could get by with it for a period of time. It was ghastly. It's just an incredibly stupid way to live your life. That wasn't the way I wanted to drink. I think that anybody that is trying to drink like that is totally controlled by alcohol because their whole life is spent figuring out when you can and can't have a drink. My God, there are other things to do. He lasted a month, which astonished him and astonished me. I never thought he'd make it. A month on that test and, of course, he cheated too, but he didn't go crazy until a month later. Then he went off and just lost it. He called up and said "Ha, ha, it's your alcoholic boyfriend." I said, "OK, he failed. Now he can do with that information whatever he chooses." But I said, "OK, I quit." This was in January 1964.

Once I stopped, I do the whole co-alcoholic thing. Now I'm going to get him to quit. I am trying to manipulate him and do everything to get him to stop, and he is continuing. I'm throwing his booze down the sink and dragging him to AA meetings, doing everything I can think of about his drinking, not paying attention to my own. At first I went six weeks without a meeting for myself and then I began to think, "You know, I better try this meeting for me." I tried to join clubs and keep myself busy. I told my psychiatrist that I thought I was an alcoholic and he said, "Oh, no, when we get your emotional problems straightened out, you'll be able to drink." I said, "I've been coming to you for four times a week for five years, when is this going to happen?" That didn't make sense to me any more. I told a family member that I thought I was an alcoholic and the family member said, "Oh God, if you are you might as well drink," and I said, "What do you mean by that?" And they said, "Alcoholics are so sick and disturbed that they have no choice but to drink." Those are some of the responses I got. Remember, this was twenty-one years ago.

I started to go to AA meetings and even there I was challenged. I was 27 and there were very few women my age, even in a major West Coast city. There was one woman that was twenty, thirty miles away. No women in the downtown meetings, no women my age at least, and not too many men my age. The point is that the men would say, "Jeanette, I spilled more than you drank, go out and drink a little more and find out what it is really like." I had somebody accuse me of being a society do-gooder, coming to try to save the drunks. Finally an older man came up to me after a meeting and said, "Do not let any of these guys throw you off. Don't listen to them." He was really helpful.

What I realize now looking back is that I had to go through adolescence at 27 when I got sober because my adolescence had been delayed in certain ways through my career and my drinking. I didn't get adolescence, I got to be grown up. Nobody cares if you're 13 if you're performing as far as they're concerned, you're an adult. So I lost a certain amount of adolescence. The other part of the delay came because the drinking began when I was just starting to date. I didn't know how to have a relationship without alcohol. Now I had to confront all this stuff sober, and meanwhile my boyfriend is still drinking. So I finally broke up with him. I knew that I had to take care of myself. He offered to quit drinking and marry me. I told him that we'd have to talk about that later if he quit. Somehow I got the strength to go through with that breakup. I asked for it, I prayed hard for it. At least I had God's will for me and the power to carry it out—and that was to get myself sober. I knew I had to take care of myself and to let God take care of the other drunks and for me to just do what I could and to get my sticky-wickets out of where it wasn't my business. I removed myself, and I loved him very much, and it was very hard. A month later he came into a meeting and he has been sober ever since. He has been sober over twenty years. Today, we are married almost twenty years and have a child of our own as well.

I have a commitment to reaching young people because I don't want other people to lose their career or something that they love like I did, to alcoholism. It took me a very long time, years, to get over the grief of what I had lost when I left the ballet company. At this time I know I have gained much, much more through my sobriety, my marriage, my family, and my work in the field of alcohol education. I'm tired of thinking of ourselves as "-ics." I think that we should understand that in all fatal diseases, of which this is only one, there is denial. We hear alcoholism called the disease of denial, but it's not. Look at cancer, heart disease. Elizabeth Kübler-Ross says that the first stage of a fatal disease is denial, any fatal disease. Addiction is a fatal disease, but in addition to that, the denial is caused by the stigma of alcoholism. If you take a group of people as I often do and say, "What's an alcoholic?" what comes to mind first thing? They say, "bums," "skidrow," "wino," "out of control," and I put that all up on the board and have an alcoholic at the top. Then I say, "What does an alcoholic have to do the first thing to recover? Admit they are an alcoholic, of course. And look at what we're asking them to admit: that they are a bum, etc." That's everybody's picture of what an alcoholic is. So my point is that as an alcoholic, I have the denial that is created in addition to the fatal disease, the stigma. Then I have a third denial, which is caused by the fact that I am dealing with substances that alter my ability to experience something. So now, I have three levels that I am dealing with. My commitment to life is to eliminate that stigma. I believe there is only one way to do that and that is to work with children. I've worked with adults, and I know how much our society has ingrained that stigma in us and how much we ingrain it within ourselves. Children have no trouble understanding that it's a disease, an allergy. I work with children from first grade on to alter attitudes and to correct misinformation. I want to help create an environment in our society that will make it possible for a generation of young people to grow up without the stigma that stands in the way of recognizing the disease from the beginning. I want them to be able to recover and live a life full of choices. I want a generation of people who know the facts and whose attitudes are informed and compassionate. We are not dealing with weak-willed, useless people. People such as myself are intelligent, sensitive, productive members of society who have been stricken by a fatal disease.

10. Anne C.

My name is Anne, and I am an alcoholic. In looking back at the things that have happened to me over the last thirty years now, I guess, I began to see more and more things in my background that, if I knew then what I know now, would have led to my recovery a lot earlier.

I was born and raised in a city in the Midwest and had a very loving and supportive family during my early years. My memories of my childhood are generally happy, although I do recall always feeling somewhat different in the sense that my interests and talents seemed to be somewhat different from a lot of the kids that I grew up with. I came from a family where alcohol was not present in the home because of the alcoholism in uncles on both sides.

I always did very well in school. Academic achievement was a virtue in our family. Productivity was a virtue in our family. Perfectionistic behavior was a virtue. I was a good kid. The teachers always had nothing but praise to tell my parents about me all through school. I also had fairly strict, religious up-bringing until I was about 13, at which time a number of Catholic kids, a different religious belief from mine, entered the public school system. I discovered at that point how my own particular Protestant background was bigoted. I discovered they didn't have tails and pointed ears. I became very friendly with a number of Catholic boys and girls and conse-quently left the Protestant Church at that time and did not return. My parents were broad-minded and didn't push the issue. I had very little experience with alcohol until high school, and even then there was very little drinking that went on in the group that I associated with. I can remember having one can of beer in my senior year and sharing it with about five other girls. That was equated with a kind of wildness and maybe some fun, forbidden fruit, but I didn't experiment with it at all. I do remember really liking the way that one can of beer felt. We were about 16 years old.

I went to college immediately from high school and also did very well academically in college. There was some beer drinking in college and I remember thinking about drinking, but because the group that I went with hardly drank, it wasn't a big part of my life. We would sometimes drink beer at a local pub, but I don't remember ever drinking enough to even say that I had gotten high. That was in the early 1950s.

I went straight to medical school to fulfill my dream of becoming a doctor. That was when controlled drinking started. The control was very little money and the enormous pressures of medical school which was more important to me than alcohol. What drinking I did do was confined to fraternity parties. I don't recall ever getting drunk, but I do remember being able to drink a lot more than my peers were without showing it. Now I know that that kind of tolerance is often a sign of the disease. But I didn't know that then, and I can recall taking care of a lot of my friends in medical school who had gotten drunk.

This ability to drink more without showing it, my high tolerance, was part of my biochemical makeup from the very beginning, I believe strongly.

I did very, very well in medical school and graduated near the top of my class and was very active in other social and student activities. During my internship I married and moved to a pleasant resort area where I did general practice for a year. My husband was a fairly heavy drinker, and our apartment was the center of many, many parties. It was then that I first became aware of looking forward to the cocktail hour with a great deal of anticipation. My preoccupation with drinking became very apparent to me. Still, I didn't recognize it as being significant in terms of the development of the disease of alcoholism, but in looking back I see that I had more anticipation for the cocktail hour that most of my colleagues and friends.

I was not yet drinking any time during the day and waited until the cocktail hour. But I began to want it to come more quickly. I began to count on the relaxation that the alcohol gave me after a day's work. I was drinking daily at that time, but not so that it interfered with my life. I also noticed that I rarely got hangovers. I could drink a fair amount with friends in the evening and wake up in the morning raring to go as far as my job was concerned. I thought this was great and a sign that I really knew how to handle my liquor, unlike some people. Friends began commenting on my ability to do this, whereas if they overindulged the night before they would pay for it the next day. I don't remember having ever had a headache all through the progression of my illness and the morning after drinking. In fact, this lack of hangovers can be another sign of the disease of alcoholism.

We moved again so that I could begin a residency program. My drinking was fairly controlled during those days. I still only drank after work in the evening and on weekends. It still had not yet interfered with any aspect of my life that I could point to, looking back. I did become intoxicated from time to time. The first time I noticed a blackout was probably two years after moving from the resort area. I was probably about 28 years old. I had been out at a party with friends and drove myself home. But the next day, I had difficulty remembering how I had gotten home. This was frightening experience, but at the time I did not realize that a blackout was a significant occurrence, or something that I should have paid attention to as far as the development of alcoholism. I then became pregnant with my first child. I don't understand what happened to me metabolically at that time, but fortunately I did not drink during my pregnancy. The thought of alcohol was abhorrent to me, and looking back, I am just delighted that I did not. Fetal alcohol syndrome was not really recognized, and it was just pure luck that during both of my pregnancies my taste for alcohol fell off dramatically. I am not saying that I didn't drink at all, but I drank very, very little. And there is no evidence in either of my children that they have any signs of fetal alcohol syndrome. A higher power was looking after me even before I knew I had a higher power.

I had two children within a very short period of time. During those years, because of the nature of his work, my husband would be away from home a great deal and didn't see either of the children until several months after they were born. I began to develop a great deal of self-pity and resentment over this situation, despite the fact that I had known full well what I was getting into when I married this man. Following the birth of my children, my drinking increased, but as with many women, the responsibility of small children served as an external control so that I was able to keep my drinking within certain limits. My children were not in any danger and were certainly always cared for as far as the material needs were concerned. In hindsight, I have to wonder when they were 5 or 6 years old if their emotional needs were met. My drinking progressed.

I completed the residency program and by now was in my mid-thirties. The children entered grade school and were doing very well. At this stage of the game, my life was such that I had fewer and fewer external controls to keep the alcoholism under wraps. My children didn't need me as much because they were in school and able to do a lot of things for themselves. I had finished my training period, so that money was no longer a limit in drinking, and I did not have to study with the degree of intensity that I did during my residency training period. I felt more free and able to indulge in what I now see as my main interest and that was drinking.

I entered private practice and was very successful, very quickly. I was able to build a practice so quickly that I couldn't imagine it. I began to be very selective about the patients I would take. My drinking by this time had progressed to the point that I was drinking daily, before I went to work, during lunch hour, and then I scheduled my practice so that I could be finished with my patients by 3:30 or 4:00 in the afternoon, so ostensibly to get home to my family. But in truth, my preoccupation with alcoholism was almost total by that time. I was 40 or 41. I was physically addicted to alcohol, and I knew it. I knew that I *had* to drink rather that "wanting" to drink. I was developing signs of alcoholic gastritis, meaning that I would vomit in the morning. My denial of what was happening to me was so great that I convinced myself that vomiting in the morning was what everybody did. I wasn't that unusual, I told myself. As soon as I could keep down that first drink I was able to function again, and without it I couldn't stop shaking.

I carried a small flask in my purse because I was terrified of going into withdrawal by not having a supply with me. I had begun hiding bottles around my house in an attempt to hide them from myself so that it would take me longer to find them. The irrationality of the disease was really catching up with me at this point. I thought that if it took me longer to find the bottles, I would drink less. This was my way of trying to cut down.

During all this, I divorced my husband and three years later met another man and married him. He was a marvelous drinking partner. The high point of the day was when he would come home from work. We would both get totally drunk every evening. My children objected more and more to this behavior. They were in their early teens. By this time I had been hospitalized on two different occasions, both times for severe vomiting, and I had also begun seeing a string of psychiatrists. They were treating me for depression and assured me that as soon as the depression was gone, I would be able to drink "normally" because I couldn't be an alcoholic. I was a professional person. I knew too much. I thought. In truth, very little attention is given to training doctors to recognize alcoholism or substance abuse in medical schools. There is some training about the end-stage medical complications of the disease, but not about the disease itself, or how to recognize it in the early stages. Given what we know about the disease, this is an appalling and tragic state of affairs. It is such a problem within the medical profession itself that is is hard to bring this kind of change about.

I saw a total of four psychiatrists during this period when I knew that I was in trouble but was not able to take care of myself. I was reluctant to contact some of the "nonprofessional help" organizations such as AA. That couldn't be for people like me, I thought. Every doctor gave me medication like Valium and Librium.

I am very, very grateful at this point that I didn't become addicted to the tranquilizers as well, as so many do. All along, I kept telling myself that alcohol wasn't going to be a problem for me because alcohol wasn't a drug, even though I knew better. I didn't want to think of it as a drug because it is legal, socially acceptable, and even encouraged by our society. I didn't take the pills extensively because pills were drugs and I was not going to be a drug addict. I was kind of a snob in that way, and today I am certainly very grateful that wasn't a problem for me too. I know a lot of people have had even more trouble when they were dually addicted. I know that many of my friends in the program have suffered from cross-addiction: Valium and alcohol, marijuana, cocaine, speed—you name it—uppers, downers, tranquilizers, all kinds of drugs.

My sister is a recovering alcoholic and during my active phases of drinking, I developed what I call "telephonitis," so that I had an astronomical telephone bill. I would call friends throughout the country and particularly my sister, who still lived in the Midwest. By the time I was drinking the heaviest, my sister had been recovering in AA about five years. Though I still have no memory of that night, apparently I called her in a blackout, really upset, and asked her to help me. She had been trying to do something for me for several years but I wouldn't let her. The next day she arrived on a plane, and took me to a treatment program. I will always be grateful to her for that. I still get choked up when I talk about it.

My sister saved my life. No doubt about it. She arrived, packed me up, and off I went to treatment for a month. It was marvelous! I was 45 then. Three months before I went into treatment I had called the central office of Alcoholics Anonymous in my area and asked for some information, "for a patient." The information came immediately in the mail and I had it sitting on my coffee table for three full months. I would walk by it and glance at it, but I could not bring myself to read it. I was a doctor. This AA business was nonprofessional, and so I kept trying to discount it in my mind. Yet I knew that people in my own profession had not been able to do anything for me. I had not been able to do anything by myself, and my sister, who had gone into treatment, was maintaining her recovery through AA. In the end, she was the one who took over and did what needed to be done. She recognized what was happening.

To this day, I can remember walking into the treatment center and feeling like two tons had been removed from my body. It was the most marvelous sense of relief. As I have said in meetings a number of times, we can surrender before we even know what surrender means in AA. I surrendered the moment I walked through those doors and admitted that I had a problem with alcohol.

During the time in the treatment I felt like I had finally come home. I was with people who understood what I was saying. I felt love and concern, and also I began coming to grips with taking responsibility for my behavior. I had been trying to do that but I didn't know how. In treatment, I finally was learning how to do that. I also learned that I didn't have to be perfect, I didn't have to have all the answers, and that it was OK to be an ordinary human being. Being a doctor didn't mean that I had to have everything I did turn out exactly right. I could make mistakes sometimes. That was a tremendous relief to me.

It was so marvelous to learn from people, to feel open enough to listen to many other kinds of people. Some of them didn't even have an education but they had a lot to teach me.

I felt that my whole life was becoming rich all of a sudden. I also learned that I wasn't essential to anybody else. That was another wave of relief to me. I had left my family for a month to go through treatment and when I came home they were fine, they hadn't starved, the house was in good shape. I could be myself, and I didn't have to be all that concerned about everybody else all the time. I was able to really put myself first, as the program was teaching me, not in a self-centered way, but simply because I was responsible for taking care of myself. I learned that unless I took good care of myself, I wasn't going to have anything to give to anyone else.

I had been told by my counselor, and all the other people I was associated with, what I needed to do to maintain my recovery after I got out of treatment. I was feeling marvelous when I left and returned home. I was told that the pink cloud wouldn't last. I was warned that my euphoria wouldn't last forever. There would be times when I might feel depressed or down, they said. Since that time I have not felt depressed. I have not felt the awful feelings that I used to feel when I was drinking. I have no more bad days or good days than anybody else. I feel marvelous, and it's been seven years since I came into the program. I have certainly had nothing that even comes close to the depression I used to have. My sense of humor is back. I love life. I see the joy in ordinary everyday things.

I was told not to return to my practice for a year, so I took off from work. I was told to go to meetings; I went on a daily basis. It never occurred to me not to do what they told me to do to maintain my recovery. I flew home late one night and was at a meeting the next morning so that I could begin meeting people in my community in AA. I was given a very healthy dose of fear when I left the program about all the pitfalls of early recovery.

I have to laugh when I look back. During my drinking days I always drank "like a lady." I never hung around in bars. My drinking was always done at home or in the homes of friends. I had a lot of fears centered around liquor stores. I used to go around to different liquor stores so that the man in the liquor store wouldn't know how much I drank. I also had a phobia about the trash collector. I worried about what he thought about me. I don't know why I should be concerned about the garbage man, but I didn't want him to know how much I was drinking either. Disposing of liquor bottles is a very big problem when you are an alcoholic, particularly when you are a "lady" about it, so I used to take my bottles to other places where there were large trash cans, to get rid of them.

About three months after I had been home from the treatment program I was walking past a liquor store. Suddenly I was afraid that I would go in and buy a bottle of booze. Then out of the blue I realized that I had a choice. It is me that would have to buy that bottle, just like it's me that has to take the first drink. Nobody can force me to do it. I felt another tremendous release and relief.

I felt very fortunate from then on out when listening to my friends in the program and their really wanting and physically craving a drink and having a lot of difficulty. During my entire period of recovery, up until today, I have not felt any craving for alcohol. Sometimes if I look at an ad on TV or see someone in a restaurant who is having a frosty drink before dinner, the thought will pass through my mind, "It would be nice to have one." But I know as long as I drank I never wanted *one* drink, I never wanted *a* drink, never. I don't understand social drinkers any more than they understand me. I didn't want the socializing that went along with the drinking. I *drank* and maybe socialized, whereas other people socialize and maybe drink. And that's the difference between me as an alcoholic and my friends who are social drinkers.

Despite the caution that my counselor gave me about returning to work, after about six months into my recovery, I'd caught up with many things I'd wanted to do and was ready to go back to do something creative in my own profession. I was fortunate in meeting another recovering physician who was working in the treatment field. We became good friends.

I met him through a recovering physician's group, which I attended regularly. He was involved in a treatment program and had just had one of his staff members resign, so he offered me a job. From that time I've been working in the treatment field. The feeling of "coming home" that I mentioned having when I first went into treatment continues through my work. I have never enjoyed the practice of medicine as much as I do now. The gratification that I get at being privileged to be a part of the recovery of other people is marvelous. I would pay to go to work with the people that I associate with every day. I feel healthy. I was sick a lot when I was drinking. I have not been ill since I've been in recovery. I'm very active physically. I play tennis regularly. I make time for taking care of myself so that I live a full and balanced life.

My children are in close contact with me. I have one child who is chemically dependent and who is in treatment. I have another daughter whom I am very close to as well, and we do a lot together. My husband has been recovering for the same length of time as I have been. And through the grace of our higher power, the program, one day at a time, we hope to continue this way. Put simply, I have been drunk, and I have been sober, and sober's better.

At the time I went through treatment, my husband decided that the best support he could give me was to begin his own recovery. He did not go through treatment himself, he just began going to AA. He and I have grown immeasurably in these past seven years because of that. We have changed from drinking buddies to real partners. We are able to communicate on every level in an extremely satisfactory way. We are both very pleased with the way our lives have gone since we began our recoveries. I feel blessed that I've had the support that I had from him, from my family and friends. My life is full. But I must remember that in order to be able to continue this way, I must give my sobriety the credit for everything I have now. If it weren't for the sobriety that I found through AA and the people in it and a higher power, I would have nothing.

11. Miriam J.

I never had a legal drink in my life. An addict and alcoholic, I began using drugs and drinking when I was 12 years old. I came in to AA when I was almost 20 and I've been clean and sober now for over two years.

I was born in New York City and we moved to the West Coast, to Los Angeles, when I was 3. All was well. My father was a successful painter, and my mother was a housewife, in those days. But somewhere along the line, she decided to do something else with her life, and he ended up leaving. When I was 5½, he telephoned to tell me that he was divorcing Mother. He hadn't even told her yet.

My world fell apart. My first addiction was to food. I became real isolated and all I did was read. The couple of friends I had always seemed to disappoint me. By the time I was 12, I was overweight, didn't have any friends, was very uncomfortable and started in private school. That's when I smoked my first joint. Within a month I was taking speed, using hash, Quaaludes, and drinking. It was pretty much whatever I could get my hands on. The only drugs I said I'd never do were acid or heroin, because those make you drug addicts. In the end I did acid and heroin, but I never shot heroin, only snorted it, because I thought if I didn't shoot heroin I couldn't really be a drug addict. Insane, huh?

People at this private school were very sophisticated and had a lot of money so access to drugs was extraordinary. A lot of kids' parents were in the entertainment business. When I was 14, one of my friends would rip off ounces of cocaine from his dad, and we would do it. Inside I was incredibly insecure and never felt "good enough" in comparison to everybody around me. But with the drugs and alcohol I could escape those feelings, that "not being good enough," especially with coke. There's a certain allure behind coke that when you're on it, it's possible to believe that you're somebody you're not—Superwoman, anyone, anything.

Drugs opened up this whole different world. I got involved with men. And I used men the same way I used drugs, as often as I could. I was extreme and not extraordinarily selective with my choices either. There was always the issue of who had the most drugs and whoever that was that's who I wanted to be with.

I started dealing within my first year of using because I had to support my habit right from the beginning. I sold Quaaludes at first because I had a boyfriend who was on them so it was easy to get them. Then acid. Pot was a hassle because it was hard to carry around. Hash was easier. Then I began to sell cocaine. It was insane. I hadn't yet turned 15 years old.

I kept journals through all this. I was always high or low, nothing in the middle. I had been an innocent child and almost within a month I had turned into a drug addict. I don't think there was ever a point that I could have stopped if I wanted to. From the very first joint I wanted another. I didn't care what it was, just more drugs. It was a nightmare.

My mother knew that something was wrong. We didn't get along. I isolated myself and I think she kept hoping I'd grow out of it. We were both in denial about what was really going on. She's now in Al-Anon herself. She had two kids, no child support, and had to work very hard. She's a very good mother, actually, and just didn't have any idea about what was going on inside me. I've only seen my father a few times since I was 5 years old. She knew I was smoking pot, but not about the other stuff.

If you're doing drugs like I was, you're covering up a lot of pain. I was miserable. I'd get hooked up with some guy, do drugs, then move on. I had no self-esteem whatsoever, which is why I was doing all those drugs. When I was 15, I had my first moment of clarity about what was really happening. I had been on a run, six solid days of doing cocaine. I liked doing it that way, but I ran out and there is nothing worse than running out. When I was coming down I realized that I was a drug addict at 15 and I couldn't stop. If they'd paid me a million dollars, I couldn't have stopped. I wrote it all down in my journal, how miserable I was, what was happening. But this is a disease of denial, and by next journal entry I'm loaded again and everything's just great.

My mom continued to worry and sense that something was really wrong. She wanted to get me out of town, out of the environment that I was in. She sent me away to an artist's camp in the mountains. I was not enthused at all. But not long after I arrived there I saw all these dancers performing outside on a platform. I wanted to do that!

Finding dance at that time in my life saved me. Had it not been for dance I think I would have ended it, but it was the one creative, positive thing in my life. I found a good dance teacher when I went back to the city, a fabulous teacher. He was also a coke addict. I danced every day. I went to school and I danced. Then I would go home and do drugs half the night. My social life only included people who drank or did drugs. If you didn't do that, I didn't want to know you. I didn't want anyone to tell me what to do and a lot of people tried. I was scared to death inside. So I danced. I was 16 years old.

By this time, my mom and I were actually getting along a little better. I was a "functional" addict and alcoholic in the sense that I could maintain myself well enough that it didn't look like I was as fucked up as I was inside. It often just seemed like maybe I had a cold or was a little out of it, but apparently I was able to hide how bad I felt inside, especially from myself. I prided myself on being able to snort enormous amounts of cocaine and make myself go to sleep when I wanted. I was also doing a lot of acid. I was seeing how much power I had in my mind, how much power I had over the drugs. I just didn't have enough power to stop or the desire either.

I took a high school equivalency test to get out of school early. Flunked it the first time because I was so hung over. Finally passed it and then moved several hundred miles north to "be on my own." I was 17. I got a job in a drug haven and really got serious about dealing. I lived in a 13-foot trailer with no running water, gas, or electricity, and my drugs. I started dealing in large quantities of drugs. My self-esteem hit rock bottom. I was working over a hundred hours a week to make more money to buy more coke and I was dealing. I rarely slept. I was always drinking by this time. My drinking had accelerated enormously. I was a white wine drinker. When I went to the bar I would drink orange juice and tequila. I was drinking daily by now and I was blacking out daily too. The kind of men I was with was in direct proportion to how bad I was feeling about myself, so you can imagine the kind of guy you might find me with. The kind of guy who's always looking over his shoulder because there are so many warrants out for his arrest or he's AWOL. Outlaws. I started carrying a gun because of all the drugs I was keeping and the kind of people I was hanging around with. I became very paranoid, some of it with good reason. I was very unhappy. I just wanted to die. I couldn't get along with anyone. I was constantly in tears. I was 18 years old. The drugs and alcohol weren't working right. My life only got worse. I had limited myself to coke, booze, and pot with some occasional heroin I snorted to come down from the coke, but it was primarily coke that I wanted. It's a terrible drug, what it does to you.

I started getting violent with the people around me. I was in the crowd that was doing the major dealing, the connections with Chile, Peru, Bolivia. It's amazing that I never got busted. Things were getting really dangerous. I started "fronting" large quantities of cocaine in blackouts. That's where you'd let somebody have some cocaine until their payday and then they'd pay you back. But because I was in a blackout I couldn't remember who I had fronted it to or how much, and come payday nobody was volunteering the information. The quantities I was dealing in and the kind of people I was connected with meant that if you didn't keep your dealing together, they would just blow you away. You were dust. Like maybe you ought to leave town right now. So I paid everybody off and got out of that job where I was around all this stuff. That was my problem, I thought—my job. Just like Los Angeles had been my problem or my dad leaving had been my problem. It was always something else. So I decided to go back to school. That would fix me.

I immediately got into a relationship with a guy that I had known before. I could function when I was drunk and he couldn't, so I thought he was gross and I had dropped him the year before. But there was something different about him now. He was straight. He looked good. He had been clean and sober for over a year. That was real attractive to me after the kind of people and places I'd been hanging out in. We embarked on a relationship that eventually led me into AA.

I was still drinking every night. We had just had a big argument when he said, "Why don't you see if you can just not drink for a month?" I said sure. No problem. *I'll show him*, I thought. Within a few days I was drunk again. We had a big fight, so I left him and hooked up with a coke dealer and went on a run again. Some people hit bottom on skid row, but that's really only about 3 percent of the alcoholics. I hit my last bottom in a big fancy house in a wealthy neighborhood with a new BMW parked in the driveway. I lay in bed drinking and snorting coke. Do a line, take a drink, wipe the blood from my nose away, do another line, take a drink.

I was watching *Lady Sings the Blues* on television and thinking how disgusting that woman was, how sick, how low. Then it hit me—I was watching myself. I knew what it was like to feel like if you don't get the drugs you're going to die. And I couldn't stand that feeling; it was terrifying. For all those years, from age 12 to 19, I had stuffed down all those feelings that I didn't want to deal with, and it was taking more and more drugs to do it. It was a dead-end street and I knew it. I had seen my boyfriend get clean, so I knew it was possible. I called a counselor at a treatment center that my boyfriend had gone to, and I told him that I wanted to come see him.

I showed up at the center to see this counselor and told him that I wanted to learn to use cocaine socially. He said he didn't think that was possible. I got up to leave but he stopped me, he said, "We'll work on it." And we did. If he hadn't said that I think I'd be dead by now. That saved me. He suggested AA, but I wasn't ready yet. I wouldn't go, but I did start into counseling and looking at my use of drugs.

I started dancing again and actually got off the cocaine, but my drinking accelerated and I kept smoking pot. Again the dancing saved me. I think I sweated a lot of toxins out of me. I went to Europe, smoking dope and drinking all the way through, but no coke.

When I got back from Europe, I ran into my old boyfriend again. He looked marvelous. He had lost weight, but he was talking about God and Alcoholics Anonymous, and I took one look at him and decided that I never should have come back. I thought it was disgusting. I was off coke now, so that meant I didn't have a problem, right? At least that's what I told him. He was talking about being clean and sober again and he'd get this kind of starry, dumb look on his face when he talked about God. I didn't want to have anything to do with him. But just to appease him I agreed to go to a meeting with him. I didn't even smoke a joint before the meeting. After all, I'm a nice girl, aren't I?

We went to the meeting and I thought everyone was a Moonie. I couldn't believe any of what I was hearing. I thought it was all an act and that after meetings they just went out and drank. I couldn't believe that people could actually be as clean as they seemed. I saw some people I knew from my counseling sessions, and I didn't like it at all. A week later I went out and drank and used coke again, which I'd sworn off of. I was just going to have a little, I told myself—but I didn't.

I called the counselor one more time and this time I went

straight into a residential treatment program. He was right. I could not use coke "socially." I'm not sure many people can. It's the only drug that laboratory animals will give up food and sex for. They'll take it until they die. And that's what was happening to me. I knew what hell was and I didn't want to be there anymore. My mother raised a nice Jewish girl and I ended up packing a gun and selling cocaine. I was way off track.

When I went into the treatment center, I was shaking so bad that I was spilling coffee all down the front of me. I was a mess. I had never spent a day clean and sober since I took my first joint. I was pissed off, irritated, resentful and angry, but I knew there was another way. The seed had been planted at that AA meeting.

When I got out of the treatment center, they told me to go to AA. They said go to ninety meetings in ninety days, and I did. I did 108 meetings in ninety days. I followed whatever suggestions were given to me, because I knew beyond a shadow of a doubt that my way didn't work. When I was in the treatment center they told me I had to stop smoking pot. They said it was a mind-altering chemical and that I couldn't have any mind-altering drugs. I said, "No, it's not, it's just like cigarettes. I've never had a problem with pot, I smoked it every day since I was 13!" So they said, "If there's no problem, why can't you stop?" I got the point. That was the end of the pot.

I found out in my sobriety that I was addicted to men. I didn't have women friends. I found them threatening. I discovered that I used men to make me feel good about myself. Even if they treated me like dirt, I was always better off, I thought, if there was a man in my life. So I latched onto a boyfriend, but it didn't last.

After I broke up with my boyfriend, I quit smoking cigarettes. Suddenly I started to eat and put on twenty to thirty pounds in the matter of a month. I wanted to drink and use, but I didn't. But the way I began to use food was just like drugs. I hated myself. I looked terrible with all the weight I put on. I wore tons of makeup, as if that could cover up how I felt about myself. I would gorge myself with food and then throw up. I was bulemic. I was back to my first addiction, food.

At 22 I knew that it was time to live by myself. And I knew that I needed to make friends with women. I finally realized that as long as I denied that I could be friends with women, I was denying a part of myself.

I started talking to other women in the program, and they told me that I had to have faith that this problem would resolve itself. Within a week of talking about it and asking other women for help, I started on a food plan that works for me today. The compulsive eating has stopped. I'm eating three meals a day and feeling better than I ever have in my life.

Now I work with a lot of women. I've started a meeting for women in the county jail. I did that because when I first thought about taking a meeting to the jail I of course thought of starting one for men. After all, they were more important, weren't they? When I heard myself say that, I realized that I had never owned my feminine side. The strong feminine side. I thought to be strong I had to be "one of they guys," doing their trip. But I have found tremendous strength in my friendships with women. It's the strength that I've found in the women in the program that's kept me clean and sober.

The miracle is that I just have to have faith, and today I have it. Today I believe that if I just stay clean and sober, one day at a time, I'll make it. It sounds hokey, but it's true. I was the kind of person your parents didn't want you to hang around with, and today I can actually be useful.

12. Mollie P.

I was born and raised in Chicago in the 1930s. I came from an affluent family in which both parents had careers, which was unusual for that time. They were both alcoholics. I had a happy childhood, though as is typical of a child of alcoholics I have trouble remembering much about it. We were sent to summer camps and the good Catholic boarding schools.

My father died when I was 17, and by that time I had had enough to drink to know that liquor did not agree with me and that it would be wise not to drink much. Being devout Roman Catholics we celebrated my father's death with a traditional Irish wake where people were inebriated for two days. I just thought we were a marvelous family, and didn't everyone drink?

I left home for college and tried to drink with my friends but I could not. It still made me sick to my stomach. Nonetheless, I had a great time without drinking, so good that I ended up on scholastic probation. I was pulled out of college and rather than stay at home, I started working for the airlines and flying. I left Chicago, got involved with any number of men and ended up marrying my first husband who was a nice, straight, older Roman Catholic. I did not want to burn and go to hell, so I got married.

I was a sitting duck for the disease of alcoholism. I had the "isms" before I ever took a drink. My insides never matched my outsides. That's how I felt from my earliest memory.

I got pregnant right away, and the next ten years of my life are a blur. I had eight pregnancies, delivered five children live, all in those ten years between age 20 and 30. By 30 I felt life was pretty dull and I needed to find some excitement.

By this time my doctor had prescribed the birth control pill.

My confessor told me that I would be in mortal sin and would be excommunicated from the church if I used it. My doctor was a Roman Catholic too, and I had had enough pregnancies and miscarriages and children, thank you. I told the priest to forget it, and I have not been back to confession to this day.

I had a proper home, all six thousand square feet of it, in the right neighborhood, with the right kind of live-maid, my nails done and my hair done weekly. I was not yet 31, and I was very much a proper matron. The other part of me was screaming for "Let's cut loose and have some fun!" so I began a series of affairs. My husband seemed to have no idea of all this. He went along with whatever I wanted to do as long as dinner was on the table by 6:30 and I had a smile on my face.

I got very involved in the Altar Society at church, and the Council on Christian Doctrine. I also got very involved with our local parish priest. Though I was still not drinking to speak of at this point, I got the priest plowed enough one night to where I was able to make a few advances, and he succumbed quite readily.

I wasn't drinking more than one or two at this time because I still would usually wind up with a migraine headache and nausea. I was born with an allergic reaction to liquor, and so I was still very moderate at this point. I was a super-Mom: Brownie leader, Girl Scout troop leader, Cub Scout den mother, room mother, and served lunch in our local high school cafeteria every first and third Friday, as every good mother did. I never said no. I was always available to do any and every carpool, soccer cookie bake, or football practice. My children always had polished shoes and were well-groomed. I felt very much a product of my time—you married, your life ended. You became the "Perfect Mother." I was shocked by my friends who gathered in the afternoons for wine and cheese. *How could they do that? Who was paying attention to dinner?* Inside I resented mightily the freedom that they had, and I chafed with all the resentment I felt toward other women. It was monumental. I did not trust them. I was also a gourmet cook. I wanted to make sure that my parties were better than anyone else's, that the silver was polished better, the crystal cleaner, the meal more superb and exotic and that everything about my home and my children was perfect. That's where I got my strokes.

I was not a warm and loving mother. I was demanding and had high expectations. I had plenty of time to run around in the midst of all this because I was superorganized and had everything tightly scheduled. The maid could oversee the children and was responsible for being sure they did their chores. My husband traveled occasionally. When he was home, there was always the "parish council" or a book club meeting that I had to get to. After a while I got bored with the priest. I now understand that he was developing an alcohol problem himself, though I couldn't see it at the time. Enough of that, I decided and moved on to someone else. Finally I decided that I wanted a divorce. I wanted to leave my husband and my children. I was tired of being so perfect. I was 37 years old.

I went out on a blind date with a man who was recently divorced himself. On our first date he said to me over the cocktail I was trying to get down, "You don't drink very much do you?" I told him no, that it often made me sick to my stomach. He said jokingly, "Well, I think I'm an alcoholic." I just laughed thinking that it was just his cute way of making conversation. After all, he was training for a race and ran all the time. He made a lot of money, belonged to the right clubs, and came from a prominent family. Alcoholics were gutter bums. They were in a different society than I ran in, and they certainly didn't attend my parish church. But something in me clicked. When he said, "You don't drink much . . . " I took that as a put-down. There must be something in learning how to drink. Now that I was embarking on a single life, I decided that I was going to have to learn how to drink, once and for all. I had moved out of my house, given my husband custody of the five children, and was living alone in an apartment. This period lasted for about eleven months.

During this time I had plenty of opportunities to learn how to drink and to run around and become wild and crazy. I dropped my image of the proper matron. I let my hair grow, took off the false eyelashes, unpeeled the fingernails, threw away the panty hose and high heels, and got comfortable. My former neighbors were absolutely horrified. If I ran into them in the grocery store, they turned the other way. I was considered a wanton woman. It was not cool to walk out on your husband and children, especially if you were a good Catholic mother. That image was already shot in my husband's mind when I insisted on getting my tubes tied after my third miscarriage. At that time, where we lived, I had to have his signature in order to have that done. He had refused. I threatened an immediate divorce. He reluctantly signed the papers, and it was done. We never discussed the matter again, and the separation occurred shortly thereafter. Eleven months later my children started to come back to me because their father was having an affair. It was more than the kids could handle.

I had started to drink, forcing myself to "learn" despite the throwing up and the hideous hangovers. Then I woke up one day and thought to myself, "You have arrived. You are no longer throwing up or having hangovers." What I didn't know was that the disease of alcoholism was progressing and was fully in motion. I was learning to build a tolerance to the drug, and my system was learning to compensate. I was no less intoxicated than I had been, I just appeared less so. The man that I had met on that blind date and I continued to see each other, having a lot of alcohol-related arguments and never relating them to alcohol. We would say that we needed to moderate, that "we're eating, or drinking or smoking too much." It could never just be one problem, there had to be multiple problems. Finally I stopped seeing Dan because I did not feel that he could handle the children, and by that time all five were back living with me. We lived in very reduced circumstances, a two-bedroom, one-bath. I had no child support, had received nothing in the settlement like the house or furniture. I was working three jobs to keep body and soul and five kids together. My three older children were in high school and worked after school and on weekends. It was truly a matter of survival.

I was devastated. Though I needed Dan, I stopped seeing him. It was too much. My drinking decreased dramatically. I was managing a bar and working at a restaurant that I partially owned, so I had access to alcohol and would drink enough after work to knock me out. But I didn't associate that with alcoholic drinking. What I drank now I had to pay for, so it was much less.

All the while I have teenage children and am trying to cope with their problems. They have been very good children. They knew what a struggle it was and they all pitched in.

Dan came back into my life. He had been drinking. He called and said, "I need to see you." I had a couple of drinks before he came to fortify myself. That evening I have a sketchy memory of being in a blackout in a fancy restaurant and bar drinking ourselves into oblivion, planning our wedding for the next day. That was Thursday night. On the next day we were married with all of our seven children, in town, dressed, plus a wedding brunch. This is typical of the compulsivity of the disease. I functioned totally under the influence of alcohol from the time he came back into my life, with little exception for the next year and eleven months. I was drunk at my own wedding, or at least hung over and drunk by the afternoon. I controlled my drinking and confined it to evenings and weekends. I was now the mother of seven children, my five and his two. We bought a house. I tried to hide all of the problems of raising my four sons from him. He had daughters and had never experienced boys. I was the middle man in the marriage. I coped with a wine bottle in one hand, my six-pack of beer in the fridge, and Dan behind me. I never wanted them all entangled. I did not feel confident that anyone else could handle anything. I had to do it all. I was back to being the perfect mother, cooking seven nights a week, even if we went out. I was back to serving lunches in the school cafeteria.

I had turned away from the God of my understanding years

before when I dropped being a Roman Catholic, but I still had a strong sense of community and that I needed to contribute somehow, now that I was "safe" again and had the mantle of respectability by being a married woman. I started to get involved in community affairs again.

The progression of my disease during this one year and eleven months that I'm now referring to was dramatic. Please notice that I did not drink for very long, for a total of about five years, two of those alcoholically. I didn't start drinking until I was 37, and I came into Alcoholics Anonymous when I was 42 years old.

I became focused on drinking, excluding my children from any emotional contact. If I wasn't concerned about my drinking, I was concerned about Dan's. By this time I thought that he had a problem. But I knew if he had a few drinks he would be affectionate. By this time neither one of us could relate in an intimate, caring way without using alcohol. The fallacy is that you can't relate intimately *with* the use of alcohol—it's like a live-in mistress. Alcohol anesthetized our inhibitions and allowed us to do and say things that we could not otherwise. There was a shallowness, emptiness in that; a feeling of helplessness. There was no way to get my needs filled.

What prompted me to go to AA was truly by the grace of a higher power I call God. Since Dan was a runner, I had become a runner. We had just finished a race and were drinking beer. Then I had a blackout. The next thing I know I'm waking up in another town in bed with my husband. Something dawned on me. It was my middle child's graduation from high school that day, just as I was waking up. Being the good mother I prided myself on being, I was shocked to find myself not there. And I was drunk again. I was horrified, helpless, hopeless, and terrified of what was happening to my life.

The next week I went away on a retreat with several women that I have been close to all my life. None of them had an alcohol problem, and they could see one in me and they tried to talk to me about what was happening. I was aware that I drank twice as much as any of them. On the morning flight home I had four Bloody Marys—not exactly social drinking.

I kept drinking when I got home. This is the only time that my children say they saw me drunk. I was in a total blackout. I said bizarre things, I verbally castrated my husband. As I staggered upstairs to bed, my necklace broke and bounced down the wooden stairs. I can still see the jade beads and the dust curls. My delusional system began to break down. I was doing things that "good" mothers, wives, and homemakers don't do. My husband was packing to leave on a business trip and gave me a look that said he'd never be back. I had destroyed him. I apologized. He didn't believe me. After he left, I sat at the kitchen table without hope. For some reason I looked up AA in the white pages of the telephone book. A gruff old man answered the phone and said, "Well, there's a meeting here in twenty minutes, why don't you just come on up here?"

I walked into that meeting terrified. I'll never forget it. I was very shaky. I went in and everybody said, "Hello, my name is Mollie, I'm an alcoholic." My palms were sweating, and I was ready to throw up. There was a man there who had just gotten out of prison. I was busy judging everybody, thinking, "How in God's name did a nice girl like me wind up in a place like this?" I left as soon as the meeting was over, got into my car and sat there and cried.

There were two very kind and loving people, a man and a woman who came down and stood by my car. They said, "Please come back, it will get better. Come and have lunch with us across the street." I couldn't do it. I certainly never went out with strangers, and they didn't look like my kind of people. He had on polyester pants, and she had on a very tacky outfit.

But there was something that drew me back, and I went back that same evening to a night meeting. Those two people were still there, waiting for me. They gave me the Big Book of AA. I couldn't believe it. I took the book home that night and the *Twelve-by-Twelve* and read them through at one sitting. I decided I would give the program thirty days. Get this problem in hand and then go about my business. That was over six years ago now—I have to laugh.

When I picked up my husband at the airport at the end of the week, I was very contrite and told him that I had discovered that I was an alcoholic and that I owed him an apology and that I needed to make amends. Underneath it all I was trying to get him back. I had an ulterior motive. I wasn't just getting sober for myself.

So I fought the program for the next two years. I stayed sober, never took a drink, but I didn't like it. Dan was very angry with me. He had lost his drinking buddy and his dearest friend. My sobriety was a threat to him and he couldn't stand it. I refused to go out every night to restaurants and bars. As we moved further apart, he grew closer to his daughters. I was furious. Being sober, I knew that I needed help, and I went to therapy for the next eighteen months. I discovered a great deal about myself and learned that I needed to get a sponsor and work the AA program just like the people in it had told me to do.

And when it hurt badly enough I started to do what I was told and began to really work the steps. I got a sponsor that I respected mightily, who had many years of sobriety, a contented and serene kind of sobriety. I had to make my sobriety the number one priority in my life. I explained this as best I could to my children, who tried to understand. My husband continued to drink, though now would go on the wagon for periods of weeks at a time.

I started to attend Al Anon, the group for friends and relatives of alcoholics to learn how to deal with my relationship with my husband and his drinking. I talked more openly with my children about understanding alcoholism as a disease. I became employed in one of the Council on Alcoholism offices and went back to school. I did a lot of research on the disease concept of alcoholism. I became skilled as a public speaker and educator on this notion and on fostering the understanding of alcoholism as a family disease. I also studied the Adult Children of Alcoholics program.

The disease model holds that "alcoholism is a primary, progressive, chronic, and if not treated, terminal illness." So declared the American Medical Association in the 1950s, and it is an understanding respected by insurance carriers who now cover treatment for alcoholism in medical policies and is held by the British Medical Society as well as others. It is a biogenetic disease. At every talk I give I am astonished at how many people still don't understand that this is a disease.

I am powerless over alcohol and my life is unmanageable, so I have learned to ask a power greater than myself to restore me to sanity, to turn me and my will over to that God of my understanding and to take a fearless and thorough moral inventory of myself and to share that with God, myself, and another human being. There is so much beauty in this program and the growth I have achieved through those first five steps has allowed the spiritual dimension of my life to return. I have often heard that to be an alcoholic one has to be spiritually dead, and I believe that. Before AA, I had decided that there was no God for me. I didn't like the God I grew up with, and I sure didn't like to find out that the priests in his church were fallible human beings. I put all that behind me long ago. But since coming to the program I have gradually come to believe in a higher power, a God of my understanding. That higher power isn't necessarily God for everyone. We all have different words we may use, so I try to be careful when I talk about this part of the program. But it's really a path of the spirit, and those who stay sober in AA know that and have put their lives on that kind of footing. I am a grateful, recovering alcoholic because of AA. I've now been sober for six years. If I did not have this disease, I would not have the incredible richness of life that I do today. I would not have the depth of experiencing and understanding pain and joy. I would not have known the variety of people that I have learned to love and cherish in all of the richness of the human condition. I was such a narrow person. I am glad to be an alcoholic. It gave me a second chance with life.

13. Marie L.

I'm 35 years old, with three children, two boys and a girl. I've been sober three, almost four years.

Growing up Latin American, I remember we partied a lot, whenever there was an occasion like first holy communions, confirmations, birthdays, baptisms, and whatever else you can think of. I got the message that drinking was definitely acceptable. Even if you were a kid, you were allowed a certain amount of champagne, which was usually served.

The first time I got drunk was when I was 13. My mom threw a party for my confirmation. I had made a vow before confirmation that I would not drink. This was a piece of paper we signed in Catholic school, and that's the first thing I did on confirmation day, got drunk. Nobody got mad at me. In fact, most of the family was drunk. There's alcoholism in my family on both sides.

I got drunk another time at 13, and both times were about my boyfriend, either I was jealous or angry. When I was fifteen, I got pregnant and married this same guy. He was nearly four years older than me and we were madly in love, and thought we were ready to be parents and all that. I quit school.

We moved out on our own when I was 16 and had already had our son. We started to drink on weekends. I had the mother role. I would take care of him when he passed out, undress him and get him to bed. When I was 17, I got introduced to drugs. The first one was grass. My brother-in-law had gone to Vietnam, and when he came back he introduced us to grass. It wasn't really "us," it was my husband. He was Mexican. He told me that women didn't do grass, he just didn't want me to do it. I felt cheated. At first it was just him and his buddies. Then one night we were at a friend's and the men went to get a pizza and left the grass. The wives decided to roll a joint and try it. We liked it right away because we started laughing, everything was funny. Being a young parent and a wife is very scary, so grass made us feel like we were having fun. So then we started smoking weed together, me and my husband. He had to accept it. Then he started selling it, and we were smoking it every day. It was getting dangerous. I didn't like it. It really started affecting our marriage. His friends would come over almost every day and smoke and drink, and since I was the wife, my part was to cook for all these guys and clean up after them, and it was a drag. I resented it. Even though I got to smoke weed, I was stuck with all the mess. He wouldn't help at all.

I was smoking more and more. If I went to visit a friend, I'd take at least five joints with me. Our marriage really began to fall apart when I started having my own opinions. I used to straighten my hair and he was used to me that way. One day I got sick of that and I just let it be curly. It was natural, right? He just flipped out. He thought I was nuts. I told him that that's the way it was going to stay. That was my first rebellious thing in the marriage. After that it was going out. At first it was just to a dance class. He wouldn't watch the kids for me, so I just took them with me. I started resenting him more and more. He didn't like me to take any time away from him. I started making other friends that were into drinking and using, even more than I was. I started going to bars with my new girlfriends, sneaking out so that my husband wouldn't know. Then I got into pills. I'd come home loaded with downers and get him up for the graveyard shift to go to work and he'd say, "Where's my lunch?" I'd tell him, "Hey, you're not handicapped! You make your own lunch." I was getting more and more defiant. We just grew apart. I packed my stuff—he didn't believe I'd do it—and just moved out.

The move was really hard on my kids, and I didn't realize how hard at the time. I was just into using and drinking by that time, into me. I felt like I had gotten robbed getting married so early, having kids, all I could think about was partying and how much time I had to make up for. That's where my head was. My disease was progressing. I still have a lot of guilt about that to this day.

Here I was, I hadn't graduated from school or anything, but I finally got a job. I just fell in with the crowd who was using; it was a huge company, and there was lots of drugs around. I started selling drugs at work. Then I found a young lady who sold uppers, and I needed that because I was always taking downers. It was a vicious cycle: get off work, drink, take downers, then take some more because all the time your tolerance is increasing, go home. Then in the morning I'd still be down so I'd have to take some uppers to get to work. I started going to fancier bars, the downtown bars, mostly on Fridays, and hanging out with people like myself who did drugs and drank like me and were dependent on other people to fix them, booze and drugs. They were Latinos like me. That was really important to me. I hung out with minority. That's who I did most my drinking and using with. Mostly Latin American like me, or Mexican, mostly women, but later on toward my bottom, men as well.

My drinking and using progressed. I met another man, who was part Mexican, and fell in love with him. From the start it was very unhealthy. We were both into drugs and the bar scene. He was several years older than me, which I thought meant he could offer me security and wisdom because of his age. I was 23 years old by this time, with two children. This was at the height of my drinking and using.

We went out to a party and I drank too much, did too many drugs and did some things I can't remember. The next day he told me that he didn't want to be with me any more. "You changed, I can't take it." I fell apart. I had a terrible hangover. I thought I could not exist without this man. I was selling Valiums at the time, so I took about fifty of them. Those suckers were hard to get down, kind of like swallowing chalk. So I called my ex-husband and told him that he would definitely have to participate in his kids' lives now, I wasn't going to be around. I told him what I had done. Well, he called the man I was in love with and they rushed over and got me to the hospital where they pumped my stomach.

That solved everything. He came back to me, my lover, not my ex-husband, and promised me that he'd never leave me again. That was at the beginning of the relationship. It was real unhealthy. So he started living with me, and we kept on using, and then I got pregnant with our first child. I did stop using drugs while I was pregnant but I didn't stop drinking. I no longer had blackouts when I was pregnant so I thought that I could take more alcohol and I did. I was incredibly lucky. My child seems to be fine to this day.

That was the best part of our relationship, having our baby. We took Lamaze classes, the whole thing. He was right there with me, it was beautiful. I thought the baby would patch up our marriage but it didn't. I realize that alcohol was such a big part of what was happening in our marriage. He began to physically abuse me. We went to counseling but he quit and wouldn't go because our counselor was a woman. The counselor told me to stop drinking. But how could I? I just couldn't explain it nor did I understand it, I just knew that I couldn't.

We were both drinking a lot and things just got worse. We'd both get crazy and he'd end up hitting me. I had him arrested the second time he did it, but I was so afraid of him I didn't press charges. It was all behind being drunk. I tried to commit suicide again. Finally we separated because we realized that we might kill each other. But even after all that I still wasn't convinced that we couldn't make it.

That last time he'd come to my work and hit me at lunch hour. He had a gun and he put the gun in my stomach. It was terrible. He was insane at that time. I was scared to death, but somehow I couldn't believe that it was over. I was really sick. I stopped using drugs and started drinking more. After six months of separation, I finally called him up one night. I hadn't given up yet. Somewhere there was that insane fantasy that we could get back together. We met in a bar and started drinking, and by the time we got home the insanity had set in. I wanted to kill myself and ran out to the freeway near my house and he ran after me. He got me and dragged me home and beat the holy shit out of me. We were both really drunk. That convinced me. It was over. I called the police, and this time I pressed charges. I followed through. I even had some of my family take pictures of me in case the police didn't. He went to jail for about four months. He had really deteriorated behind the alcohol and drugs. I was 28 years old by this time.

Still I didn't stop drinking. I didn't think drinking was my problem either. I started back to school and was doing really well there for a while, until I fell in love with another guy, and we broke up. Then I fell apart again. Was going to bars more, in the worst neighborhoods of the city. There I met a guy who introduced me to cocaine. I found out that the more I snorted coke, the more I could drink, so that's what I did.

By this time my daughter had taken over my role as the mother in the family and took care of everybody while I'm out drinking. This insanity had gone on for so many years that she just accepted the role, and I expected it of her. The other children expected it too. My oldest son had gone to live with his dad. He had gotten entirely out of hand and was into drugs and alcohol too. I couldn't deal with him.

I met another guy at one of these bars that was like a guardian angel to me. He loved me so much—he was a perfect co-alcoholic! He watched out for me. I would be in bars drinking late, and my kids would call him and say that I wasn't home, and he'd go looking for me and find me and get me home. I was constantly in blackouts by this time. I wouldn't know where I was, who I was with. I had quit school by now. Well, this guy who looked after me told me that he thought I'd become an alcoholic. He told me that he would give me anything I wanted if I would just go talk to this woman he knew. I said that I would go when he agreed to give me a gram of cocaine after I saw her.

I went, and this woman gave me the twenty questions about whether or not alcohol might be causing a problem in your life. She gave me the AA Big Book, a schedule of all the meetings around, all kinds of AA literature. She told me that I looked very depressed and that she was concerned about me. I didn't like that. I didn't like her telling me that at all. She also gave me a list of places I could go for help, like a thirty-day program or a recovery house, different places like that.

I continued to drink and use, but I was getting more and more depressed. My daughter was angry with me. She would ask me please, if I could just stop drinking and using for the weekend, she would do anything I wanted her to do. But I wouldn't do it. I wouldn't give it up for a weekend. That was absurd. I couldn't. So she started leaving for school and didn't kiss me goodbye or say anything. One morning after she left I was walking down the hallway where we have a place to put notes. And pinned up there was a note from her to God saying, "God, please help my Mom stop drinking."

That got me. That reached me. I didn't stop drinking yet, but I felt worse, full of guilt and remorse. I really hated myself. I couldn't understand all this. I felt like I was mentally ill. So I called up one of those numbers that lady I'd gone to see had given me. It was a women's alcoholism center, it turned out. They asked me some questions over the phone and then told me they'd like for me to come in for an interview to see if I was qualified for the program. I was really nervous but I went. They asked me some very simple questions, like how long I had been using weed and how long I had been drinking. I never had stopped to think about those things, and I realized that I'd been doing it for years. I saw that it was something I couldn't control. I had wanted to stop many times, so I'd substitute weed and say to myself, "Well, I won't drink." I'd smoke a joint, and then as soon as I was stoned I'd say "Fuck that, what am I trying to prove?" And I'd start drinking again. It never worked. They helped me see that. Well, I qualified for their program, and they wanted me to start on Monday. That was a Friday. The condition was I had to arrive having been clean and sober for seventy-two hours. I said OK to that.

I really thought that they were going to teach me how to drink socially, so it wouldn't be such a problem. I didn't know what I was getting into. But I wanted my daughter's love so badly that I was willing to agree to anything. So right after the interview I went to a bar and was telling my friend the bartender that I was joining this program and that I was going to stop drinking. She served me beer. I drank half of that beer and then I was thinking to myself, "What am I doing? I'm going to join this program, why wait to stop until tomorrow, why not start right now?" And I did. I didn't finish that beer. I told myself, "That's enough." And it was. I haven't had a drink since that day, thank God.

I went to a party that weekend and took two bottles of club soda and some chips. Got there early and left early. I had it all planned. I loved to dance and I danced and had a wonderful time. When the evening wore on and I started noticing drugs and more and more booze, I split. It was real important to me that I did that. I had a really good time too.

I told all my cousins that I'd quit and they didn't like it. They were still drinking and using. I had been real popular with them because I always had drugs and I was always turning people on. That was a big change. I also made the mistake of expecting my friends to understand, and they didn't. They didn't like it either. I was their cocaine connection and I had to deal with that. I started getting on everybody's cut list, and pretty soon I found out that I really didn't have any friends except for one woman who was totally supportive the whole way through.

They had child care at this alcoholism center. It was just for women. I'd go five days a week for six hours each day. You had to participate in all the groups and go to AA meetings right there in the building, and then there were a couple of meetings outside the building, so you could leave for a while. I did that for three months.

About one month into that program, I told my mom that I was an alcoholic and she said, "No, you're no alcoholic. You don't have to go to that place." It upset her. I told her that nobody was forcing me, that I had been miserable and that I didn't want to live like that anymore, that it had been awful. She felt like it was a reflection on her. I tried to explain to her that it was a disease and that I just happen to have it, it didn't have to do with her. That was hard for her to understand, but she tried.

After a while, my cousins who like to party at my aunt's house would start coming over to see me and ask questions. "How did you stop? Do you still have cravings? How many meetings do you have to go to? Is this for the rest of your life? Do you think I could do it? What made you stop?" And I'd tell them.

All those relationships, now they are for real. Now when I see my cousins and they hug me and kiss me, it's because I'm me, not because I have cocaine or wine or grass. That feels really good. My family loves me the way I am now.

My oldest son was able to come into the program and I know that it was because I am recovering myself that I was able to help him. He's 19. I had lost custody of him during my drinking, and when I was in the women's alcoholism center he wanted to come back and live with me. He did, kept using, then finally went out on his own because I couldn't have him around drinking and using. Finally he got beat up and ripped off, and he asked me to put him into a hospital program we'd heard of for young people. It was really hard, but thank God he did it and now he's in AA. That's really nice. I've seen him grow so much, and he's been great help to me as well.

My daughter is involved in her own recovery process as well. She started using and drinking too when I was so bad, and I never knew it. Naturally the longer you're sober, the more aware you become. After I was in the program awhile, I started noticing things about her and I forced her to get some counseling at the women's alcoholism center that I had been to. At first she didn't want to do it, but I told her that she had to go. Whatever she did with what she got out of it was her business, but I wanted her to go. Well, she went and kept it up for a year. It's really helped her a lot. I'm really proud of her. Of all my kids.

I tried to turn the women I used to drink and use with on to the program once I got sober but they resented it. I just lost them altogether. They're still out there. At times when it gets hard, like a divorce or something, one of them will call me. A lot of times drugs and alcohol are involved so I suggest that they go to Al-Anon. They can take that a little easier you know, to think that they are the friend or relative of an alcoholic or addict, than to look at their own problems with the stuff. A lot of people come into AA through Al-Anon, people who aren't ready to admit yet that they're addicts or alcoholics.

I don't see many other Latin American women at meetings. I know that there's a lot of fear in admitting that you have a problem with alcohol. And with our culture, the family is so important it's almost like you fear what your family's going to think. They think it's a reflection on them. "If you're an alcoholic we must have done something wrong. You can't be an alcoholic. What does that say about us?" In our culture there is so much pride. It's almost like they are too proud to admit it. It's a sign of weakness if you ask for help. I was brought up with my mother saying to me, "You're born alone, and you're going to die alone. You don't need anybody." That attitude has held me back a lot, and I'm still getting rid of it.

I remarried in sobriety, and after a year I knew that we needed some counseling. I was afraid to bring it up because my husband is Mexican and I know that, Mexican or Spanish, the traditional person does not ask anybody for help. Oh, you might ask a family member, but that's it. Finally I had to say something. It was, "Go to counseling or forget it." I gave him a week to decide. He said, "OK, but I want you to know that the only reason I'm going is because I love you so much. Men don't go to counseling. I'm only doing this for you."

When we went to Mexico to meet his mother I was really excited about going to an AA meeting there. He got angry. He told me that if I wanted to go to a meeting he would have to go with me because women do not go to meetings.

In that culture, you just don't admit that you have a problem, particularly women. Men can have a problem, but I guess it's that traditional thing about men keeping their women in line that's still really going on in Mexico. I noticed that women there didn't seem to do anything without consulting their husbands first. It's almost like they have no voice. That goes for the Spanish culture in this country too, it's not just Mexico.

I've noticed that most of the women I know who've come into the program who are Spanish have come in single. They've had to let go of that relationship because it is a put-down for the man. I have a girlfriend who is white and an alcoholic. Her husband is Mexican. She wanted to go to a meeting with me and finally did and he was really angry. He told her that he would rather she got involved in some religion to stop drinking than to go to AA. And that is what she has chosen to do. I saw her about three months ago and she was really obese. She used to be a beautiful woman. She doesn't drink anymore and she goes to church all the time and she's miserable. He still drinks, of course.

Since I've come into AA, the one thing that's been absolutely wonderful for me is that now I can believe in the God of my choice and that there are no conditions on who or what that is for me. When I start noticing that I find a man attractive, I'm not committing a sin against my God. Sometimes I even have a conversation with God when that happens and say, "Thank you, thank you for letting me know that I'm human, thanks for letting me enjoy that," instead of feeling guilty like I did with the God of my childhood. That's been such a gift for me and for my children, having a loving, unconditional God.

I'm separated again, but we're going to counseling and there's a good chance we'll work things out. I go to about four meetings a week these days, and I'm secretary at a Narcotics

Anonymous meeting. Once a week I go to a mental health program that helps me deal with my emotions, and then every two weeks my kids and I go to family counseling.

The rewards of being sober and being in the program, with my children as well, is so wonderful to me, even in the times when I've been in a lot of pain like with the recent separation. I know that I'm not alone, and I can go to a meeting and talk about what's really going on with me. When I'm by myself here in the house, I remember that God's with me now and that I'm going through what I need to go through and that it's all a growing process. The pain isn't there for nothing. I've learned that. It forces me to grow, to look at myself, to change. All this awareness has come to me because of Alcoholics Anonymous. I can really see the difference in people who are trying to get sober on their own and the people in AA. I'm grateful to be in the program.

14. Leah G.

I'm 50 years old and have been sober for sixteen years. I came from the East Coast, grew up in Boston and New York. I came from a perfectly normal family. I had an average middle-class upbringing. My family was stable and stayed together. I had grandparents, aunts, uncles. No one drank or was abusive. Nothing happened to me that was particularly frightening or traumatic. I was not abused. I was never denied or deprived in any conceivable way. And still, I'm an alcoholic. It's a disease. It didn't come from having had a broken home, an abusive father, or a lack of love and attention. None of that is there in my story. It doesn't take that kind of background to produce alcoholism. Everyday folks, even Jewish women like me, suffer from it.

I started to drink when I was 16 years old. That first drinking episode characterized what my drinking was to be like for the next eighteen years. I got drunk, which I found terrifying, and I tried very hard to be sober against all of the alcohol that I had put into my body. That was my pattern. It was a crazy-making situation. The physical effects of alcohol were so frightening to me that I was probably only drunk a couple of times in such a way that was obvious to other people. I never passed out. I was what is referred to as a "high bottom." I didn't have to lose everything before I realized that I needed help.

Yet I drank a lot, all the while resisting the physical and chemical effects on my body with everything I had. The insides of my teeth are worn thin from gnashing them to stay conscious when I should have just passed out. Or sometimes the fear was so strong that I would just dig my nails into the palms of my hands and not have that next drink. I was at war inside myself.

Like many women, I was a very functional drunk. I went to college, graduated with a bachelor's degree in dance and went immediately to New York to begin dancing professionally and working. Shortly after graduation I married a man who was an incredibly supportive co-alcoholic. He encouraged my drinking and was himself a child of an alcoholic, though he himself did not have a problem with alcohol itself. I now understand something about the alcoholic family system and realize that he needed to be connected to alcohol. I was his connection. We were a perfect match. He got to take care of me like he had the alcoholic in his family.

So there I was, married at 21, dancing and drinking. Five years later I had my two children. They were 5 and 6 years old respectively when I got sober at 34. I was functional till the very end. It amazes me that so few people even knew that I had a drinking problem.

My beds were made, my house was clean, my children were fed and tended. I didn't black out or get drunk in ways that people could see. I was very present with my kids, though inconsistently so. I did everything I thought I should do. I functioned in my art, I was a good wife and mother, I had friends. I denied and hid my alcoholism in the fact that I functioned. I did my drinking alone at night generally, for at least seven or eight years.

I would sit up alone in my house, which was an old railroad flat in New York City. My husband was in the arts, so he was conveniently out almost every night of the week. He was a workaholic and often didn't come home until after midnight. I kept my bottle of sour mash bourbon in the kitchen at one end of this long flat and myself in my bedroom at the other end. I would start drinking about five in the afternoon and continue on through the evening, especially after I had gotten the children to bed.

I have a sadness even still about reading stories to them at night and knowing that as I opened the book for the next chapter that I couldn't remember what I had read them the night before. I can almost feel them, lying on either side of me, my arms around them, a perfect picture of maternal love and caring, but I wasn't there. I was acting "as if" and the sadness of my alcoholism was sometimes in those subtle little things that they never even knew, but I did. I would say to them, "What happened in *The Hobbit* last night?" and they would tell me, and we would go on reading.

After they were asleep, I would drink more heavily. Towards the last year, every night became a nightmare. I would drink to the point where I had thoroughly terrified myself and I had to stop. I would walk down this long hallway of our flat. It was eighty feet from the kitchen to my bedroom, almost a city block. I would start leaning against the walls and have to use my hands to guide me down that corridor; I was losing my equilibrium. Then I could stop.

I never took the bottle with me to my room. I made myself make that trip down that hallway all the way to the kitchen in order to get a drink. Then I would have to come all the way back to my bedroom. I would often have the glass in my hand but never the bottle. I separated myself from it. That way I could deny what I was doing and hide it from myself.

By the end of the night I would sit, propped up on my bed. I was afraid to close my eyes because then the room would spin and I would have that terrible feeling of loss of control. So I would sit there and watch movies on television with one hand over one eye so that I wouldn't see everything double because I was drunk.

I would sit there like that and say to myself, "I'm a regular person doing a normal thing—just a woman watching a movie in her bedroom at night." That way I denied that I was actually drunk and too afraid to go to sleep. The stories we tell ourselves! My hand was like an eye patch. I would usually do that until I felt safe enough to fall asleep. Or sometimes I would just go in the bathroom, stick my finger down my throat, and throw up so that I could get sober enough to lay down and not have the room spin. Then I could go to sleep.

It was exhausting. It took being insane and scared to live like that and have the energy to maintain all the myriad of little coping mechanisms we develop as alcoholics. You hear stories of a mother lifting a huge automobile when her child is about to be crushed and that's how I was. My life was this two-ton auto that I was holding up. Then I would flex my muscles and say, "See, I'm strong. Everyone is in one piece. I have children, we do things together. I am in one piece."

One night I fell at two in the morning while I was trying to hang up a picture in the bathroom. I was drunk of course, and lost my footing on the back of the toilet, fell off, and barely missed breaking my head open on the bathtub. It was one of those queer, startling moments in which a voice came to me and said, "You fell because you were drinking. You were a quarter of an inch away from splitting your head open because you are drunk." It was like a headline, but I ignored it, blocked it out. I didn't remember until I was sober that I had had that thought. And there were a lot of other moments like that, moments when I knew what was happening, but I couldn't face it. I scalded my youngest child when he was six months old by sitting him in the tub and turning on the hot water. He had a second-degree burn. I can still see the red welt running down this baby's back, and I said to myself as I saw it happen, "If you hadn't been drinking this wouldn't have happened."

But the need for alcohol was stronger than the awareness that I was in trouble and that I was hurting people, including myself. I drove drunk as well. A guardian angel, somebody, kept me from ever hitting anyone when I was in a car.

I felt desperate by this time, suicidal. I thought that I was losing my mind. So I went to a psychiatrist. I told him that I thought that there was something wrong with my drinking, that it frightened me. He replied, "What do you mean there is something wrong with your drinking? I have a glass of wine or something to drink every day at lunch. You don't have that kind of problem. What do you think you are, an alcoholic?"

And I said to myself, "Thank God. This man is a medical

doctor, a psychiatrist. He knows what he's talking about. I am safe. I am not an alcoholic."

He never asked me about how much I drank or what was frightening about my drinking and I, for one, never brought the subject up again. I was this nice Jewish woman. We both needed to see me that way. He just said, "See, I drink every day and I am not an alcoholic." That was what I wanted to hear.

Later I went to a different doctor who put me on Librium because he thought I wouldn't drink if I was on Librium. The combination of the two made me very sick, but then I discovered that the Librium would cure my hangovers, so I took them in the morning and drank at night.

As the disease progressed, my fear of loss of control grew. Anything I couldn't be in control of terrified me—planes, buses, trains, subways, boats, and elevators. I was riddled with fear.

I continued to dance all this time, dance and teach. I had developed this mechanism by which I could talk to my students holding my breath. Since I drank sour mash bourbon I knew they could smell it if I got close to them, so I would take a deep breath in and talk to them and give them some physical correction about their dancing while holding my breath. I wouldn't exhale. It was horrendous. I had begun drinking earlier in the day. I gave up performing. I was in a dance company in New York and I quit. Of course I had good reasons, like a back injury. But in truth, it was becoming less and less possible to drink and dance. So I chose to drink.

I was totally lost. My life lost its focus. I rented a studio one day, and stood there in front of the mirror alone under the neon lights. I was 34. I began to weep. I saw myself in the mirror, and I was an old woman. My skeleton peered through the flesh. I didn't stop drinking at this point, but I went back into therapy and started to get honest about my drinking. I don't think the man knew much about alcoholism, but he did his homework. One day out of the blue, he came in and said, "Leah, would you consider going to Alcoholics Anonymous?"

I just remember sitting there in total silence with nothing to say. I felt as if I had exhaled for the first time in thirty-four years. In my heart I said yes to myself. I felt as if I had finally come home. That was the beginning of the end of my drinking.

I went to an AA meeting right away, but didn't stop drinking. But I knew that I was an alcoholic and there was relief in that. I could hold on to that fact. It had a name. All that craziness had a name. It was a disease. It was alcoholism.

I kept going to meetings, but I didn't understand or listen. I was filled with arrogance. I thought I was superior to all those little slogans you hear at meetings, like "One Day at a Time," "Easy Does It." I thought they were so stupid. This went on for four months, and then one night someone was telling their story, and they said, "Today is the first day of the rest of your life" and with that I got sober. I never took another drink again after that. Those words that I thought were so foolish and simple-minded were the beginning of my spiritual recovery.

I began to listen. It was the people next to me telling me their stories that kept me sober. It was hard for me to deal with the language you run into in AA, with some of the images and ideas. I confused religiosity with spirituality and often thought to myself, *This just isn't for me.* But nothing else had worked, and somehow I knew that I needed to be here, whether I understood, agreed or not, so I just kept coming back.

My marriage fell apart as sometimes happens when one person gets sober. My husband didn't like me sober and had no interest in his own recovery from his part in the disease as a co-alcoholic. That relationship had helped me become the alcoholic I was. It was a harbor that I needed to leave, and I rejoiced in being sober and finally able to make a healthy choice. Being alone with my kids was not easy, but I had an incredible amount of support from people in AA. My kids were AA babies. I would put them in their pajamas and they would toddle across the street with me to my home group, which was just across the street in Manhattan.

I was probably four or five years into my recovery when I began to realize that I had had a spiritual recovery and that I couldn't have stayed sober if I hadn't. Something changed, nothing monumental that I could put my finger on. But now I was consciously hungry, thirsty, seeking with awareness what my spiritual life was about and what it was going to be. It was a very exciting time. I knew that I was no longer alone in the world in a way I hadn't understood before. Someone said that "Spirituality means turning towards life. Practicing alcoholics have turned away from life." My life had taken another turn.

I began working in the field of alcoholism, doing a research project for a large treatment center in New York City. I continued to go to meetings, as I do to this day. I remember sitting around the table after a meeting one night laughing with several other women friends who were also Jewish, saying, "If there's no such thing as a Jewish alcoholic, what are we doing here?" There were eight of us, just the women alone, at that one meeting. I never heard that story that Jews aren't alcoholic until I came in to the program. Then it took me another year to realize that I wasn't sitting in synagogues, I was sitting in church basements. Why? Because there was such resistance to owning up to alcoholism in the Jewish community that many synagogues were not open to AA meetings. I have been to one synagogue in the sixteen years I've been sober and going to meetings all over the U.S. and around the world. I hope this is changing.

Alcohol work continued to be important in my life, but it became crucial to me to find out if I was still a dancer. I moved across the country and structured my life in such a way that I could really dance again. Dancing was first, and working was secondary. I got back in to performing and teaching and making dances. I had a small company for a year or two. It was exciting, discovering dance again, pushing out my boundaries, taking on things that I would have been terrified of before. It felt risky and wonderful! I was still a dancer. Yes, this is still who I am. OK.

Then I began to do more work in the field of alcoholism and women's recovery. I kept dancing, but I was asked to direct a women's residential treatment program. I became aware of how terribly few women were in treatment, of how limited the treatment facilities are for women and other issues we face in recovery. Today I am in private practice as a counselor and continuing with my dancing. I just turned 50 years old.

When I first got sober, I remember clinging to this little seed, this pinpoint of light that I somehow knew was there. It was inside of me. Over the years that light has expanded and grown and it not only encompasses me but it goes outside, way beyond me. I feel filled with it and also held by it. It started out as such a tiny prick of light, and now it's a wonderful kind of brightness. I suppose that's what I was looking for in the bottle but it wasn't there. Today I have a kind of joyfulness and peace because what I was looking for is within me and all around me. That's what the program of AA has given me.

15. Harriet B.

I was born on a reservation in the Midwest, and I lived there until I was about 7 years old. Then I was sent away to a Catholic boarding school. My mother moved to the city to work in a defense plant. I stayed at the boarding school until I was 11, and then I was sent to a sanatorium for tuberculosis. My brother had died of TB at the age of 7. Somehow the welfare department became involved and decided that I might have TB too. My brother had died of it while he was in the sanatorium. The only thing I remember is that I was subject to TB. I was there for about a year; later on, I found out I did not have it.

Pretty much of what I remember about my childhood was being under the guardianship of welfare people, always being shuffled off someplace, not being totally brought up with my mother. I don't know whose doing it was; I just was always being sent away someplace. Both my parents were alcoholics.

I spent summers back on the reservation with my grandmother. I am Chippewah and French, so my mother looked white. When she moved to the city, she passed. I felt ashamed to be an Indian. I had gone to public school for one year; after that, Catholic school for one year and then they sent me away again. That was to the sanatorium where my brother had died. I got the idea that it was not good to be an Indian. I kind of shut down that part of myself because later on I went away to Indian boarding school in South Dakota, and I remember having a real difficult time adjusting. First, I had been with my grandparents and all my cousins back on the reservation, very traditional Indians. My grandparents and my cousins spoke Chippewah. My mother knew it but wouldn't speak it in the home. So I was torn between two worlds, my cousins speaking Indian and I'm not, I being raised in an entirely different culture and being assimilated into it. Talk about confusion! By the time I got to this totally all-Indian school in South Dakota, I am going through all sorts of changes. It was a government school, and you could only speak English. That reinforced my feelings that "I don't want to be the Indian after all. Period. I dropped that part of myself, all of it, anything that had to do with the Indian culture. The government school convinced me that it was not a good idea to be an Indian.

Later on I began to feel the difference. By the time I'm in my late teens, I have a lot of white friends and I live in the city. I take on white attitudes, I don't have anything else. And I took on those attitudes toward other Indians. During that time, the only Indians I saw were drunk or at least drinking. I was really embarrassed for my grandparents when they came to visit. I got married to a white man when I was 17.

My first drink was when I was about 11 years old, and I got real giggly. That was about it. It was not a part of my life until later on. I became pregnant right away, got right into being married, being the young urban housewife, and drinking wasn't a problem. My third son was born, and I had no connection with the Indian community at all. My mother had dropped away all vestiges of her background and been completely assimilated into the white culture. My own life was pretty much like everybody else's life who was on a regular block in a middle-class neighborhood. I didn't feel any different. We were pretty much wrapped up in our family. I drank occasionally with our friends.

I took my husband back to the reservation where my grandparents lived. It had been maybe about fifteen to twenty years since I'd been back. It was the first time that I realized that I was still Indian.

We walked into this little cafe on our way to my grandmother's, somewhere in the middle of nowhere, to stop and have a bite to eat—and they wouldn't serve me. This was in the 1960s. They wouldn't serve me. I was carrying my third son, who had just been born, and I was with my white husband.

My husband was absolutely appalled. The waitress came over and said to my husband, "She can't eat in here." My husband said, "What? What do you mean she can't eat in here. Of course she can." "Not here." "Why not here?" "We can give you food to go. You can eat here, but she can't." And my husband said, "Oh," and that really brought home to me that I wasn't white, I was Indian—shock upon shock.

We got up and left. My husband couldn't stay there another minute. He had never seen me in an Indian community, so now our situations were reversed. He was the only white in the Indian community. That was real different for him. We spent about ten days there. I wasn't close to my grandparents by this time. I was in the beginning, up until I was about 12 or 13. Moving away broke that connection with them emotionally. And then there were my feelings of shame about being Indian. That incident in that cafe didn't help any, just brought it all up again.

So still, drinking wasn't a problem. We did drink, we had couples over to our house, parties and stuff, but nothing serious. That didn't change until we moved cross-country. Then my drinking increased. I was 32. I hadn't wanted to move.

I have five children, and I had four by the time we moved. There were a couple of isolated incidents with my drinking that happened just prior to our move here. Warning signs. But I didn't know what they meant. The personality change. When this incident happened, I couldn't believe that I was the same person, that this had happened. It again goes back to not the quantity of alcohol consumed, but how it affects you.

We were at a New Year's Eve party having a great time. Then something changed. I saw this other person just take me over. I became obnoxious. I got into a fight; I bit my husband. He was just stunned, shocked, he couldn't believe it. We had gone to this party over at a friend's house. We were part of a group of about seven young married couples that rotated parties, and we had all been friends for a long time. Everyone was shocked. Well, after that I chose to drink very little at all, because I couldn't believe my behavior. It scared me, and it was an isolated incident. I hadn't even been drinking a whole lot, but it didn't matter. That's just what happened.

By the time I was 37 years old, I had had my last child. She was 2. We celebrated, had a party, and I blacked out. It was really traumatic. It was the first time that ever happened. My husband said, "Don't you remember what went on that night?"

And at that point I had been this status drinker. I drank Chivas Regal. This had to do with the feeling that drinking better liquor would make me equal to everyone. And I really noticed that, after that cafe incident, and having spent those ten days on the reservation, and seeing a lot of poverty at a level that I hadn't known, ever. I was an only child and had never experienced poverty like what I saw the people in my tribe going through.

And the reservation wasn't anywhere that I had remembered it. I had great feelings of shame, and it was real painful for me to be there and see my people. When I came back, I chose not to be an Indian again, with all resolve. Just *chose* it. It was too painful. I did everything I could not to acknowledge that I am Indian.

One argument my husband and I had somewhere along the line was about this dilemma. It wasn't so much him as it was me. I said, "When I married you, I didn't become white." I was resentful. He said, "I never expected you to become white." So all those mixed feelings kept coming up.

We moved across the country. Our drinking increased and it became a regular weekend thing. I didn't want to move. My friends were all back in the Midwest, I was quite happy there and my husband wasn't. He didn't want the winters. I did everything I could to sabotage our moving. He finally said, "I'm moving with our children, and you can come if you want to." So he gave me ten days, because I had been dragging my feet.

We moved from an eleven-room house to a four-room. I attempted at one point to get involved in the community. I volunteered at an Indian health center, but it didn't work. I didn't have to work and was just at home with the kids. I wasn't drinking during the week. Then I began to have physical illnesses. I got pregnant with my daughter. It took me two years to really adjust to the move. I didn't want to be here, and every opportunity that I had, I blamed my husband for moving us. Our marriage began to go steadily downhill. I began seeking out help, family service support groups, marriage counselors. My husband moved up the career ladder. He's quite good at what he does and was just becoming part of that whole corporate scene. His drinking increased, and mine decreased.

I was being a super-Mom. My boys were in Boy Scouts, and I became very active with them. I was involved in all sorts of parents' groups at school. In addition, I was a perfectionist about my household duties. I was overachieving right and left. I was constantly running from one thing to the next, dragged my kids with me, and everyone else's. My daughter became the treasured little girl. I starched and ironed all her dresses, she had a whole closet full of them. My kid's shoes were always polished and gleaming. My husband didn't have to do anything, truly. I bought all his clothes, even his underwear, he didn't even have to replace a broken shoestring. My sons were pampered as well. I remember I ironed forty-eight shirts at one count during this time. I often worked until 2 A.M. to get this all done; I don't know how I did it. This, of course, was before the drinking took over. Cleaning out the stove was a major event. I was a fanatic. Finally when my daughter was about 5 or 6 months old, I chose to leave. Left the kids, the baby, everything. I had been in therapy, and I was trying to hold it together, and it seemed like a whole lot of stuff I tried to hold together. Too much. I began to drink at the bar. Now I was drinking *at* people and I was drinking for relief, to get the pressure off. But I was still not drinking on a daily basis.

The separation lasted about three months, maybe four at the most. We got back together; I went home, and we wrote up a contract agreeing that neither one of us would drink for a year. And we stayed with that agreement. We had no other support system around us, we isolated ourselves. We just stopped drinking. All of our new friends were drinkers, so there was no one but just the two of us to rely on. After that year, we went back to drinking. When our year was up, we said, "Let's walk down to the corner bar and have a drink." So we started drinking again. But for me now it's taking less. The disease had progressed, but I didn't know it.

So for the next two years, Saturdays start running into Wednesdays. I couldn't believe it, I was possessed with drinking. We began keeping liquor at home. I had always wanted to reestablish the social system that I had back in the Midwest, with the couples about our age, and the children our children's ages. We would go to these friend's house, bring the children, and stay up most of the night playing cards. I wanted that back again and couldn't get it. I was trying to reestablish that system, hoping that I could get back to that place where drinking was not a big thing.

But it wasn't working. This drinking was more intensified. Sometimes we stopped drinking or cut down during the week. But by now the children are now beginning to act out, my youngest boy begins to act out—he begins shoplifting, running away, all kinds of things. The other children are not yet showing anything. My husband is still doing well at his job, stopping in the bar to relax, then coming home. I begin to work in a bar, so now I am not coming home. I start with one drink and don't come home until 2 A.M. I come home, and I am loaded, all the time. I get jobs as bartenders, and the house, the furniture, and everything is a mess. Finally all the kids are acting out.

I stop drinking for a while and become a binge drinker. I don't drink for six to eight weeks at a time. But I begin to set it up so I have to go out. I need a night out to drink. I can't stay stopped. At first I had friends, but later on they became a problem for me. They were interested in doing other things besides drinking. I was into drinking. All the time. Something is happening. I sense it. I see the house beginning to look seedy, and I tell myself, "It's their fault." I felt like I was trying to keep the ocean back from running up on the sand. Everything is slipping away, and I am like this mad woman, running around, going to a support group, doing therapy to get it all back the way it was, and nobody's cooperating. I don't drink often, but the times that I do are disastrous. My husband drinks every day, but he is maintaining control and I can't. I'm furious because he, after two or three drinks, can say, "I am going to go home, I'm tired." I start off with one drink and I have to run the full cycle until 2 A.M. And all the while I am trying to control my drinking. I don't understand any of it. It was a horrible way to live. When I look back at that time, I think, "God, how did I survive?"

I couldn't stay drunk and I couldn't stay sober. I was driven by this compulsion. Yet for a time I would just hold off. At one point prior to my coming into the program, I stopped drinking for eighteen months. But still I had no support system; I went into deep depression, and I would get terrible muscle spasms. When I look back, I think that I almost created illnesses—I mean, major surgeries—just to get somebody to pay attention to me. I knew something was wrong, and I wanted somebody to fix me. In one year I had four operations: partial hysterectomy, a gall-bladder operation, a therapeutic abortion, and my appendix removed.

I didn't know that I was sick. I looked at all the things I was doing in terms of being in a support group, being a conscientious parent, and yet my children were still acting out. I was about 40. I am considering suicide a lot. I was seeing a therapist. Every once in a while we'd have family session, and somebody would bring up the fact that I was Indian, and I would go off, lose my temper, become enraged. I was in absolute denial about it. My kids would come home and say, "Mom, we are Indian, aren't we?" and I would say something like, "Yeah, so what? Who cares?" "Well, Mom, could you tell

us a little bit about . . . " "I don't know anything about it."
And if someone would tell me they had Indian friends, I would
say, "You know what? I don't really care." I did not want to
discuss being an Indian. For one reason, I was ashamed to be
one, and the other was that I was ashamed that I didn't know
anything about being Indian, so I chose not to discuss it.

So what brought me into the program was the house had
now turned to garbage, the kids turned to garbage, my marriage turned to garbage. And I am not feeling much more than
that, and I was saying, "What's happening?" I'm not happy
at home, not happy at this part-time job that I got. I am
working in the bar, but not drinking there because the drinking is different. It's worse. I have to be very careful, to drink
maybe only on Friday night, because I cannot stop. But I can't
drink on Saturday or Sunday, because nothing will go down
or stay down. I have such a terrible reaction now. That's how
controlled, absolutely insane I became. From whatever night I
chose to drink, I couldn't drink for however long it took me to
clear up to get well again, four days. If I drank again, I could
look at being sick, pure insanity.

So I began to ask the question, is this what life is all about?
What happened to my big dream? In the *Twelve-by-Twelve*, it
says that by an act of providence, God is here; mine was a
mugging that got me into a program. I had sat down one night
for my last drink. Five bottles of beer. I was laughing and
talking on the outside, and inside I was having this interior
dialogue saying, "What is this all about? Where do I go from
here? This is a dead-end street." I walked out of the bar that
night, and I saw this guy coming toward me very casually. He
gets within striking distance of me and stomps my foot. I had
taken a year of karate, and I saw the guy walk up, smash my
foot, and then I just watched him run off with my purse. I am
still lucid, and I am saying, "What happened?" That night
was the beginning of the end.

For two weeks I had to sit in my house. My foot was broken,
and my whole world crumbled around me. My children looked

at me contemptuously. I hadn't been drinking since that night, and they said, "It doesn't make any difference, you were drunk." And I said, "But you don't understand, I only had five bottles of beer and I was on my way home." They said, "We don't care, you are a drunk and that's it."

I finally called my therapist and told her I wanted out of here right now and I don't know how to get out. And she said, "You know we never talked about drinking, maybe you would like to check out being an alcoholic?" And I said, "I don't care. Just get me out of here, I'll go anywhere." So she recommended this program with the U.S. Public Health Department. Ironically, she said they would accept me because I am a Native American; me who isn't interested in being one. So I thought to myself, "OK, if that gets me in, I'll go for twenty-eight days."

That program brought up to my consciousness that I am Indian. I don't want that. So now I am dealing with my alcoholism, I am dealing with the denial of being a Native American. Where do I go from here?

What I suffered in that place was the "pitiful, incomprehensible, demoralization" they speak of in the Big Book. I wanted to die, and I couldn't. It was horrible. It wasn't until I read the Big Book of AA that I found those words that described my experience. I considered suicide again. I was fortunate to get another good therapist. And that is how I got into Alcoholics Anonymous.

My marriage dissolved completely right after that. It was already well on the way. Two days after getting out of the treatment program, my husband left. Six months later, I chose to leave my family. I was 44 years old.

I called my husband a month before I knew that I was leaving and told him what I was going to do and asked him to come back and take care of the children, which he did. He took custody. He moved back in, and I moved out. It has changed my relationship with my children for the better. What

we have now is much more real, much deeper. It is chosen—
not expected so much.

I moved to a hotel, and as shocking as that sounds, it was
truly the beginning of my life. When I moved to the hotel
room, it was like a return to the womb. I am now almost four
years sober.

The most crucial part of my recovery has been my return to
the Indian community. It was very traumatic. I had been sober
for a little while when I read an ad for an Indian street fair. I
thought, "What the heck, I'll go."

I had a friend with me that day fortunately. I remember it
just as it happened. We walk around the corner to the fair,
and I'm engulfed with waves of sadness that's rising up out
of my lower belly. I am overwhelmed with feelings, and I'm
breathing deeply, and I feel myself choking up and beginning
to cry. I turned to my friend and said, "I don't know what's
going on, I don't know what's happening, I just can't help it,
but I think I'm going to cry."

The closer we get, the tighter my throat gets, the more my
eyes well up with tears, and I am in a lot of pain. I have never
had an experience like this. We look around as we walk up to
the fair and we see these very Indian-looking people. I come
to the first booth, and I finally burst into tears. I had to go off
by myself and sit down on the sidewalk, I couldn't just stand
there. My friend was saying, "What's wrong, what's the matter?" And I am crying from the inside of my soul, just sobs,
convulsing with them and I said, "I don't know if I can stay
here, this is too painful. I don't know what's happening." That
wall of denial about being Indian was coming down. I had
made one more attempt to go around and be, and it was too
painful, so we left after I purchased one item from that booth.
I took it and put it away. A couple of years later I ran into a
woman that I had been in a parent support group with and
she was Indian. She had always known that I was Indian and
I knew that she was, but I stayed away because I did not want
anything to do with Indians. When I ran into her after that

fair, she invited me to lunch at the Indian health center that I work for today. She wasn't in AA, but that isn't all of what goes on here. I was reluctant to come, but I also knew that I needed to come. I needed to find out where I stood because there was a piece of me still missing. I had been sober for a while and was working real hard on myself, but I somehow felt like I'd been left in isolation. When I agreed to come, I don't know what I expected Indian people to do or how they would be different, but I found myself absorbing them like a sponge does water. I was thirsty.

We came here twice. I was not very comfortable, but I was curious. I rarely said anything, but I watched. I made no attempt to get involved in the community here. My friend kept inviting me to community events and I always said no, but finally this one time I said yes. She had invited me to a big pow-wow around the first of the year. It was the first time I had been to one in many, many years, perhaps since I was a child. We were sitting in the stands when the Indians made this grand entry on horseback in all their regalia and I began to cry.

Again I said, "I don't know if I can stay, this is too painful." And she understood. I just sat there and cried. I ended up staying for the entire thing. She even got me out there to dance one time. At first I couldn't, and I went back and sat down for a while. Then a little later I tried it again, and we went on and danced. This time I stayed. It was a whole new awakening for me. And I knew that this had been the missing piece in my life, the part I needed to become whole, to become who I am, Indian.

When I walked into the halls of this Indian center as an employee not long after that, I had no reservations at all. It was like I walked into a glove, it fit. Here there was a grand-mother and grandfather for me, a brother and sister, mother and father, it was family, I walked into family. This was the place for me to be and I knew it. It wasn't even the job, it was the relationships that I needed, the claiming of my heritage which is great.

This has all been a real growing, a growing into myself, into being whole and valuable. I worked the steps of the program a lot in the beginning, but now it feels like they work me. That is the difference. When the hard times came, did I work a step? No, the steps worked me. That was my spiritual awakening. Yes, I had learned them, familiarized myself with them, but they came up and were lived out of my heart. I don't know how to explain what I mean by that, it's just a feeling you get about the steps when you see them working in your life and you know that you didn't do it, some other power is at work here.

When I was trying not to be Indian it was such a big deal; now that I am, it is just part of it all, part of the whole that makes my life complete.

If you're Indian and I'm white we have different problems. That's a lot of how Indians come into contact with AA: they can't relate to the white world. But if I can have the *Big Book* taught to me by another Indian, then I can relate.

There are not too many Indian women who are very visible in the program so some people think that Indian women don't have such a problem with alcoholism. That's not true. Typically the Indian women getting sober are not going to be so visible. They tend to keep a very closed, low profile and they really need support. It all ties in with the lack of self-esteem that runs through any alcoholic, but particularly women. And if you're Indian or a woman of color, the problem is compounded. I got real active, because that's part of where I came from, organizing Cub Scout troops, PTA's, parents' groups. That's my white background. I have another woman friend who is Indian and has fifteen years sobriety and is very visible as well, but she is also totally assimilated into the white culture.

Not long ago I was secretary of a large meeting in the city. It had about a hundred and fifty people in it, but no people of color besides myself. Being a secretary was a year's commitment for this particular meeting, so I took it on and began to bring in speakers from different ethnic groups. It was a wonderful experience. I just finished that commitment a few months ago. People came up to me afterwards and thanked me. They said, "I'm so glad you brought in all the different ethnic groups you did because we don't see a lot of them." The picture's slowly changing.

I don't think that I have any more spirituality because I'm Indian. People have asked me that—isn't that odd? I got my spirituality through the program. That's the whole purpose of the Big Book, to give you a foundation and a belief in a power greater than yourself.

16. Eleanor E.

My name is Eleanor, and I'm an addict alcoholic. I was born in South Carolina, an only child in a family in which my father was an alcoholic, as well as several other close relatives. I had a half-brother, nineteen years older than myself, my mother's son by a previous marriage. He was off in the military while I was growing up. I loved him very much nonetheless. When he got out of the service he was drinking heavily. At one point he was gone for three years, and we ended up finding him in Chicago at the Salvation Army. This was a big disgrace in the family.

From the time I can remember, I remember alcoholism. In the South everything is hush-hush, never discussed outside the home. I lived in a small town in which most people were black, the rest Caucasian. My father owned the liquor store in town. We always knew who drank. Most people didn't drink socially. Drinking was done in the home, behind closed doors. Very prominent women in town would send their maids into my father's store to buy their liquor for them. When my father came home at night, he and Mother would go in the kitchen, close the door, and have a couple of drinks together, from a shot glass. Rarely did they mix a drink. From the time I was 5 or so, I always got to sip my father's drink. I liked that.

I always felt different, even as a child. I was the kid who never fit. And I had everything. I was spoiled rotten. I was the kid who always had money, new toys, a jeep when I was 10 to drive around our summer home on an island, charge accounts. When I was in the first grade my parents sent the maid to get me from school. She carried me home on her back while all my other friends were walking. That made me different and yet it made me special; and that part—being special— I liked and cultivated for the rest of my life.

My parents vied for my attention, competed with each other. My father would tell me that if it hadn't been for him I wouldn't have been born. I was torn between my parents. My mother was wonderful and made all sorts of marvelous fancy, lacy clothes for me at the same time my dad was going out buying me boots and footballs. I could always get what I wanted from my dad. I learned to manipulate at an early age.

My parents lost a child the year before I was born. They had a boy who was born dead. They dressed him up and photographed him out in a bassinet in the yard, just like he was alive. I have pictures of that today. Apparently I came along the next year by accident. I was wanted once I arrived, I knew that. I went everywhere with my dad. I became his little boy. He would say to my friends, "When Eleanor was a little boy . . . " so much that as a child I thought at some time I *had* been a little boy.

By the time I got to high school I was a poor student. I'm very tall, and I played basketball. I was the star of the team, and I loved it. I never had to go to class. Women's basketball was big at our school. So my parents sent me away to a girls' boarding school in the South in the tenth grade. There I immediately developed my first crush on a woman. She was a senior, a rebel, and the most popular girl in school. She was like a big sister for a while, but then we had a total affair, which I instigated. This was to become a pattern with me.

I had never read a book on homosexuality. I didn't know anything about it, but I knew how I felt about this woman. We got caught. The teachers found a letter I had written to her. The letter didn't prove anything, but they contacted my parents anyway and they came to the school one Sunday morning and took me home. But first they took me to a medical doctor to have me examined to see if anything was wrong with me physically. I never admitted anything. I denied it all. They kept me at home for about six weeks and then took me back to school. I did not want to go back, because I knew that everyone would know what had happened. They made the girl who had been my lover move out of the dorm and in with her family, and they moved me into the librarian's house, on campus. Again I was separate, a special case.

We continued to see each other anyway, but I begged my parents not to send me back there, to let me come home and go to public school. They did. I dated all the time, had lots of boyfriends, but I continued to have crushes on women. When I was in the eleventh grade, my parents left town and had one of my teachers stay with me. I had an affair with her too. Again, I started it.

I went away to a women's college which they didn't like because they were afraid that my relationships with women would continue. I didn't know how to study, made very poor grades. I just wanted to be a P.E. teacher. My mother kept telling me I was masculine, but I never was. I was just tall. All the boys were always shorter than me. I used to stoop over to try to be like everyone else.

I had started drinking in high school. I was 13 when I got drunk for the first time. I was at a house party with some older people and I got drunk on "Purple Jesus"—grape juice and gin. Threw up on everything. My father came to get me the next morning and carried me out saying, "Honey, I guess you are just going to have to learn to drink. Don't worry about it, it's not bad, we're not going to punish you. You'll learn." He also told me that I would learn to like Scotch, to like martinis like a lady, what the finest liquors were and that you didn't mix them with anything. I grew up with alcohol being OK. It was the only thing in my life that was OK. Once I began to drink, I could get rid of that feeling that I always had about not being able to fit in, about being different. I drank all through high school and on into college.

My homosexuality progressed. I got married for a year after college and that didn't work out. I continued to see women. I thought I was really sick, and that someday I would get well and no longer be homosexual. I didn't know any other gay people. Every woman I had an affair with, I brought out, and

I always made them think they were the first one that I had had an affair with, just like that first time. I continued to see men and dated a lot of guys as well. I could have a good physical relationship with men, but I could never have the emotional relationship that I had with women. Women were my best friends as well as my lovers. To me that was a wonderful combination.

I moved to Houston, Texas, and discovered that I was hardly the only gay person in the world. It was a real melting pot in the late 1950s. I'm 22 at this point, have only lived in small southern towns, so I really came out in full bloom. I went through all the role playing that was going on, tried to fit in the bar scene, but I didn't understand a lot of what was going on. In those days you had to be classified as a "fem" or a "butch" if you were gay. Neither one of those fit either, but at least it was closer to what I felt like. I began to meet people who were like me. Still, I was unhappy—the fit was miserable. All my life I never confided in anyone, just shoved everything down. I didn't know life was any other way; I didn't know why I was on this earth or why I felt as badly as I did.

I began to work in the medical profession and worked for a wonderful doctor who turned out to be an alcoholic-addict.

I had back surgery in 1961. Up until this point I only drank. But then I got addicted to morphine. I was on it for seventeen days. They got me off of it by giving me Librium. Given that I worked for a doctor who was also an alcoholic as well as a drug addict, I had no trouble getting whatever drugs I wanted, so I got into morphine and codeine after my surgery.

Whatever pill was available to me, I got hooked on. I took Valium when it came out. My drinking progressed. I still had control over that. I was very disciplined about getting up and going to work. I was a workaholic. I worked my day, then came home and got drunk. Drugs progressed too. And everyone drank in Texas—pick up a beer on the way home, didn't you?

Eventually I moved. I was still working in the medical profession and had access to all the drugs I wanted. Every doctor I ever worked for was an alcoholic and addicted. They still functioned. The first one in Houston is dead now—he blew his brains out.

I would get codeine in the big bottles that they store it in in the pharmacy, and all the Valium I wanted. With a bad back, I had more surgery and a partial gastorectomy and so again I was addicted to morphine, as well as Preludin (speed) and sleeping pills by now. Sleeping pills didn't do anything for me. I could take six Nembutal and I was just rummy. I had a massive tolerance. I kept drinking more and more.

I finally stopped working for doctors and got into medical sales. It was one of those fields that had been closed to women. I broke into it and did very well. Now I was on my own. I made a lot of money, my career flourished because I was so disciplined, always driving myself. Then I decided that it would be fun to open a little restaurant on the side. I'd always wanted to do that. Now I was my own boss, had a lot of money and some spare time, so I did. I thought it would be like a hobby. We served thirty lunches a day, and I had six employees.

The restaurant turned out to be a smash hit. All the theater people in town hung out there on a daily basis. It was written up in *Newsweek* and *Vogue* magazine. I never meant for this to happen. I was now doing three hundred lunches a day, in a liquor bar, open for dinner and I was doing two hundred dinners, seven nights a week. It was more than I could handle; I didn't know anything about the restaurant business. It was successful in spite of me. It *looked* successful—I wasn't making a dime. I had loans all over the place and couldn't pay them off—should never have expanded. I had bartenders that were dealing drugs. I was drinking from morning until I fell asleep at night, and I didn't know it. So I started using cocaine to keep me on my feet and from looking loaded.

My father killed himself in 1970, the same year I opened the restaurant, and what I discovered was that that gave me permission to fall apart. He was finally gone, and that meant I didn't have to live any more if I didn't want to. I could kill myself if I wanted to—I didn't have anything more to prove. I hated the restaurant—it came to that. I had to be out there smiling; I made the place by hand carrying everyone to the table. Everyone knew me and we had great service, and I was sitting down drinking with them all day, going from table to table. I gave them what they wanted from me.

I got to the point where I knew the business was failing, and I knew I couldn't make it, couldn't stop drinking or using. So there was one way out, and it was no big deal. I would just do myself in. So I went home one night, and just didn't know how to live in the world without the drugs and alcohol and was scared to death. No Dad any more, either. So that night I took about twenty Nembutal, about sixty Valium, and had been drinking all day. I really intended to die. But I was found and taken to the hospital, and I was thinking when I woke up, "Goddamn it, can't I even do this right?" Got out of the hospital and they wanted me to see a psychiatrist, and I said, "Absolutely not, and I want my hospital records changed." And they changed them to say that it was just a reaction to drugs and alcohol.

I went home and was stumbling around the house, and the phone rang. It was a celebrity and she said, "Darling, you've got to come to the restaurant, I have this new boyfriend you've got to meet." So I was back over there with a drink in my hand. I continued to function with cocaine. That's the way it went for a long time.

Finally, I knew I couldn't make it with the restaurant. I had hired some restaurant people, and they told me that maybe in five years I'll start making money. Consequently I closed the doors to what looked like a very successful place.

I moved in with a new lover who was very successful in her field. She did not want me to work. For me, that was crazy, because the first year I was scared. I was scared to death, because I had gone into bankruptcy and didn't want to show my face. The next two years all I did was sit home and take care of the construction of the new swimming pool, and deal in some of the property we bought and resold. I was doing some interior design, and she was into that too.

I was going crazy, sitting home drinking all day. I couldn't be in the sun by the new pool without putting Valium in me, so I started using cocaine again. That made it possible for me to look all right by the time she got home at night. We'd have a few drinks and often spend the evening entertaining with dinner parties. I managed to hang in there because of the cocaine. It made everything perfect.

With all my free time, I ended up getting very promiscuous. I started up another serious relationship with another woman on the side. I finally convinced the woman I was living with that I should start a small business just to keep myself occupied. She agreed. That gave me an excuse to come home later and later at night. I came in very late one night, loaded. It was 2 o'clock in the morning and out of guilt, I think, said, "Well, I guess I'm an alcoholic, so I'd better go to AA." I didn't want to go to meetings or stop drinking, I just needed a cop-out.

I began going to meetings with a group of people that I thought were just like me. They had big cars, the right kind of clothes with designer labels and I seemed to fit right in because I had all those things too. They seemed to like me, and I couldn't see that AA was any different from anything I'd done before, except now the people I hung out with weren't drinking. My lover got very upset and began to complain, "At least when you were drinking, you were at home." That was all I needed. That was my out, the one I was looking for. I stopped going to AA and drank and used for another three years. Finally I ended this relationship because I couldn't drink or use enough to stay in it. We had been together six years.

I just moved right in with the other woman I'd become lovers with on the side. She too was an alcoholic and addict, and I got to drink and use all I wanted to. So did she. But by now my disease had progressed to the point where I could never get enough. It was bad.

Despite my interior chaos, my business was doing well. I had a wholesale-retail showroom of lighting accessories. I managed to do well with it until the cocaine took over my life and stopped working for me. At some point it turned and began to work against me. I became paranoid. I would get up in the morning and take twenty milligrams of Valium. When I went into the bathroom and looked in the mirror, my face looked like it was melting away, just like on an acid trip. If I had any cocaine around, I would use it and it would keep me on my feet and allow me to pour my first drink at 7 A.M. After about three straight shots of vodka, I could put on my makeup and my face had stopped melting. I would dash out of the house and down to my business, all the time running on guilt and fear. By the time I got there I couldn't even go out front and see people. So I hired other people to run things for me and I just stayed in the back, drinking and using cocaine all day. My life was completely falling apart. I didn't want to live and I didn't know what to do. I was afraid that I couldn't die.

I had also started a manufacturing company with my new lover. That was still going pretty well. But then we would get loaded and get into violent fights. Sometimes I'd go back down to our factory to sleep at night after a fight. I slept on a cot. There were rats running around on the floor all around me, but I couldn't even get up off the cot. I'd get up in the morning and try to bathe myself in the sink in order to get down to my lighting store and keep that image going. I was dying inside, but I couldn't die. I had $60,000 in cash at that point, from the sale of a house that I owned, and within that year I ended up spending $40,000 of that on cocaine just for myself. I had completely lost control.

Again I tried to kill myself, and took every drug I had around. Again I was saved. My lover found me, called the paramedics, and they took me to the county hospital. I woke up and my first thought was, "My God, I can't do this either," and me next thought was, "How dare she bring me to a county hospital! Doesn't she know who I am?"

I talked myself out of being put in the psychiatric ward where you're supposed to be kept after something like a suicide attempt. Having been around the medical profession, I knew the right things to say. I took a cab home, paid the driver and could hardly wait to get out of the cab to get to the drugs again. I couldn't believe it.

It was clear to me that I couldn't do this any more. My lover's mother had been in AA for twenty-seven years. I called her up and said, "Please come get me and take me to a meeting." While I was getting dressed, my lover woke up and asked me where I was going. I told her that her mother was taking me to an AA meeting. She got up, got dressed, and came with me. And there we were at the meeting, reeking of booze. We were awful. Two nice women who'd been raised properly and had everything, and we were a mess. I have a lot of empathy today when I see people walk in the door of their first meeting.

My lover stayed sober from that point on but I didn't. Not only was she going to AA but also to Al-Anon, so that she could learn how not to be a co-alcoholic for me. I kept slipping. Finally hit my bottom, blacked out, threw up, fell out of my car on the street. Meredith, my lover, dragged me into the house and just left me there, and that was the right thing to do.

God must have been there with me that day because I don't even remember dialing my sponsor's number, I didn't even know that I knew the number, but I did. She said she'd come right over. While I was waiting for her, I drank a bottle of hot champagne. By the time she got there, I was wandering up and down the street. I was a wreck and I knew that I had to get sober. This time I wanted to get sober for the right reasons.

I had a lot of wonderful friends that stayed with me, twenty-four hours a day, for the next several days. They took shifts, moved me into a new apartment, and I started going to meetings right away. I was going to two meetings a day which I did for a long, long time. I didn't know what to do with my life. My businesses were ended. I had a little money in the bank, enough to live for a couple of months and that was it. I was looking in the paper one day and saw a job advertised for a part-time x-ray technician. I had done that, years ago. I hadn't worked in the field for twelve years. I called; turned out that the man hiring was someone I'd worked for years ago, and he said he'd hire me immediately. The job was five minutes from my house.

AA meetings and the program became my priority. I knew that I couldn't die and so I'd have to make the best out of life. I no longer had a choice. All I did was work and go to meetings. And more meetings and more meetings. I made enough money for the basics, and that was all, and that was fine. I got all the rest from AA. This time when I started back to meetings I made it a point to seek out people who really wanted their sobriety, who worked the steps and didn't just talk about it. I knew this time I had to change.

I went to a meeting at a place for gay women and I felt like I didn't fit in there. The women were all just off the street and were really tough. I walked in, in my wool skirt and cashmere sweater and pearls, and stood out like a sore thumb. They elected me the secretary of the meeting. I didn't know what to do. My sponsor taught me a really important lesson right then and there. She encouraged me to take the commitment and said, "Eleanor, you have to learn to love the unloveables before you can learn to love yourself." I stuck it out for the six months, got to watch these kids getting sober, worked with them, and it was fantastic. I really grew to love them and learned a great deal from that experience.

Through a friend in the program, I found out about a job as a fashion buyer for a big department store. I had never done anything like that before, but I got it. There was a lot of drinking around me, but I never drank or used again. I got on airplanes and did not drink. When I got to where I was going, I would get on the phone and find out about meetings or just talk to someone at the local central AA office while everyone else was out drinking. I stayed sober.

Now I do interior design on my own and once again have my own business and am very successful. The woman who was my lover, who went to AA with me, and I are back together. She's still in the program and we have a wonderful relationship that's now eight years old. I have freedom. I go to gay meetings, I go to straight meetings. I feel like I fit no matter where I am today. I can be who I am, and I am totally accepted for that. AA has saved my life and the promises in the Big Book are all coming true: "We will intuitively know how to handle situations that used to baffle us, our fear of financial insecurity will leave us." I still have financial insecurity, but I have lost the fear. God takes care of me today. He didn't let me die. He runs my life. I just do the footwork. I show up; what happens after that is up to God. My life is a miracle. I want to live. I'm happier than I've ever been. Look at us—sitting here talking now over a cup of coffee and a glass of water instead of Bloody Mary's and a line of cocaine. It's incredible. I don't have to impress anyone any more.

17. Pearl J.

I was born in Burke County, Georgia, in 1921. I was adopted by an aunt and uncle when I was about 16 months old. We moved to the Midwest, where I grew up.

My mother died when I was 4, my natural mother, that is. I never could figure out why I was the one she gave away, because I had two sisters and a brother that stayed at home. I thought there must be something terribly wrong with me as I grew up. The truth was that I was a very sickly baby, so sickly that they thought I was going to die. I needed constant care. We lived in the backwoods in Georgia and there was no place to work except the fields. It just wasn't the kind of situation I could survive in. My aunt that raised me never had a child of her own and she wanted me. So Mother let her take me with her to the Midwest.

My aunt, who became my mother, explained all this to me. She loved me, wanted me. But that wasn't enough, I decided. I must have been ugly to be unwanted like that by my natural mother. That's how I felt inside.

I grew up with a lot of drinking. During Prohibition my mom made beer and wine, which was legal, and my dad made moonshine, which was illegal. My mother was nervous about that because they had a wood stove up on the top floor of our house, and they cooked the mash on that wood stove. It took a lot of fire to cook those big vats of mash, and it takes a lot of heat to run liquor. They'd be running liquor in the summertime. "Why would anybody have that much smoke shooting out of a chimney in July?" she'd say, and worry that they'd get caught, but they never did. They had parties, and I saw people drinking, and I could see what alcohol did to some people, how it made them do crazy things, how it changed them. I knew from an early age that it was liquor that was doing it and that it was causing a lot of trouble in people's lives. I made up my mind that when I grew up I wasn't going to drink—ever, because I might be one of those people that liquor made do crazy things.

I don't remember my first drink as such because my mother was a great believer in the hot toddy. If I had a cold or a stomachache, she would put a little liquor in some hot tea with lemon juice and honey and sugar, and it tasted good. I remember getting that warm glow. At Christmas the kids were allowed to have a little glass of wine, but it was the hot toddies that I remember. I used to say that I had a stomachache when I didn't have one just because I wanted that little toddy.

When I was 16, I went to my older sister's house and she gave me a glass of blackberry wine. She had company over. I drank it down like you drink a glass of water, and I got my first charge from alcohol. I felt all this pain that I had been carrying all my life and didn't even know that there was a pain there, was gone. It was completely gone, and I was delighted. I ran out in the back yard and got on my bicycle, and rode around and around the block, and I rode fast, and it felt so good!

I went back to the house and felt very embarrassed but I didn't know about what. I wasn't relating what I did to the alcohol I drank. It was obvious to everybody else why I was running around like that, but not to me. That's my alcoholism. I just couldn't relate the two things.

That was the first time I got a real release from alcohol, and it was total. For me that was a one-shot deal. Never since has alcohol completely taken away that feeling of unworthiness, ugliness. I tried, I gave it everything I had to get that feeling again, that total release from the pain, but never since that one time did it ever completely obliterate it again.

I grew up in a middle-class Jewish neighborhood. Most of the time I was the only black kid in my class. I was never in a class with another black kid until I got to high school. There were only about eight of us in a grammar school of 1,500 kids. The school was predominantly orthodox Jew.

As a minority I always felt that I had to protect myself against this majority of people. I learned to manipulate and get people to do what I wanted them to do. Some people even say that's part of the disease of alcoholism. Well, I was good at it, and I started young. When I was in the eighth grade, I organized a student strike, and it worked. That was back in the days before kids were doing such things. I wanted to control people and situations, it seemed like it was necessary, because if I didn't control them, they might hurt me.

I dropped out of high school to get married at 17. I married a wino, a 26-year-old wino that I'd known for about a month. I was drinking sweet wine by this time and my dad's drinking had become pretty heavy so I wanted to leave home. My dad was a drunk. I didn't drink any hard liquor then. My husband had this sweet wine, and we drank that for a couple of months, and we talked sweet nothings, and then I acquired a taste for gin. That was all for him. I went back home to my parents within three months. We just drifted apart.

Then I took up with another man and had my son by him. I didn't want to marry him. I'm just glad I got my son. That man was a heavy drinker. I was working at all different kinds of jobs. I always wanted to be a housewife. That was my big ambition in life was to be at home, take care of the house and have a lot of kids, be a good wife, good mother. Well, as I told you, I didn't want to marry this man, and our relationship had broken up by the time my son was 6 years old. I was still doing odd jobs, and at this point, during World War II, I worked in a nightclub, and I was drinking every single night.

My pattern was to be a periodic drinker, and that's what I did for thirty-four years. I had these periods of time when I would stop drinking altogether. If I had done something that I felt guilty about or was hurting somebody else or myself too much, I would stop. Then I would go into depressions, real deep depression, sometimes. Before I ever got to AA, I had stopped drinking for a whole three years at one time. Never touched a drop. Other times it was for two weeks, six months. I could stop and start. But that's not what I was doing when I went to work for that nightclub, I was drinking every night. I never had a high tolerance for liquor like some people, and there I was drinking every night. That's the first time I can remember a blackout.

We got off work about 3 A.M., and I came to standing in the ladies room crying, looking in the mirror and I didn't know how I got there or why I was crying. I went out and asked the bartender what happened to me. He said, "You don't know?" I said, "No. Tell me." "You slapped one of the customers," he said, "and he slapped you back and you ran into the bathroom."

I had been getting fearful, afraid of things I couldn't figure out. I love cats, but I was afraid of cats and if one came near me I'd panic. I was afraid to go home. My son was staying with my mother since I was working nights and I was afraid to go home. I dreaded it. I just couldn't. I thought I was going crazy. I didn't know what a blackout was. I couldn't handle this sudden loss of memory and things happening that I didn't know were happening. I walked several blocks that night, to the county psychiatric hospital and walked up to a young intern. I couldn't stop crying. He said, "What's the matter." I said, "I'm afraid." "What are you afraid of?" he said. But I couldn't talk, I was crying so hard; so he gave me a pencil and a piece of paper and said, "Write down what you're afraid of." I wrote, "I'm afraid of life."

He asked me if I wanted to stay there at the hospital and I nodded yes. They admitted me and I stayed for almost two weeks. I felt better, but I still didn't want to go home. So they asked me if I wanted to go to the state hospital, but they explained that I would have to be committed. So there I was going before a panel of judges and doctors allowing myself to be committed to the state mental institution because I didn't know what was wrong with me.

They put me in a receiving ward, and almost every single

one of those beds was occupied by a self-admitted alcoholic. When I told the women in the ward some of my story, they said, "Oh, you're an alcoholic," and I said, "No way am I an alcoholic!" (This was in the 1940s, remember.) AA was around, and one of the doctors in the ward was a self-admitted alcoholic and drug user and member of AA himself. The women in that ward had a copy of the Big Book of Alcoholics Anonymous. I was exposed to AA right away, but it didn't penetrate. The women told me that I was an alcoholic. I read the Big Book, read the Serenity Prayer; but I was in a deep depression and I was seeing a psychiatrist every day.

One day I took him the Big Book when I went in to see him. I told him that I liked what I had read and that that's what I wanted. He read it and said, "If we could all do this, we'd all be gods." This is what the psychiatrist told me. So we talked about sexual fantasies and my mother and things like that, but we never talked about drinking, ever. I was transferred to another ward and they scheduled me for electroshock treatments.

The women on the ward told me again, "You're an alcoholic, you don't need shock treatments." But that just made me mad. I said, "Oh, you know better than the doctors, right? Alcoholics just want everybody else to be an alcoholic." I had several series of electroshock treatments, and after about six months I was better. I was recovering from the deep depression I had been in and I was released.

Just before I left, one of the staff doctors came in and warned me about drinking. She said that if I go home and just don't drink that I would be OK. If not, I'd become like my 60-year-old roommate, "Bernice, she can't even get down to the bus stop without getting drunk, so we keep bringing her back. She never gets as far as the bus to get back to Chicago." I carried a resentment against that doctor for the next twenty years. I was going to show her. I'd gone through six months of shock treatments and I was *cured*.

I went home and I didn't drink for three months. She did scare me. By that time I hadn't had anything to drink for nine months. I was 28 years old. I started to drink again. I got depressed. I started hearing voices, also called "auditory hallucinations." I got scared. I went back to the hospital. They diagnosed me as having an anxiety neurosis with schizophrenic reactions. I hadn't heard any voices since I stopped drinking, but I didn't put that together. This time I had insulin shock. Electric shock is just a sideshow. Insulin shock is the real horror. After three months my depression was gone and I went home. I never went back to the hospital after that. I just continued believing that I had a very serious psychiatric problem. I continued to have severe depressions over the years.

I married again, another drinker. That marriage lasted for twenty-three years. We had one daughter. We drank together some, but he was a daily drinker, and I was still a periodic. I think that's what saved us and let us manage to keep a roof over the kid's heads. He was an entrepreneur, he'd get into something and make a lot of money, then bang, it was gone. Chicken one day and feathers the next. Sometimes we had an apartment, sometimes a house. Meanwhile my alcoholism had continued to progress and I was getting very paranoid so I decided to divorce my husband.

I got out of bed one morning with all my clothes on and my shoes still on. My panty hose was laying over on the chair, so I picked them up and started to put them on over my shoes when I saw what I was doing. *I'm going crazy*, I decided. *That man is driving me crazy.* Everything was his fault, right? I got to the point where I had to get everything out of my life that interfered with my drinking. He never complained, mind you, he bought liquor for me. I just didn't have time to be a wife. Occasionally I'd have to pick up a pair of socks off the floor and that cut into my drinking time. My daughter was away at college, my son was an officer in the Air Force by now. So I was at home alone.

Now I could drink the way I wanted to for the first time in my life. I got a good settlement from my husband and I didn't have to work. I had no responsibilities. I was fifty-one years old. All I had to do was call up the liquor store and have them bring my booze and drink. This is it. I finally made it.

This didn't last too long because soon I took the phone off the hook, let the hedges grow up tall and cover the front windows. I was hiding in my own house drinking. I began to drink daily. My drinking scared me because I couldn't stop. I contemplated suicide.

Then I went to work as a community volunteer. I was able to stop drinking for the six weeks of orientation. At the end of that I had one drink. The next day I drank again, and the day after that. Then I did something I said I'd never do, I drank on the job. There I was supposed to be counseling kids who were seriously damaged emotionally when this girl called me one day, wanting to leave her foster home. I picked her up and we went to lunch. She didn't even notice, but I had to be sure and find someplace where I could get a drink. I drank on a job you don't drink on, and I just couldn't go to work after that. I stayed home and thought about suicide again. I'd tell myself that I wasn't going to drink that day. Today's the day I'm going to go out and do all those things I'd been meaning to do, and all the while I'm walking to the refrigerator hoping there's a cold beer in there and hoping that there wasn't because then I could postpone the drinking just a little longer. It just got worse. I had a rope strung up in the cellar across a beam and I was going to hang myself. I finally admitted to myself that I was an alcoholic and that I had to drink. That depressed me even more.

I admitted that I was an alcoholic, but no way was I accepting it. I was going to kill myself. *I can't be an alcoholic*, I'd tell myself, *I'd rather die. I'll hang myself if I can't control this thing*, and I wasn't controlling it any more.

I decided to give a party first and have some friends over on a Saturday night. I was a booze fighter from day one. I never belted liquor. I'd drink an ounce of liquor and I'd mix it with whatever was on hand; I didn't care what it was, I diluted it. I'd drink that, then watch the clock and drink another ounce.

But what was happening now that the disease was progressing was that I wasn't able to get enough alcohol into my system to keep the DT's away. I had hallucinations. I kept going in and out of the DT's. And of course the voices were there, almost constantly during this period. But I never shook, that's what people who can't handle their booze do, they shake. Well, I shook inwardly. Inside I would have this terrible shaking and quivering, and it took alcohol to get rid of it.

I did not consume a lot of alcohol in comparison to what a lot of people can tolerate physically. I never could tolerate large quantities of alcohol. Being an alcoholic and having to drink, I learned early on that I couldn't handle any quantity. So I diluted my drinks and stretched them out over long periods during the times I was drinking. That way I could maintain a certain level of alcohol in my system. That's called "maintenance drinking."

My friends came and went, and from Sunday morning through Monday morning I walked around my house and drank. I had liquor in every room, set out, just sitting there, a glass here, a glass there. I would walk from one to another, just sipping. By this time, I could not get six feet away from alcohol. I had to be physically near the stuff. I was dependent on it. I walked from room to room saying, "Oh, God, oh God," I said that over and over.

Come Monday morning I went into my bedroom where I had a bottle of gin that I hadn't opened. I unscrewed the cap and poured an ounce into a glass. I could pour an ounce of liquor without measuring it, I had done it so many times. I poured that gin into a shot glass and looked at myself in the mirror. I don't have any words to describe the revulsion I felt when I looked at myself in that mirror. Then I looked at the glass in my hand and at that moment I knew that if I were to drink that gin, I couldn't guarantee where it would take me. That's the first time in my life I had thought about alcohol in that context, because I always told myself, *Well, I'll take this drink first, and then I'll be able to do what I want to do.* But it didn't work out that way. But I was never aware that it wouldn't work out that way because next time it was going to be different. It was always *going to be* different, so when it didn't work it didn't matter; next time.

But now I knew that I had it all backwards, that if I took that drink first I didn't know what would happen. I understood that here inside somewhere deep down and almost simultaneously I said to myself, "I am powerless over alcohol." I took the first part of the first step of Alcoholics Anonymous without knowing it. And in the next breath, I took the second part of that step because I said, "God, I can't live like this any more." My life was completely unmanageable.

It was 2 o'clock in the morning. I went to the phone and called Alcoholics Anonymous, and a woman answered and said, "You having trouble with alcohol?" and I said, "Yes." Then she asked me if I was willing to do anything to get sober. I said that I would do anything. She said she'd have someone get in touch with me, which they did. A woman called and said that she would take me to an AA meeting. She said she called me two or three times that day, I can't remember. She was going to pick me up that evening, and here I was with liquor all over the house. I didn't want to drink though, I knew I didn't. I was in my nightgown and a housecoat, so I went out on my porch and potted plants all day.

When it was time to go to the meeting I went into the house, put on a wig, some dark glasses, and threw on a caftan over my nightgown and that's how I went to my first meeting. The lady came and picked me up and took me to the back room at the local Congregational Church where I was living in Massachusetts.

It was a very small meeting that night. There were three people that I remember particularly that were in the back, talking about the first three steps of AA. I identified with every single thing those three people said. I knew I was in the right place. When I was standing in line waiting to get some coffee, a fellow asked me if this was my first meeting. I nodded yes, and he said, "Welcome home, you don't ever have to suffer like that again."

I thought, "How does he know how I suffered?" But he did, I could tell from the way he said it. He knew where I was. That was the beginning, and from then on I kept going to AA.

I got a sponsor who told me to call her every day. I called her two–three times a day. I was having a hard time, but I didn't tell anybody. I was hallucinating, but I kept dragging my body to meetings. They told me to go to ninety meetings in ninety days, and of course I was going to get well three times as fast so I went to three meetings a day for ninety days because I wanted to be OK right now. After sixty days, the hallucinations got so bad that I finally went to a friend of mine who is a Catholic priest and talked to him. I collapsed in the rectory and they rushed me to the hospital, where I was diagnosed as having the DT's. I was there for three weeks and received the medication I needed to save my life.

DT's are the most severe form of withdrawal from alcohol. A lot of people die from them, so I'm not kidding when I say that they saved my life there. They lasted for well over a week. Not only did I see things and hear things, but you feel things too, like bugs crawling on you. It's awful. Every morning I got down on my knees and asked God to keep me away from drinking alcohol today. Even though there was no alcohol in the hospital for me to get, I did this because it was suggested to me in AA. And every night I got back on my knees and thanked God for keeping me away from alcohol.

They released me after three weeks and the first place I went was to an AA meeting. There were people there for me, saying "Welcome back!" I got better from that point on. I went to a step meeting where I found out about how to work the steps of the program, about three or four of those a week. Most of the meetings are open-speaker meetings, where someone tells their story, just like I'm telling you mine right now, but it was recommended that I take in at least one step study meeting too.

I got as far as the Third Step in the program, where it says that I'm to "turn my will and my life over to the care of God, *as we understand Him.*" But I didn't think that God liked me enough for me to trust him with my will and my life. I no longer thought that killing myself was a solution. That's what I'd always told myself before, if it gets tough, I can always blow my brains out. But I had taken the Second Step of the program, and I was being restored to sanity. So it was like this wall behind me. I was backed up against this wall. That was sanity. That Second Step tells us that we "came to believe that a Power greater than ourselves could restore us to sanity." I couldn't go back. I knew that I couldn't kill myself, but how in the hell are you to go forward? I could not turn my will and my life over, so I was just going to die. I thought I was going to die and I didn't want to die alone. I called my friend that was the priest and asked him to come over right away, which he did. I wanted to make my last confession and let that be the end.

Well, he came over and picked me up and we drove around in his car. We must have driven for about three hours while I talked to him and told him some of the awful things I had done in my life and about the awful person I was. I was hyperventilating, and at first he asked me if I had asthma, which I did not. And once he knew it wasn't something like asthma, he had enough experience with people like me to know exactly what I was going through. Rebellion. I was dying from rebellion. It was that third step, and I wasn't going to take it. He finally got me to quiet down a little bit and he said, "Repeat after me 'I can't, God can, He will.' " At that point I realized that what I'd been saying was, "I can't, God can, but will he?" There's a big difference.

I said, "He will," and I kept saying it. My friend took me home and told me to go in the house; "God's in there, and he's going to take care of you." I said, "Hell, no, not him again, I'm not ready for him yet. I don't want him in my house. It's OK, he can stay in the car, we can ride around with him, but in my house? I don't trust him that much yet." But I did go in, and I did feel better. From that point on, I never experienced fear to the degree that I had up to that time.

When I did my Fourth Step, I wrote an autobiography. I never knew what the Fourth Step was until I did it. I never knew what any of those steps were until I did them. I didn't know I was taking some of those steps at the time I was taking them, like when I admitted that I was powerless over alcohol and that my life was unmanageable. I didn't know that I had just taken the First Step of AA. I just knew that that was the truth.

When I looked at that Fourth Step, where we "made a searching and fearless moral inventory of ourselves," I saw that it was my story and nobody else's. I saw that I had had a miraculous, spiritual experience and that it was just my story, nobody else was in there, just me.

Today my children who had been alienated are back with me. My ex-husband is one of my best friends. I used to have a lot more in the way of material things before I came into AA, and I've had a lot of medical problems, unrelated to my alcoholism, since I got sober. I was unable to work altogether for three years because of those medical problems. But with the Twelve Steps it has been possible to go through all these difficulties, and I've been sober now for over eleven years.

Sobriety is its own reward, that's what I'm saying. I am recovering from the disease of alcoholism, and everything has been possible because I was willing to take a few simple suggestions.

When I finished the Fourth Step what I saw, for the first time, was myself. That was what I had lost. The Fourth Step was like my higher power saying, "Pearl, meet Pearl." He introduced me to me. When I came to AA I was broken in body, mind, and spirit, and God put me back together again, through working the program of Alcoholics Anonymous. The doctors couldn't do it, the psychiatrists couldn't do it nor could the priests. Nobody could put me back together again. So when I looked at the Fourth Step and saw what my disease had done, I had no doubt that I was powerless over alcohol. Drinking was the symptom of the disease. I drank because I had to drink, I drank because I had no choice, none whatsoever. Once I saw that, about 90 percent of the guilt surrounding my drinking was gone. I used to tell myself that I really didn't have to drink and that I had just done it in order to get up the courage to do some things I knew I wasn't supposed to do, but that wasn't true at all.

I have a disease that tells me I don't have a disease, and I saw beyond a doubt that I drank because I didn't have a choice. I saw that I didn't like booze, never had, mixed it with anything so that I didn't have to taste it. I didn't like the way it made me feel, but I had to have it because I was addicted to it, physically and mentally, and I was spiritually bankrupt.

Today I have a choice. I can choose to drink or not, and any day I had that choice, I didn't drink, one day at a time.

My sponsor told me that my answers are in the Big Book. It tells us to "remember that we deal with alcohol, cunning, baffling and powerful." That's so true. I went along, doing the steps, like it's suggested in the Book.

I made an appointment with my friend, Father Bill, at 9:30 A.M. on a Thursday morning to do my Fifth Step where we "admit to God, ourselves and another human being the exact nature of our wrongs." Those are the wrongs we see when we do our Fourth Step and take that moral inventory. Well, I had written over sixty pages, and I began to read, telling him the things that I'd only planned to take to the grave with me. I closed my notebook at 2:30 P.M. I had no idea of the time that had passed. I looked up and he was looking at me, and he told me some good things about myself. At that time I was still very negative about myself, and I didn't see much good in me. But I trusted this man, and I was willing to take his word for it that there were some good things about me that I hadn't yet been able to see.

I left there feeling like, *Here's a person who knows everything, about me, and this person loves, respects, and even likes me.* I had hope again. I was off to a fresh start. What a relief that brought.

The Sixth Step is "becoming willing to have all these defects of character removed." I got bogged down in what I call the "paralysis of analysis." "How in the world do you become entirely ready to have all these defects of character removed?" I asked my sponsor. "By doing the first five steps. Go to the Big Book." That's where the answer was. You do those first five steps in order to become entirely ready. Then the Seventh Step is to humbly ask God to remove all these shortcomings. That's when I started carrying on conversations with my higher power. I talk with my higher power quite candidly. He's with me all the time. I'm so glad he's got humor and patience.

Then I had to deal with the Eighth Step, and I turned again to Father Bill, and he taught me the most about that. We're supposed to make a list of all the people we have harmed and become willing to make amends to them. I had a lot of resistance to writing down the names of all the people I still had resentments against, for example, but he pointed out to me, "You don't have to do anything but write their names down." And after I did that I gradually became "willing to make amends to them all." I began to realize that there is no such thing in my life any more as an insignificant human being. All people are important, regardless of what their station in life may be, even those people that have harmed me.

I began to see how I had categorized people according to race, religion, the way they dressed, where they went to school, their politics, the usual. Up until that point there were some people I considered insignificant, of no importance to me because they didn't fit my description of what a real person was supposed to be. Well, the Eighth Step took that away, and now there are no insignificant people, none whatsoever. I'm doing this for my recovery. I'm not doing these people any favors. If there's anybody on that list that I'm not willing to make amends to, that jeopardizes my sobriety. Suddenly that person has become very important to me. In the Ninth Step I made face-to-face amends with those people that I could contact directly. It's spiritual experience. I didn't know what I was going to say until I was sitting there actually facing the person. It wasn't until I was sitting there across from my ex-husband that it ever occurred to me that I had harmed him. I thought I had all these things that I was going to tell him I was sorry I had done. But when I sat down to talk, something else altogether happened, and I understood for the first time how I'd hurt him.

The Tenth Step I do is daily inventory. The Book tells us that in order to stay sober we "continued to take personal inventory and when we were wrong promptly admitted it." I find that doing this on a day-to-day basis helps me keep my side of the street clean. It's easy for me to take my inventory because I know me now. If I try to take your inventory, there are too many pieces missing, I don't have all the information. I can't judge you. But I can take a look at myself now that I know who I am, where I came from and where I'm going and that makes life pretty simple. I only have to deal with me, with what I'm doing or not doing, not what you're doing.

The Eleventh Step says that we "sought through prayer and meditation to improve our conscious contact with God *as we understand Him*, praying only for knowledge of His will for us and the power to carry that out." So when I wake up in the morning, the first thing that enters my mind is *Thank you God, for enabling me, an alcoholic, to wake up this morning sober.* I get down on my knees and ask the God of my understanding to give me one day of sobriety, today. I ask God to restore me to sanity and to take care of my will and my life. I ask God to remove all my self-centered fear, to help me help myself today and to help another human being.

I was told and I found it to be absolutely true that you cannot do the Twelfth Step unless you've done the other eleven. When it says, "Having had a spiritual awakening as the result of these steps . . . " that means the other eleven steps. No doubt about it.

I used to always be depressed, full of terrible, negative feelings and fears. One day I woke up,and the first thought in my mind was that everything is OK. I went to the phone and called Father Bill. It was about 6 A.M. I said, "God is good," he said, "Yes, Pearl, I know." I said, "People are beautiful." He said, "That's all the truth there is." That was the first time I ever knew and believed that everything is all right. And I remembered back to how many times when I was drinking I had thought, that if I just take one more drink everything would be all right. Or if I just get that job, everything will be OK. If I can just change my husband, everything will be OK. If my kids would behave, everything will be OK. One more drink, and everything will be OK. But here I was that morning, convinced that everything *is* all right through my own experience. That was my spiritual awakening. Now it doesn't take a hell of a lot of faith when you're convinced through experience. That's not faith, that's concrete living evidence, and I am the concrete living evidence.

Ever since that day the uppermost thought in my mind, regardless of what is happening around me, is that everything is OK. Trying to carry the AA message to the alcoholic who still suffers and practicing these principles in all our affairs is the action part of the Twelfth Step. Talk about accomplishment! I may not ever write the Great American novel, I may not find a cure for cancer, but I have something, or I have been given something. I have been given a willingness to carry AA's message to those who still suffer. God can use me as an instrument as long as I'm willing, to save hundreds of lives. To me, that means I'm worth something. If God thinks I'm worthy of carrying this message, I don't care what people think.

I'll be 64 years old soon, 64 years of borrowed time. My people have convinced me that I was so sickly nobody thought I'd live past my first year. My mother used to tell me stories about all the people who would say to her, "Why would you want to take a dying baby on your hands? That child can't live." Then she'd name off all the people to me who are dead now that said that, and we'd laugh. What I've gotten through AA at last is myself. I got me.

18. Jean C.

My name is Jean C., and I'm an alcoholic, I've also been known to take a few thousand pills and smoke a little dope. I was sober in AA for thirteen years, and then I went out and smoked a little dope and got drunk again. I was in and out of the program for five years and have now been sober twelve years. So altogether I've been around AA now for thirty years and I've learned a lot about sobriety this second time around.

I had a lot of loving, laughter, and tears in my family while I was growing up. I can't say my childhood was unhappy because I was unconscious most of the time. I was always trying to figure everything out. Somebody, please tell me what's going on. I never did figure it out. All the pictures of me in my mother's scrapbooks show me scowling. I was cursed with a baby sister who was born when I was 18 months old, and that's when I needed my first drink. She had curly, blond hair and baby blue eyes like my father, and I hated her. My mother spent the next ten years saying, "Go and help your sister study, go take care of her, do this, do that, and she's so pretty!" I became the "smart one." That's a curse, to be the smart one, because I wasn't smart. I had to study like hell to make those grades. My sister became an alcoholic too, a periodic. She was in AA for four years before she died. We finally got to be real sisters to each other, thank God. Mother continued to maintain that there was no alcoholism in our family.

Mother was a marvelous woman nonetheless. She could have run Ford Motor Co. She was a powerful Victorian lady. My father was a little Irish engineer who was a genius and invented all this stuff for the oil fields, and he was a liar. Well, I became like my father. You become the parent you can't have.

The whole focus of my upbringing was "be nice and be a

lady." To this day I still catch myself saying to my grown sons, "Be nice." It's a great tragedy to be that way. I didn't know how to live. AA taught me that.

I started drinking when I was in college. I was in a sorority and most of the girls drank. I wanted to be just like them. I didn't care what they drank, I just wanted to be one of them. I went home one day and got into my father's bar. There was a whole bottle of Manhattan mix. I poured myself an iced-tea glass full of it. I did not drink for the taste, I drank only for the feeling. I chug-a-lugged half of it and then drank the rest of it and just slid down the wall. One of my sorority sisters came in the front door and found me and said, "What is your mother going to say? Oh, my God."

That was my whole life, "What is my mother going to think? What will she say?" My sorority sister pulled me up off the floor and got me into the shower, and every time I'd try to get out she'd slap me. It took a long time to sober me up. That was the beginning.

I finished college, went to graduate school and married a nice man. Nice girls marry nice men. My Victorian heritage prepared me to do that very well. Of course at the time I didn't know that his favorite hobbies were broads, booze, and television. We had some fun together, but not much. The marriage was based on the fact that we had read a few of the same books, he was an excellent dancer, and I was physically attracted to him. It was one of those marriages that never went anywhere. Never flowered, never bloomed. We had two sons. I was miserable in that marriage and continued to drink more and more intensely for the next thirteen years.

I went to lots of psychiatrists, hoping that they would diagnose me as crazy. I would rarely talk about my drinking with any of them. This went on until the disease had progressed so far that I was drinking two fifths of liquor a day. I'd have to have one fifth in the morning just to calm my nerves and stop the screaming meemies from running up and down my back. Before the day was over, I'd have another fifth. It was awful, horrible! This only went on for a few weeks at the end before I finally realized that alcohol had turned on me. I had lost my best friend. I couldn't get drunk and I couldn't get sober.

I had read the Yale Study On Alcoholism. I knew what was wrong with me. I wasn't crazy. I was an alcoholic. I had suspected this for some time, but I didn't want to admit it. I wanted to be crazy rather than be an alcoholic. When it turned on me like it did at the end, I called Mother and told her that I had to have some help for my alcoholism. In those days there were a few treatment centers, but we couldn't find one that took women, they just took men. Finally we found a sanatorium for psychotics and people with advanced senility that would take me. There was an old man there who looked just like Charles Boyer who had had a lobotomy. He followed me around all the time like a dog, scared me to death. That place put an end to my drinking nonetheless.

I came into AA in 1954 straight out of that funny farm. They'd locked me up with a bunch of those senile old ladies, and that scared the hell out of me. Kept me sober for thirteen years. It makes me so happy today to see all the treatment centers that we have now all over the country. We have been locked up in back wards with crazy people, tucked away, everybody ashamed of us all this time. It was difficult. We are so lucky to be alive today when we are finally dealing with alcoholism for what it is, a disease. Today we have hope and recovery. We don't have to end up in the back wards, thanks to AA.

When I came to AA in 1954, I was in love with the people, I was in love with the action. I went to AA morning, noon, and night. In those days we'd have three speakers at a meeting so that you could stand at least one of them. They always put me in the middle between two men. They'd make me write out my talk before because they wanted to be sure I talked nice. One time I said, "Hell" from the podium, and everybody got mad at me. I was supposed to be good. I was fed up with being nice.

By the time I was ten years sober I was Queen of the May,

King Baby, in love with AA people and I talked a lot, but I didn't say anything. I was getting phonier and phonier. And I started to read myself right out of AA. I got bored. I got into metaphysics which I had always been interested in. I got involved in studying the Kabala and spent three years on that. I got into it really heavy. I studied Zen Buddhism, I became involved in the Rosicrucian Order. Alan Watts was a close friend and stayed with us when he was in town. I mean, I was really into all that stuff. I entertained Paul Tillich when he was here, all sorts of people involved in the spiritual world. But all of this stuff that I was doing was out of spiritual pride. I was trying to know God and I wanted a quicker, easier way to God, and your way in AA was too damned tough.

AA is the only organization I know of that has twelve steps that give us a simple recipe for *experiencing* God, not knowing about him. Each one of us has a different higher power. But I didn't understand that then. I started getting migraine headaches and they gave me tranquilizers. That was part of the slip that was to come too, those tranquilizers. I got hooked on them too. In those days nobody understood how addicting those things can be. They're only just now beginning to accept that in the medical profession, and there are a lot of doctors out there still pouring them down people.

I went down to Mexico to see a friend of mine who's a good woman but she can't stay sober. Whenever she wanted to get off the booze, she'd smoke marijuana for two or three days and then she'd get sober again. Well, there I was and she had just gotten some marijuana in and she kept saying, "It's got some marvelous stuff in it, some hashish. You've got to try it. Come on, Jean. The Big Book doesn't say anything about smoking dope." I told her no, that I didn't want to do that. She said, "Take one drag." I took one drag and the floor tilted and I had the feeling. I'm not hooked on alcohol or pills or grass, I'm hooked on an instant change of feelings. Doesn't make any difference where it comes from. I can't look down on people who do heroin or cocaine, because I'd have done it if it had been there, baby. So there I was, smoking this joint, and six weeks later I was back at home at a party with an old beau and they passed a tray of vodka drinks and the waiter said, "Would you like one?" and I said, "Thank you," and picked up that drink just like I did this cup of coffee I'm drinking now. The old me was back in spades, and I was off and running.

I thought that old self had died, but I met her after thirteen years of sobriety and she was strong. She's patient and cunning and baffling and powerful, and she came back into my life with the attitude of "God, aren't you marvelous? You don't need to put up with this crap about not drinking any more."

But I was not working the steps. I was not going to three to five meetings a week like I do now and that I hope to do for the rest of my life. I was not living by the principles of the program. I was back in control, and my old self took over and I let her. I was in and out of the program for the next five years. At one point I had eighteen months of continuous sobriety, but I just couldn't hang on to it. Another time it was six months. I went into treatment twice. After the first treatment program, I thought I was going to be all right, but then I came home and got so depressed I couldn't stand myself. My marriage was so ghastly. I just didn't have the tools to live with my situation. So I got ulcers. I was counseling and doing AA work and lecturing and being miss smarty-pants. I was trying to save everyone and you can't save anybody, so finally I went back into treatment. Those five years were unmitigated hell.

When I developed ulcers over that eighteen-month sobriety, I got into the elixir of Demerol. I was in horrible shape. One of my AA friends came to see me in the hospital. I was lying there in bed with cigarette holes burned in my sheets and my nightgown, and I'm smoking and waiting for my next pill, and she said, "Jean, you're going to die. You'd better go back into treatment." After she left, I called up the center in Minnesota and asked if I could come back and they said yes. I walked in more bankrupt, more lost, more paralyzed with fear than I had ever been. I didn't want to have to walk this walk again. I kept saying to God, "How can you possibly ever use me again? I'm a total wash-up. I'm wiped out, scared to death." By the time I got back there, I was afraid to drive down the freeway, afraid to ride in an elevator, I was afraid of everything.

They had me work the first five steps of the program again and I found out some things I'd never known before. There was nothing intellectual about it; I *experienced* them. The first time I went into my counselor's office he helped me see that I had never taken the last half of the first step—admitting that my life was unmanageable. I had no trouble admitting that I was powerless over alcohol, that first part; it was the second part that got me in trouble. I thought as long as I didn't drink that I could control this and control that, control, control. But he helped me to see that I had never understood the Serenity Prayer. He said, "It's simple. When you say, 'God grant me the serenity to accept the things I cannot change' that means everything outside of you. You cannot change your mother, your sons, you can change nothing. When you say, 'Grant me the courage to change the things I can,' it refers to the fact that I can change me, I can change my actions and my attitudes. I cannot get a good attitude without changing my actions. I cannot think myself sober." Then he explained that "the wisdom to know the difference" is to ask God to always help me remember to "know the difference between those things I can change and the things I can't."

That explanation has stayed close to me and gotten me through some really tight places these last twelve years. I had a hard time with my new concept of God because I did not want the church God that I had known. I wanted something different but I didn't know how to get it. So this counselor told me to get the attributes of my higher power from the group. "The group is going to be your God for a while." So I started watching. What did the group give me besides acceptance? They gave me sharing and caring—I could go on and on about what that group gave me. So today I have a higher power that has no eyes, no arms, no face, just a universal power that is filled with love that has mercy on us all, because most of us would be hanging by our toes if we didn't have mercy. I got humor again. I learned to laugh at myself that second week back in treatment, and I will never forget it. I knew that Methodist Church God of my childhood didn't work, that's why I was studying all this metaphysical business; but like I told you, that was straight out of pride. Taking my idea of a higher power from the group itself was marvelous. Now my higher power has monumental attributes and grows every year. Something beautiful comes out of beginning over that way.

Back in the 1950s and 1960s we didn't talk about alcoholism as "the feeling disease," where I was from. But when I got into treatment in Minnesota they told me that I had a "feeling disease." They said that I'd never been in touch with my feelings. I denied that. I said, "Oh yes, I have." And the counselor said, "Will you look at your hands? You are clutching the chair." And she said, "How do you feel?" and I said, "Mad." "That's a pretty good word," she said, "How about angry?" And I said, "Yes, that's what I am, I'm angry." Then she asked me if I'd ever shown that to anyone before and I said, "No, it was inappropriate."

In my generation, with a Victorian mother, nice little girls never got angry, never got out of line, and they all turned into ladies. That was one of the nice reasons I loved drinking. I did not want to be a lady like my mother. I wanted to be a whole, lusty woman. That's what I wanted to be.

When I did a Fifth Step at the treatment center, I did it with a Catholic priest. You don't have to do it that way at all, that was just how I chose to do it. Anyway, here we were going through my "moral inventory . . . admitting the exact nature of our wrongs" and he asks me about lust. We were going over the seven deadly sins, and it was next on the list. I told him, "Lust, hell, I am 50 years old. I didn't find out about lust until I was 40 and I'm not giving it up right now."

Those counselors and people there were wonderful to me.

My counselor helped me see that I was very, very hard on myself. He said, "Did you know that God is in the judging business, not you? You've been playing God in and out of AA for the last eighteen years." That hit me like a ton of bricks. I was totally unaware of what I was doing. I was unconscious. That has held me close. Every time I start judging one of you of course I start hurting myself. Now I stop and say, "Listen, God, forgive me, because that's your business, and that's not fair." I've learned not to judge me but to care about me, and to ask God to pull me up out of whatever problem I'm into.

Another thing they taught me to do just before I left the treatment center was how to write in a daily journal. I have a notebook now, and every morning I pick up and date the top of the page. Then I write in, "Dear God, please help me to stay sober today and help me with whatever character defects I'm working on." Then I go down to the bottom of the page and I sign it. I look at that empty page and I say, "God, it's your day, let's go." I've just taken the first three steps again. At night I come back and write down a feeling, a high feeling and a low feeling because I did not know what feelings were. I couldn't identify them and they told me that I had a feelings disease. I had to get lists of feelings out of books so that I could begin to identify them. Well, I started doing this when I got home from treatment and I'm scared to stop here some twelve years later. I'm still writing in my journal, though not in as much detail. My journal has turned out to be a God journal. Let me tell you what it has meant to me. It has meant an emotional sobriety that I never dreamed possible. I didn't even know there was such a thing. I don't have it all the time, mind you, but I do some of the time. I have that peaceful place inside that makes me happy, makes me feel content, makes me know that life is worthwhile. It has gotten me through some very tough, tough places.

I discovered in this second sobriety that I had to get rid of a lot of things. I had to get rid of a lot of women I was sponsoring because I found out they weren't serious about working the program and they were dragging me down. Back to that realization that we can't save other people. I told all the people I was sponsoring that I wouldn't work with them if they didn't keep a journal on a daily basis. That got rid of half of them. Another thing I had to get rid of was my gurus. I had all kinds of great heroes that I worshipped in and out of Alcoholics Anonymous. I began to see for the first time that we are all exactly the same. Every one of us in the program knows what I mean when I say "lonely," or "filled with self-hatred and fear and complete despair and hopelessness." We've all been there. Those are words and feelings we all know. I got rid of my gurus and then I could look to you because I have learned and accepted that God works through people.

I didn't want God to work through you. I would have never gone to you in the past and said, "Help me." If I got into a bad place, I'd go to a psychiatrist. Why should I go to a woman who didn't have any sense in the first place and ask *her* for help? Let me tell you that when you get on your hands and knees and crawl back into sobriety like I did, and they tell me that God works through AA people and especially AA women, since I'm a woman, I'd better get on with it. I used to have this very shallow attitude towards other women. It was sort of chic, I thought, to say, "Well, I just do better with men," implying that I was good with the men, which wasn't true at all. I've learned to trust women, really gotten to know women. I've got a woman sponsor this time around as well as a man whose been sober for thirty-six years. And now I know that God works through you. I learned after that slip that my old self never dies; in fact she's gotten more subtle as the years go by, narrower and narrower, until she can be like a knife. So I better check out things with others. You may not be receptive to me, but I will talk to a couple of people and I'll say, "I want to tell you how I feel about something, I want to divorce my husband." And you say, "What for?" And you start making me think. And I will listen to you, and I can tell if it feels right, not if it feels good, but if it feels right. You are making me be honest with myself, and I know that God has used you to talk to me.

People don't realize it but AA is really a spiritual path. I read Gurdjieff, Ouspensky, all sorts of esoteric spiritual masters. Why was I reading those damn books to learn how they experienced God, when God was saying to me, "Baby, you have got to do this for yourself. Their way isn't going to get you down the pike." But no, my spiritual pride was so strong, so powerful, I just kept going until finally I saw that AA gave me a way to experience God on a daily basis.

In my journal that I was telling you about, I find that I keep saying, "Listen, God, I can't do anything about this. I'm powerless one more time. My life is unmanageable, I can't handle this, you have got to help me." Everything I think we ever learn is back to that First Step. I write down in my journal what I want help on. And if I don't get some help pretty soon now for what I asked God's help for, then I call you up and I say what's bothering me. I don't care how little the problem is, it can make a big enough stack for you to trip over if you just keep stuffing it down inside.

I was filled with unexpressed feelings, ready to explode when I came back into AA. I was a walking, talking mess of resentments. But through the tools of this program and helps like keeping this journal, I can have some emotional sobriety and I love it. I try to keep my side of the street clean and take care of my problems in today where God is and not drag that stuff around from day to day. It's important for me to be able to wake up in the morning and not be mad at somebody. I have enough trouble when I wake up in the morning anyway. I've got my old self and my new self. The old self, the destructive self starts off reminding me what a hard time I have. And all of the sudden I snap out of it when my new self comes into play. I've had enough bad days. I don't need them any more. That's my new self, "into action," with a positive attitude. If I'm feeling bad, I'll call you and see how you're doing and get out of myself, put some energy and concern out for somebody else, and pretty soon I'm feeling better before I know it.

I had no daily routine when I was thirteen years sober. Now I have a daily routine. One commitment is to my higher power for not less than three to five minutes in my journal. Now that's pretty damn simple. If I forget it and wake up at night, I get up and write in it. If I'm on a trip and I don't have it with me, I'll write on another piece of paper and stick it in there when I get back. If I forget a day, I go back and fill it in. It's my covenant with my higher power, and through it I've developed a whole new kind of relationship with God.

Relationships can be a real problem. How do you get them to work? I ran across a paragraph that Bill Wilson, one of the founders of AA, wrote in a letter. It changed my life. My goal is to have emotional sobriety and to cease fighting anything or anybody. Back in 1958, Bill wrote, "If we examine every disturbance we have, great or small, we will find at the root of it some unhealthy dependency and its consequent unhealthy demands. Let us with God's help continually surrender these hobbling demands."*

All I have to do is get rid of my demands and dependencies. They told me that the first time I was in treatment. They did a personality profile and said if I didn't get over my unrealistic expectations I'd get ulcers. Eighteen months later, when I went back into treatment, I had ulcers. I lived all my life on fantasy and hopeful expectations of things to come. Never did I live in the present moment where God is. Well, I didn't know what to do with all this, so I went and talked to an old-timer at my home group and he said, "Jean, are you aware that you squeeze everything? People, places, things, everything." He said, "Ask God to help you to see people as they are, accept them as they are and quit squeezing them." So I used that as a prayer for the next two years, almost verbatim. Every now and then, I'll get in a tight place where I'm expecting too much from life or from you, and I go right back to that little prayer.

I wrote that prayer in my journal over and over until it was

* A.A. Grapevine, "The New Frontier, Emotional Sobriety" by Bill Wilson, 1958.

emblazoned on my mind absolutely. That way, if I was squeezing something or being overly expectant my unconscious would say to me, "You're squeezing." I've practiced that for so long now that it still does it. Oh God, how I miss squeezing. I really do miss it, but I'm much more comfortable.

I discovered that nothing can fix me. That's really the crux of recovery. I always wanted Mother to fix me, ministers to fix me, psychiatrists to fix me, treatment centers to fix me. But the last time I was in treatment, it finally got through to me that God and I were going to have to do the work. I was going to have to experience this higher power on a daily, maybe hourly basis. Not once a week like church on Sunday or once a month, but daily. You know we don't talk much about self-discipline in AA, but I know what's out there for me if I drink again and I don't want it. So I'm willing to do a few very simple things every day to keep my program and to keep my old self from taking over. That old self never dies, she just sits there, like alcohol, cunning, baffling, and powerful, waiting to pull me apart.

Another thing of Bill Wilson's that really turned me around was the practice of prayer, meditation, and self-examination. He said, "The maintenance of my sobriety is daily. Prayer, meditation and self-examination, these three intertwined or in balance provide an unshakable foundation for life." Now, that's powerful! I had prayed myself drunk, I had meditated myself drunk, but I had never done self-examination. That's why that's so important to me. If I had done something and needed to make amends I could see that, on a daily basis. If I was hurting, that would come out in the journal. See, if I go to bed clean and I wake up clean, it's a whole 'nother ball game. That comment of Bill's on self-examination combined with prayer and meditation, and his paragraph on demands and dependencies, have done more to help me maintain emotional sobriety than anything. I never had that before in that first thirteen years of sobriety. I certainly didn't have it the next five years I was in and out of the program. I've really only had it about the last six years of this second sobriety. It's some kind of serenity. It's a place that I can to to when all hell's breaking loose, and ride it out.

Every day of sobriety gets you ready for what will happen down the road. Life is tough, and it's also perfectly beautiful. When the tough times come, how do you cope with them? You use the same thing you did to quit drinking. Not long ago when I had to have brain surgery, all I did was tell God that my life was unmanageable and please give me the courage and the strength to get through this thing. Sure, I was afraid, but let me tell you, I always get about five or six people that I can trust to really pray for me and then I just float, I get along real fine.

My sponsor from out in West Texas, Kay, she's my best friend in AA, been sober thirty-two years. Those West Texas AA people, back in the 1940s, they were driving from West Texas to Fort Worth just to get to a meeting. Out there from Alpine to Amarillo is a day's drive, but I got news for you. If you were drunk up there or about to get that way and you needed help, they'd drive. Those folks thought nothing of driving 100–200 miles to get to an AA meeting. Their homes were just like Bill and Lois's. Their kitchens were the kind where people just dropped in, sat around the table and drank coffee, and the marvelous thing is, they still do that today. Kay always says to me when I call her up with a problem, "Jean, what step are you working on?" She puts me right back where I need to be, working the steps. Now when some of the girls I sponsor call me up, I do exactly what Kay does to me, I say, "What step are you working on?" And they hate me. They say, "Oh, but you don't understand, my life and my man and my this and my that, it's my relationship problem," and I say, "The only thing I know is, here's your problem and here are the twelve steps. When you work the steps, your problem goes away. How's that?" That's the question I have to keep asking myself, "What step are *you* working on?"

Those first nine steps are about ego reduction in depth and

this ego reduction will make you comfortable. I didn't understand all that until about two years into this second sobriety
when I was getting high on my lows.

There is a classic line in AA that they used to say to us,
"The last thing you are going to give up is your pain." And
the time came both in my first sobriety and in this new one
that I really got high on my pain. A friend of mine in AA
who's a nurse came over to me and said, "Jean, I found out
what's wrong with me. I am important when I am hurting. To
tell you the truth, I get high on my pain." I said, "Oh, my
God, in heaven, that's what I've been doing all these years."
And by that time I had been around AA twenty years. "I am
just like you."

Well, once you know the name of the game you can't play it
any more. When my old self would start up with how hard
my life is—"poor me"—this new self says, "Hey, are you
going to listen to that trash?" and I go back and get me a good
attitude. The only way I know to get a good attitude is to
accept the fact that the old self still lives and I don't have to
stay there. I can get into action. So AA also means to be
absolute action and acceptance, "action and acceptance." There
is no attitude adjustment without action to move you into
acceptance. Then I can get a good attitude, after I've taken
some action.

There was a doctor who came up to me at one of the meetings after I got home from treatment. One of those folks you
hate but he's so bright you have to listen to him, and he said
to me, "You're the most I-centered woman I have ever heard,
and if you don't get other-centered you're going to get drunk
again." And I thought to myself, *You son-of-a-bitch!* but I never
forgot it, and I went about my business learning how to get
other-centered. Number One, I learned to sit in a meeting and
listen even if I didn't like the talk. Number Two, I learned to
call you up and say, "I hurt," and then listen to you about
your pain. It is important to get out of the hurt, to get out of
the pain.

New things are coming out about alcoholism every day now. I have been shocked, really shocked by all the incest business and molestation that we women are beginning to talk about. But you know, I've been locked up in psych wards with women who were incest victims, and they weren't necessarily alcoholic. They just went crazy from it, they felt so dirty. One woman told me that she had felt filthy all her life. I had such compassion for her, my God, but that experience told me that no matter what terrible thing we've been through whether it's incest or rape or even being raped by a gang—oh, I've heard it all—it doesn't have a son-of-a-bitchin' thing to do with my alcoholism. It's a disease, it's biochemical. Some people have it and some people don't, and even if terrible things happen to you, that's not what makes you an alcoholic.

The biggest difference in this sobriety and the last one is that I have learned how God works through people. Hell, I wanted a direct pipeline to God. They really hit on me about that in treatment. They pushed me to work on getting a conscious contact with God as I understood God and told me that it was not to be the God of my childhood. I had to get away from that.

I've taken to making a real study of the Big Book with my sponsor. We read it and discuss it often. I go to lots of meetings. I stick with other people who really work the program, and I'm working the damned twelve steps as hard as I can. In Texas when we tell our story we start off by saying our first name and our sobriety date so we don't ever forget that last drunk. These days I say, "My name is Jean C., and by the grace of God and the fellowship of this program I've been clean and sober since so-and-so, and through no little effort on my part." I have really had to work at it. After six years this second time my life began to turn around and it's turned around ever since. I've done things in these last six years that I never could have done before, didn't know were possible. So now I'm up to twelve years again, for the second time, and I wouldn't trade these twelve years for anything.

19. Rachel V.

I was born in the South. I went to a Catholic girls' convent school for the first eleven grades and led an extremely sheltered life. The attitude toward the body that I grew up with might best be described as considering the flesh "an occasion of sin," particularly the female body. Best to subject it to harsh discipline. The saints whose lives I read about and was fascinated by were praised for mortifications of the flesh. I was so caught up in the notion of penance that I became afflicted with scruples and would not let myself take a drink of water until I was so thirsty that I had no other choice, and then I would feel guilty for not waiting longer. How were all the poor souls in purgatory going to get to heaven if I wasn't offering up penance for them? If I were really good, I would have worn a hair shirt underneath my navy-blue uniform. I wanted to become a nun.

My family's attitudes did little to alter this perception. I was taught not to cry, to displace pain by getting angry at whatever had hurt me such as the tree I had just fallen out of. But somewhere in the mix, I took on a kind of toughness myself that in sobriety I see now was a sham. I'm still trying to get rid of it. I was always ready for a fight. I used to take great pride in the fact that I could beat up anybody in the neighborhood, at least until I was 12.

My idea of a good time was playing football, a fight, a bicycle race, or a day exploring the abandoned gravel pits nearby. I hated dolls. Give me the woods or the creek anytime. I was a very good student and wore braces for years.

I attended a large state university and made a big splash. I got into the top sorority on campus, was elected president of my pledge class, was selected as one of the "ten most beautiful," sweetheart of one group and another. It was a shock to find myself accepted, not seen as the oddball that I had always felt like. The change from my sheltered convent school upbringing was tremendous. I was very uncomfortable. I had begun drinking the year before, as a freshman, and to my recollection drank no differently than anyone else. However, I do remember throwing up out the window of someone's car on my way home from a dance after a big football game. That's the only drinking episode I remember. I had not drunk in high school.

At the university I met a fellow tormented Catholic. We had a strong sexual attraction to one another, but I was filled with guilt about my body and was overwhelmed by the instant campus popularity. So I broke up with my beau and left, completing my education at a tiny Catholic university with very little social life.

There I met a fellow from another Catholic university and fell in love, or so I called it. He was tall, blond and blue-eyed. We went to daily mass and communion together, and he never tried to do anything but kiss me goodnight at the door. I thought that was great. At long last, I had met my match in unreality. He was pure and holy, it would be just like the nuns said love should be, and so we planned to get married. That way I'd get my freedom, my sexuality, and the Church's blessing. I was 19, and after all, he had a new Ford convertible.

We hardly knew each other. He went to schoool outside the state so we didn't really date. We corresponded. At vacation he asked me to marry him. He came home the next year for a big church wedding. At that point in time, my drinking was not a problem, but as I look back, I can see that I was an alcoholic waiting to happen. I had an enormous denial system firmly in place. The night before my wedding, my husband-to-be slapped me across the face for smoking a cigarette. I called off the wedding. Frightened and shocked, I did not want to believe what had happened, so I didn't. I managed to convince myself, with the help of other members of the wedding party who witnessed the episode, that the man who slapped me was not really the man I was marrying. I went through with the wedding that next night and left for my honeymoon in Paris. Two days later he started slapping me around in our hotel room. I had made a terrible mistake and I knew it, but having married in the Catholic Church, I thought I had nailed my coffin shut. There was nothing I could do. It never occurred to me to confide in anyone or ask for help.

I became pregnant right away and had my first child. During the pregnancy, the violent episodes continued sporadically, after which my husband would become suicidal. He tried to kill himself twice, and the third time tried to kill our child and me with him. At that point I knew something was terribly wrong. The maternal instinct came to life and I asked for help. A priest advised separation and counseling. Now I was pregnant with my second child. I separated, then went back to live with him briefly once he had agreed to counseling. Again violent episodes which resulted in my being hospitalized, about to lose my second child with whom I was five months pregnant. I had to drive myself to the hospital. The car was almost on empty. I was bleeding on the white upholstery. My baby was in the back seat crying. I will never forget handing the filling station attendant the only money I had—a dime. I made it to the hospital and we managed to save the pregnancy. But I was so stubborn about the finality of marriage I would listen to no one, not the doctors, not my father. Finally a priest got through to me and told me that not only could I get a divorce, I had to get one and that I had grounds for an annulment. I could still be a practicing Catholic. The church didn't expect me to risk my life and my children's. I filed immediately. I was then six months pregnant and 21 years old.

That's when I began to drink as I recall. I needed the anesthetic that alcohol provided. That's what it did for me and that's how I used it. I was lost, shattered by the whole experience.

I moved back with my family and had my son three months

later. His sister was 13 months old. I had no child support and no money of my own. My family saved us, especially my grandparents; they took care of the children. Pride, insanity, God only knows why I remained silent. I told everybody I was "fine." I was not going to let anyone know how bad I felt or how scared I was. Not only was I going to hide it from everyone else, it was most important to hide it from myself.

I didn't date, still waiting for the annulment for which I had filed. I tried to find work and could not. Then I was offered a fellowship to graduate school. I took whatever work I could get on top of teaching freshmen and taking a full graduate load myself. But no matter what, I could not support myself and two children. I began to borrow money, and I drank. All my friends drank like I did. Beer after classes, beer after work, beer on the weekends. Pitchers and pitchers of beer.

The day came when I either had to come up with the money to send a priest to Rome to plead my case for annulment or wait the minimum of seven years it took to travel the routine channels to the Vatican. Instead I chose to leave the Church, a decision more momentous for me than the divorce. Now I was going to run my own life. My drinking continued daily.

I remembered now my grandfather telling me that he had removed twelve beer cans from underneath the seat of my car and asking me if I didn't think maybe I was drinking too much. Of course I did not. I saw no relation between the insane feelings I was having, the constant thoughts of suicide, and my drinking. I drove down the highway with my eyes closed to see how long I could stand it before forcing them open again, just in time. I thought I was losing my mind. Finally I was in so much pain I called a psychiatrist for help. He gave me amphetamines. I saw him weekly for the next two years. I continued to function, though I don't know how, beginning my day with speed and drinking at night.

Somehow I managed to finish a graduate degree. I packed up my children and went back East, continuing to drink. I was no longer taking speed since I no longer saw that doctor. Now

I understand I went into withdrawal. I had become addicted to speed, though I didn't know that then. I fell in love, had an affair with a man that I enjoyed thoroughly and felt absolutely no guilt about it whatsoever, only delight. To my still Catholic mind, that meant that I had become a whore. So I refused to see him again. I thought I was having a nervous breakdown and became severely suicidal. I went to yet another psychiatrist who confirmed my worst fears. Yes, he told me that I was hanging on by my fingernails and that I needed to be institutionalized for at least a year. I told him that was ridiculous. Who would take care of my children? He shrugged his shoulders and assured me that there was little chance I could make it on my own. I was desperate for help.

I called an old beau, my drinking partner from graduate school, in a state of hysteria. He hopped on a plane, flew to New York and said, "Let's get married." *Yes, I thought, that will fix everything. That's what I'll do.* We got engaged to marry the following summer. I stayed on in the East, got a university teaching job, and continued to deteriorate emotionally. I had no clue as to what was wrong with me. I saw yet another psychiatrist who assured me that my problems were just about getting married again. He said that it wouldn't matter who I married after my first experience, any wedding was bound to be upsetting. He prescribed Valium. So now I was taking Valium and drinking and was deeply conflicted about remarrying. Finally I decided to go through with it. My children would have a father and would no longer be from a "broken home." I had been filled with guilt and fear about their not having a normal family. They were 3 and 4 years old.

Being married only made things worse. We moved to a new town after the wedding. I knew no one. He traveled a lot. The children had a father in name only. I continued to drink and now had no job that I had to pull myself together for. I was hopelessly undomestic. I got pregnant again and was furious at his continued absences. Now I wanted to kill myself *and* my children. It would be terrible for them to have their mother commit suicide, so I would simply "take them with me." But there was enough sanity left in me to at least know that such thinking was crazy. At this point I drank daily, but confined it to late afternoon and evenings.

I wanted to think that my husband was the problem. If he would just stay home, if he just wouldn't use drugs, if, if, if— anything to avoid seeing myself. He drank like I did, so of course I didn't see that as a problem.

I tried to pull myself together. I went to another psychiatrist, went back to graduate school, and started work on a Ph.D. I met people, became active in the community. But nothing alleviated the insanity I was caught in. Worse, I had gotten myself into another battering relationship. After a few months of marriage, I found out that this husband had a violent temper; but this time when I got hit, I fought back. I became violent as well. The cycle of violence continued. Going from one abusive relationship to another is a familiar story in alcoholism. The children became terrified of the fighting and the beatings they witnessed.

In the middle of all this my third child was born.

The next six years of marriage were a constant round of battles, not worth repeating. We kept moving. I kept drinking and avoided my own problem with alcohol. I thought I was willing to look at myself because I went to counselors and psychiatrists. But I don't ever remember talking about drinking as one of my problems. Despite the chaos and the progression of my disease, my career blossomed. I was still maintaining a good cover. We were written up in the local paper as the successful professional family. It never occurred to either one of us that my behavior was totally off the wall. I'd smash out windows in my house with my bare fists. I took a bottle of Valium and overdosed. I threw myself out of the car as he turned the corner. I told him I hated him but could never remembering saying it. Inevitably, I had been drinking.

I was going to make this marriage work. I was going to fix it, whether he liked it or not. By separating and threatening to divorce him, I forced him into marriage counseling with me. At the least sign of willingness on his part, no matter how awful things were, I would get back together with him. I had no self-esteem whatsoever and completely humiliated myself in these dogged attempts to "save" my marriage. I had been divorced before and I wasn't going through that again. Now there were three children who needed a father. Then a fourth move and attempt to start over, when my children confronted me about getting a divorce. "We can't stand the fighting. Please divorce him. That is terrible." I hated myself and drank all the more for having stayed in a marriage so long that it took my children to get us out of it. I poured myself a good, stiff drink and filed the next day.

Six months before this it had occurred to me that I might, just maybe, have a drinking problem. We had gone home at Christmas and I remember looking through some old family photos. I had come across a picture of one of my relatives who was a practicing alcoholic in those days, and who had been very good-looking in the photograph. I couldn't believe it was the same person these twenty-odd years later. Something clicked. For a moment I saw it, I saw that what had happened to him could happen to me. For the first time it occurred to me that maybe alcohol had something to do with the chaos that continued to fill my life. The denial system had begun to crack.

When we got back from Christmas vacation, I went straight to a counselor and said, "I think maybe I have a problem with alcohol." She said, "Oh, so why don't you stop drinking for six months?" I seemed to have no trouble not drinking for those six months, if I even lasted that long. So I convinced myself that my problem wasn't alcohol. But I was already drinking again by the time my children confronted me about getting divorced. The divorce only gave me license to drink more.

Those months without alcohol had done something, though, no matter what story I told myself or who I tried to make wrong. Deep down I suspected that I really did have a problem with alcohol and I spent the next five years trying to prove to myself that I didn't. I spent a great deal of energy on *not* drinking.

I know now that social drinkers don't have to stop drinking to prove to themselves that they don't have a problem. If you think you've got a problem, you probably do. But I didn't know that at the time. I even went to an AA meeting at this juncture to convince myself that I was really willing to look at this drinking business. I deceived myself with a surface "honesty." But all I could see were people drinking lots of coffee and smoking cigarettes. They were unhealthy, I decided. I didn't drink coffee or smoke. I wasn't like them.

I don't think I heard a word that was said about alcoholism, I was so busy looking for reasons why I was *not* like these people. I had survived my second divorce. I lost weight, let my hair grow long, took up running. I was attractive, healthy. I couldn't be an alcoholic. They were older, wrinkled up, wore trench coats, and drank cheap liquor out of bottles in brown paper bags—didn't they?

I couldn't find a regular job. I had three kids at home ages 5, 9, and 10, and no help with child care. I hadn't a clue how to survive.

I took off into the wilderness, into the woods. I ran wild rivers, climbed mountains, hiked into desert canyons. I looked everywhere for some peace but could only find it in snatches and moments. Wild places soothed me and gave me whatever kind of precarious balance I had, but nothing could heal me, and I couldn't heal myself.

There would be periods when I wouldn't drink at all. I worked very hard to control it. I was crazy about my kids and, no matter what, I couldn't make everything OK for them. I was an utter failure. I had failed to provide them with a father.

Something had to give. I went to a tiny desert monastery in an attempt to reconnect with the Catholic church. But at the mass I found I could not bear the language of the fathers. It was painful to hear how as a woman I was excluded and forgotten by God. The world was for man's use, and I just wasn't one.

Though I couldn't return to the church, the experience told me that I must, upon my life, find a spiritual path. There was no turning back, no way to ignore that part of my being anymore. I had begun the journey.

I went into therapy again. I took up running longer distances. I went back into the wilderness, whenever possible, with or without my children. I turned to Buddhism, became a Zen student, rising at 4:15 A.M. for morning zazen and service. I began to feel better from time to time. I set up an elaborate system of checks and balances within myself. If I had been to the monastery for zazen and run three miles in the afternoon, I could stop in the neighborhood pub and have two beers or two glasses of wine. Sometimes that worked. There were times when I could stop just at the right moment before crossing that invisible line into inebriation. I would feel pleased with myself, take those times that I was able to stop as proof that I *could* drink. "The idea that somehow, someday he will control and enjoy his drinking is the great obsession of every abnormal drinker. The persistence of this illusion is astonishing. Many pursue it into the gates of insanity or death." (*Alcoholics Anonymous* (The Big Book), p. 30). I was on my way down, but little did I know it. No matter what I did or how I improved, nothing lasted.

I had blackouts, more and more of them, but hardly recognized them for what they were. I had had them for years without realizing it. Having a blackout meant that I "functioned" but had no memory at all or only a spotty memory of what I did or said. Alcoholism is a progressive disease, and ironically just as I thought I was controlling my drinking "better" with my system of checks and balances, my tolerance was changing and I was progressing downhill rapidly. I would cross over that line, call my children, way past their dinner hour when I could no longer tell myself that I would just be a "little" late for dinner and tell them to fix something for themselves. They had done that hours before. I would arrive home and they would be asleep. Filled with remorse and self-loathing, I would tell myself that I must stop at two, or better yet, stop drinking.

One night near the end of my drinking I tried to choke a man. I was in a drunken rage and in a blackout. I had had good reason to be angry, so when he told me about it the next day I glossed over what I'd done as justified. Within another week I was again drunk, enraged, in a blackout and finally "went to sleep." I woke up thinking that it was the next day, but it was six that same evening. I had once again verbally abused and hurt everyone around, this time my daughter. She caught a lot of my self-hatred because part of what I hated was being a woman and she was just like me. There was something terrible about having a woman's body. It's a silent teaching that's passed on from mother to daughter, and I was passing it on to her as surely as my mother had passed it onto me, and hers to her. I can't tell you what that silent teaching was, but every one of you that's either received it or passed it on will know what I am talking about.

There was no way to justify my behavior toward my daughter. She was completely innocent, unlike the man I had attacked a week before. I was completely wrong, and I knew it. She refused to accept my apology, and I knew she was right. She was 14 years old. The only way to apologize was to change my life. I was on a downhill run, picking up speed and I now knew it. I was destroying everything and everyone in my path.

I reached out and called for help. I telephoned an old friend who used to regale me with his drinking escapades. I knew that he had stopped. How did he do it? Alcoholics Anonymous. He asked if I knew anybody in AA and, thank God, I did. A woman I admired, respected and could relate to had told me she was in AA. Stephanie was brilliant, successful and on the cutting edge of a lot of movements I admired. I called her up and told her I thought I had a problem with alcohol. To my surprise, she assured me that she thought so too, from what I had told her about my life. She got out her meeting directory and told me when and where the next meeting was that was closest to me. "Get yourself over there!" That was four years ago, to the day of this writing.

I was relieved.

The first thing that struck me in that meeting was the complete candor of the speaker. I'd never heard anybody talk with the honesty and humor that this man had about his life before and after coming into AA. It was incredible. People came up to me after the meeting and gave me their phone numbers, made sure that I had a meeting book, and encouraged me to get to a meeting every day, offered me rides.

The candor and humor I encountered in that first meeting I kept finding in AA. I loved it. I loved the people, all different kinds. But I was still in denial and kept looking for every reason to prove that AA wouldn't work for me. People told me that alcoholism was a terminal disease. Many people seemed relieved by that fact, but I was disgusted. I was a "New Age" thinker, and there was nothing incurable. I was a neo-Puritan and wrote off illness as a psychological problem. Disease was a cop-out. I thought the whole idea was terribly depressing.

People kept telling me I *had* to read the Big Book of Alcoholics Anonymous, that I had to work the steps of the program and that the book would tell me how. I went to meetings where the book was read and discussed. I was horrified. I decided that it was written for men. Every description of the alcoholic was of a white middle-class male. It had a chapter entitled "To Wives," but no chapter "To Husbands."

I felt alienated by the language, lost, locked out as though sobriety was for someone else. There was a lot of mention of God, whom I wanted nothing to do with. I was a Buddhist now. I didn't believe in God. Not only was God mentioned, but God was always described as "he." More of the patriarchy. I was a maverick. How could I go along with this book? I was told that it was like the Bible to AA and that if I was going to stay sober I was going to have to read it. I complained in meetings. Another friend pointed out that as much as I wanted to be critical of the Big Book, it was important to notice that I was still sober. Over six months of sobriety had passed, despite all my intellectual and political misgivings.

The first two years of my sobriety remind me of a line from a Woody Allen movie—"Eighty percent of life is just showing up." I just kept showing up. I didn't understand AA, I was still critical, but I knew that it worked, so I hung on. Besides, the stories I heard at meetings were terrific. I loved the people I met, and I knew that something authentic was happening in the meeting rooms whether I approved of their use of pronouns or not. I saw people come in and change 180 degrees. I saw others go back out and drink again. Some never made it back sober.

Talk about people going back out again drinking, and the insanity of the disease never really hit me until a friend of mine committed suicide. Elizabeth and I had come into the program about the same time. She had everything going for her. She was active in the program. Then she wasn't around for a couple of weeks. Shortly thereafter, I saw her one night at a meeting and she told me that she had been drinking again. She had gotten very busy at work, too busy to get to meetings and one night decided that she could handle a glass of wine. That went OK so she drank again the next night, no problem; but by the third day she was on a run and couldn't stop drinking. She stayed drunk for three more days. When I saw her that night at the meeting, she was relieved to be back in the program, but greatly demoralized by her slip. "Don't ever drink again, Rachel. It's worse than everything you've heard people say. At first it seemed OK, but within no time, it was worse than anything before I ever came into AA."

I listened, but I didn't really hear her until I walked into a meeting the next week or so and another friend came up and asked me why I hadn't been at the funeral. "Funeral, what are you talking about?" I said. "Didn't you know Elizabeth committed suicide? Shot herself in the head?" Julia said.

Her death has kept me sober many times. She has been a teacher for me, bringing home the truth of what I had been told about this disease, that it ends in death or insanity. Elizabeth had been drinking again when she blew her brains out with a .38 pistol.

I went through a long period of being suicidal myself after about two and a half years sober. I was convinced that I was one of the people who can't make it. I was in a black hole, and I couldn't get out of it. I dreamed that I had killed myself. It was a terrifying time and it went on for several months. I kept going to meetings. I kept hearing people share their experience, strength, and hope, and through others I was able to keep that flicker of hope alive. I did not give up. I kept talking to people, kept acknowledging how I felt. I hated telling everyone how terrible I felt. But gradually it changed. Very slowly. One day I just didn't feel like killing myself any more. I was on the other side. Driving to a meeting after that, I wanted to tell Elizabeth, "See, it changes, everything changes, it would have changed for you too . . . " So I have to tell you. She can't hear me any more.

After some time passed in AA, I was able to hear the phrase "God, *as I understand him*," a phrase added to the Third Step so that anyone and everyone could find a way to connect with a power greater than herself or himself. After three years, I noticed that there's a chapter in the Big Book, "We Agnostics." I read that I could be an agnostic and still have a spiritual experience. I didn't have to go back to the God of my childhood. "The Realm of the Spirit is all-inclusive. . . . When we speak to you of God . . . we mean your own conception of God" (*Alcoholics Anonymous*, pp. 46–47).

Gradually my morning meditations shifted from zazen, an emptying of the mind, into a dialogue with a higher power. It took a long time to admit that what I was doing was praying. I wasn't a Christian. I was horrified. Now I can laugh at that.

In meetings now I say that I'm promiscuous with God. I call on everyone: the Blessed Mother, the Lord Buddha, God the

Father, Jesus Christ, Tara, the Holy Ghost, my Grandmother, Inanna, Kwan Yin, Isis, Ishtar, Kali, Sophia, the Shekhina, anybody and everybody. I need all the help I can get. I'm sure that God understands. My life is evidence.

I've begun to let myself look at my Christian roots again. I've found medieval Christian mystics who addressed God as "Mother," like Julian of Norwich, Hildegarde of Bingen. I've found the Black Madonna, a Catholic remnant of the pre-Christian worship of the Great Mother Goddess. Looking for the female side of God is a way of coming to peace with myself as a woman, finding the female body which I thought so terrible, inhabitable by God.

I began to study the Big Book, its history, and the development of AA. The Big Book is a compilation of the experiences of the first hundred alcoholics who got sober. AA wasn't trying to tell me what a higher power had to look like. I began to notice that Bill W. had taken a great care to use many other phrases to describe God besides "he," such as "Supreme Being," "a Creative Intelligence," "a Spirit of the Universe," "the Great Reality."

I have begun to marvel at the Big Book. I can now accept the fact that it was written in 1938, when there was only one woman member of AA with any continuous sobriety. The principles given in the first 164 pages continue to work regardless of sex. I live with the language by looking at it in its historical context. In meetings I read "she" as well as "he" or use "they." I have marked up my book to read that way, too. I say, "Our Father/Mother" at the end of the meetings if the Lord's Prayer is said.

Getting sober has meant getting in there and looking into the dark places. That's been the Fourth Step for me. I'm in the middle of doing it a second time. The longer I'm sober, the more nooks and crannies I see I have. Little dark corners, twists. A labyrinth. I call doing the Fourth Step "eating the dark." In the Fifth Step, I found out that even darkness is good. Sobriety doesn't change having good days and bad days.

It's just that now I can have a bad day and remember that it'll change before I know it. Today I think God keeps my life on the edge so I'll pay attention.

Children raised in an alcoholic family, like my children, learn ways of coping that let them survive the chaos, but cripple them later if they don't come to understand their behavior. It's taken all four years for my kids to begin to understand what I've been trying to talk to them about all this time. They've all been to counseling, and are beginning to undo and heal some of the damage. Their initial response to my announcement that they might need to change too was greeted with the comment, "Hey, you don't drink any more. There's no problem. You're not an alcoholic. It's got nothing to do with me." Slowly, slowly the entire family system is beginning to turn around. Feelings they've been sitting on for years are popping out, and it gets a little wild, but it's fabulous. We just get closer and closer, the more old hurts we get out. My children have been the greatest teachers of forgiveness, of which I still have a lot to do. The steps of the program give me a way to have and sustain intimate relationships, something I could never do before. Today I have a loving, gentle and sober husband.

Alcoholism is full of irony. Never before have I understood so fully what mystics of all traditions have been trying to tell us: there is no separation between body and soul, mind and matter. Alcoholism has taught me this through my own experience. It is a physical disease for which the only known recovery is a spiritual transformation. On one level alcoholism is a hunger for spirit, for God. Carl Jung pointed that out to Bill W. in a letter years ago. My disease was a distortion of my search for God. We are all hungry for God. It's no accident that alcohol is also referred to as "spirits." What I hungered for, thirsted for is God and for whatever reason, biochemical, genetic, emotional, I used to look for that spirit in the bottle or through a drug. What I wanted was communion, our common union, and that's what I've found through the help of AA.

If You Think You Have a Problem

Several paths are open to the person who thinks she might have a problem with alcohol. A simple and free beginning is to call Alcoholics Anonymous, listed in your local phone book and begin to attend meetings. It is also worth noting here that alcohol is a drug, only one of the many available today. If you think that you may have a problem with drugs instead of alcohol, whether they are prescription drugs from your doctor or street drugs (for the sophisticate perhaps I should say "recreational" drugs), keep reading. Multiple addiction or cross-addiction to both drugs and alcohol is very common these days, much more so than when AA started. Some old-timers in AA have been known to hold the line and say that AA is for alcoholics only. But more and more people discover that as you try to get off what you think is your drug of choice, be it cocaine, marijuana, or heroin, your alcohol intake goes up to take up the chemical slack. Just because you think that drinking isn't a problem for you, but you have been a little concerned about your use of, say, marijuana or Valium or cocaine, for example, it still would not hurt for you to check out AA meetings or look up Narcotics Anonymous (NA). There are increasing numbers of programs such as NA that are modeled after AA and use the same Twelve Steps. More and more I am coming to understand that chemical dependency is the issue, whether it's alcohol or drugs. Sobriety means freedom from *any* mood-altering chemicals. Many people achieve complete abstinence and sobriety through AA's Twelve-Step program of recovery.

Others go into recovery from the disease by entering a treatment center, of which there are thousands around the country. Treatment programs are often a minimum of twenty-eight days spent in residence at a treatment center. Treatment can be much longer depending on your problems, your insurance coverage, and your pocketbook. Most reputable treatment programs prescribe complete abstinence and recommend active participation in your local Alcoholics Anonymous program for continued sobriety. Most assume that alcoholism is a chronic illness for which there is no cure. Teaching people to drink socially is not generally a goal of a reputable treatment program. There is common agreement in the field that for the alcoholic, a goal of abstinence from alcohol and all other mood-changing drugs of addiction is the foundation for recovery.

Some communities have recovery centers where daytime recovery programs are available and residence is not required. This can be helpful for women with families and child care problems.

Your local Council on Alcoholism can refer you to treatment programs in your community, or you can write to the National Council on Alcoholism for information on local resources. Often members of the clergy are familiar with community resources for alcoholism as well. Your doctor should be knowledgeable in this area. If not, find one who is.

Resources and Books

The following sources of information and books have been useful. This list is by no means definitive, but it will give the interested reader some places to start to learn more about alcoholism, addiction, and the resources available for recovery and treatment today.

RESOURCES

Alcoholics Anonymous World Services, Inc.
Box 459
Grand Central Station, New York, New York 10163
(212) 686-1100

Estimate of 42,000 groups, with over 1 million members worldwide. It is an international fellowship, with meetings going on all around the globe.

If you are a friend or relative of an alcoholic, you may want to contact your local Al-Anon Family Group. Your local AA office can guide you to an Al-Anon group or contact:

Al-Anon Family Group Headquarters
P.O. Box 182
Madison Square Station
New York, New York 10159-0182
(212) 683-1771

Both AA and Al-Anon have many publications and educational materials available as well in addition to meetings. They are open to everyone. There is no age limit. Al-Anon also sponsors the Alateen program as well as meetings of Adult Children of Alcoholics.

National Council on Alcoholism
12 West 21st Street
New York, New York 10011
(212) 206-6770

The National Council on Alcoholism maintains affiliates in more than seventy cities throughout the United States, which provide treatment information and referral sources. It is also a good source of information and publications on the subject.

CompCare Publications
2415 Anaplis Lane
Suite 140
Minneapolis, MN 55441
(612) 559-4800

Hazelden Institute Educational Materials
Box 176
Center City, Minnesota 55012
(800) 328-9000

Johnson Institute
510 First Avenue North
Minneapolis, Minnesota 55403-1607
(612) 341-0435

Rutgers University Center for Alcoholism Studies
Rutgers University
P.O. Box 969
Publications Division
Brunswick, New Jersey 08903

National Institute on Alcoholism and Alcohol Abuse
U.S. Department of Health and Human Services
National Clearing House for Alcohol Information
P.O. Box 2345
Rockville, Maryland 20852

BOOKS

Alcoholics Anonymous (The Big Book). 3rd edition. New York: Alcoholics Anonymous, World Services, Box 459, Grand Central Station, New York, New York 10163, (212) 686-1100, 1976.

Twelve Steps and Twelve Traditions. New York: Alcoholics Anonymous, World Services, 1976.

Jan Bauer. *Alcoholism and Women, The Background and the Psychology.* Toronto, Canada: Inner City Books, 1982. ICB, Studies in Jungian Psychology, Box 1271 Station Q, Toronto, Canada M4T 2P4, (416) 484-4562.

Ernie Kurtz. *Not-God, A History of Alcoholics Anonymous.* Center City, Minn.: Hazelden Publications, 1969. Hazelden Institute Educational Materials, Box 176, Center City, Minnesota 55012, (800) 328-9000.

"Pass it On," The Story of Bill Wilson and How the AA Message Reached the World. New York: Alcoholics Anonymous World Services, 1984.

Sharon Wegscheider. *Another Chance, Hope and Health for the Alcoholic Family.* Science and Behavior Books, 1981, 701 Welch Road, Palo Alto, CA 94306.

Claudia Black. *It Will Never Happen to Me; Children of Alcoholics, as Youngsters, Adolescents, Adults.* M.A.C. Publications Division, 1982, 1850 High Street, Denver, CO 80218.

Each Day, A New Beginning, anonymous. Hazelden Publications, 1983. Very good collection of daily meditations for the woman alcoholic.

Jean Kinney, M.S.W., and Gwen Leaton. *Understanding Alcohol.* New York: Mosby Medical Library, New American Library, 1982.

Peace Pilgrim. Ocean Tree Books, P.O. Box 1295, Santa Fe, NM 87405-1295. This is a model of the spiritual life of anonymity.

The Twelve Steps of A.A.

1. We admitted we were powerless over alcohol—that our lives had become unmanageable.
2. Came to believe that a Power greater than ourselves could restore us to sanity.
3. Made a decision to turn our will and our lives over to the care of God *as we understood Him.*
4. Made a searching and fearless moral inventory of ourselves.
5. Admitted to God, to ourselves, and to another human being the exact nature of our wrongs.
6. Were entirely ready to have God remove all these defects of character.
7. Humbly asked Him to remove our shortcomings.
8. Made a list of all persons we had harmed, and became willing to make amends to them all.
9. Made direct amends to such people wherever possible, except when to do so would injure them or others.
10. Continued to take personal inventory and when we were wrong promptly admitted it.
11. Sought through prayer and meditation to improve our conscious contact with God *as we understood Him,* praying only for knowledge of His will for us and the power to carry that out.
12. Having had a spiritual awakening as the result of these steps, we tried to carry this message to alcoholics, and to practice these principles in all our affairs.

The Twelve Traditions of AA

1. Our common welfare should come first; personal recovery depends upon AA unity.
2. For our group purpose there is but one ultimate authority—a loving God as He may express Himself in our group conscience. Our leaders are but trusted servants; they do not govern.
3. The only requirement for AA membership is a desire to stop drinking.
4. Each group should be autonomous except in matters affecting other groups or AA as a whole.
5. Each group has but one primary purpose—to carry its message to the alcoholic who still suffers.
6. An AA group ought never endorse, finance, or lend the AA name to any related facility or outside enterprise, lest problems of money, outside property, and prestige divert us from our primary purpose.
7. Every AA group ought to be fully self-supporting, declining outside contributions.
8. Alcoholics Anonymous should remain forever nonprofessional, but our service centers may employ special workers.
9. AA, as such, ought never be organized; but we may create service boards or committees directly responsible to those they serve.
10. Alcoholics Anonymous has no opinion on outside issues; hence the AA name ought never be drawn into public controversy.
11. Our public relations policy is based on attraction rather than promotion; we need always maintain personal anonymity at the level of press, radio, and films.
12. Anonymity is the spiritual foundation of all our traditions, ever reminding us to place principles before personalities.

Taken from *Twelve Steps and Twelve Traditions*, copyright © 1953 by Alcoholics Anonymous World Services, Inc. Reprinted by permission of AA World Services, Inc.

Adapting the Steps and Traditions

Because of the difficulties I have had with the description of God as exclusively male, I have crossed out the "Him"'s and "He"'s in the Steps and Traditions in my copy of the Big Book, and inserted the word "God" so that there is no reference to God as being one sex or another. This feels a lot more comfortable to me and serves to remind me that God is neither and both and a lot more than I can ever imagine on top of it all. That way my God can be a female Buddha or Jesus Christ if I want; or an Inner Light, like the Quakers describe.

The point as I take it, is that we are each to develop our own relationship with a power greater than ourselves and who and what that is, is to be proscribed by no one. I use the word God only because we roughly understand the territory that attempts to describe. Not having such a concept tied to sex reminds me that the power that I am attempting to describe is without limit.

AA World Services in New York gave me permission to print the following adaptation of the Steps and the Traditions. By printing them again with the few changes required to make the concept of God more inclusive, you can see for yourself what a conceptual difference a few marks can make.

I am certainly not the only woman in AA who has marked her Book up in this way. Many others have found this helpful as well. I have been told that this kind of change in the language will be a long time coming in AA as a whole, so I thought I'd start with my own book.

Rachel V.

The ~~Twelve~~ *adapted* Twelve Steps of AA

1. We admitted we were powerless over alcohol—that our lives had become unmanageable.
2. Came to believe that a Power greater than ourselves could restore us to sanity.
3. Made a decision to turn our will and our lives over to the care of God *as we understood Him.* ~~Him~~ *God*
4. Made a searching and fearless moral inventory of ourselves.
5. Admitted to God, to ourselves, and to another human being the exact nature of our wrongs.
6. Were entirely ready to have God remove all these defects of character.
7. Humbly asked ~~Him to~~ *God* remove our shortcomings.
8. Made a list of all persons we had harmed, and became willing to make amends to them all.
9. Made direct amends to such people wherever possible, except when to do so would injure them or others.
10. Continued to take personal inventory and when we were wrong promptly admitted it.
11. Sought through prayer and meditation to improve our conscious contact with God *as we understood Him*, praying only for knowledge of ~~His~~ *God's* will for us and the power to carry that out.
12. Having had a spiritual awakening as the result of these steps, we tried to carry this message to alcoholics, and to practice these principles in all our affairs.

The Twelve Steps reprinted for adaptation with permission of Alcoholics Anonymous World Services, Inc.

adapted

The Twelve Traditions of AA

1. Our common welfare should come first; personal recovery depends upon AA unity.
2. For our group purpose there is but one ultimate authority—a loving God as He may express Himself in our group conscience. Our leaders are but trusted servants; they do not govern.
3. The only requirement for A.A. membership is a desire to stop drinking.
4. Each group should be autonomous except in matters affecting other groups or AA as a whole.
5. Each group has but one primary purpose—to carry its message to the alcoholic who still suffers.
6. An AA group ought never endorse, finance, or lend the AA name to any related facility or outside enterprise, lest problems of money, outside property, and prestige divert us from our primary purpose.
7. Every AA group ought to be fully self-supporting, declining outside contributions.
8. Alcoholics Anonymous should remain forever nonprofessional, but our service centers may employ special workers.
9. AA, as such, ought never be organized; but we may create service boards or committees directly responsible to those they serve.
10. Alcoholics Anonymous has no opinion on outside issues; hence the AA name ought never be drawn into public controversy.
11. Our public relations policy is based on attraction rather than promotion; we need always maintain personal anonymity at the level of press, radio, and films.
12. Anonymity is the spiritual foundation of all our traditions, ever reminding us to place principles before personalities.